THE MAN
CALLED
BROWN CONDOR

THE MAN CALLED BROWN CONDOR

The Forgotten History of an
African American Fighter Pilot

THOMAS E. SIMMONS

A Herman Graf Book
Skyhorse Publishing

Skyhorse Publishing books may be purchased in bulk at special discounts for sales
promotion, corporate gifts, fund-raising, or educational purposes. Special editions
can also be created to specifications. For details, contact the Special Sales Department,
Skyhorse Publishing, 307 West 36th Street, 11th Floor, New York,
NY 10018 or info@skyhorsepublishing.com.

Skyhorse® and Skyhorse Publishing® are registered trademarks of
Skyhorse Publishing, Inc.®, a Delaware corporation.

Visit our website at www.skyhorsepublishing.com.

10 9 8 7 6 5 4 3 2 1

Library of Congress Cataloging-in-Publication Data is available on file.

ISBN: 978-1-62087-217-8

Printed in the United States of America

Dreadful is the mysterious power of Fate

— Sophocles

Table of Contents

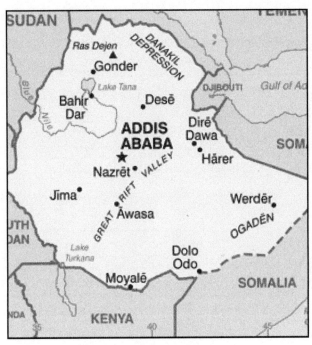

Ethiopia

Chapter 1

Africa, 1954

ON MARCH 14, 1954, A YOUNG ETHIOPIAN IN A RURAL VILLAGE lay badly injured. An urgent radio message requesting delivery of whole blood and medical supplies was received at the Lideta airport, Addis Ababa.

A handsome, trim, fifty-one-year-old American, former commander of the Imperial Ethiopian Air Force, volunteered for the mercy flight that would cross some of the most rugged terrain in all of Africa. It would be a fateful decision. His name was John Charles Robinson.

As the colonel walked from his flying school office toward the L-5 Stinson, Biachi Bruno, an Italian engineer, caught up with him and asked to go along as copilot. With a nod of his head and a smile, Robinson granted the request. Biachi read the smile as a silent recognition of the irony of the former Ethiopian colonel and an Italian aviator flying together. Less than twenty years before, Italian pilots had tried their best to kill the colonel.

The flight in the small, single-engine former US Army observation plane would take two hours. By land, in a four-wheel-drive vehicle, the same trip could take two days or longer—and that was if the roads and trails had not been washed out or blocked by landslides. Even in the mid-twentieth century, a donkey could be the most reliable mode of surface travel in much of the mountainous country.

The two men waited impatiently until a packet containing two units of whole blood, surgical supplies, morphine, and bandages arrived from the hospital. Biachi loaded the packet into the baggage compartment behind the rear seat of the two-place tandem Stinson, climbed in, and fastened his seatbelt. Colonel Robinson took the front seat, started the engine, taxied to the runway, and conducted the pre-takeoff check of engine, instruments, and flight controls. Satisfied, he ran the engine up to takeoff power and released the brakes.

Because the capital city is situated at an elevation of 7,600 feet above sea level, the 185 horsepower L-5 climbed slowly in the thin air. They would have to reach a minimum altitude of ten thousand feet to clear the ragged ridges, saddles, and passes that lay along the route between mountain peaks reaching above fourteen thousand feet, some snow-capped year-round. Because the snow existed near the equator it was called "tropical ice."

Air travel across the rugged terrain of Ethiopia is and has always been the kind pilots find extremely demanding and risky. Even in the 1950s, there were few modern radio aids to aerial navigation. The colonel did not need them. He knew the rough terrain of Ethiopia better than any pilot alive. Twenty years earlier, his life had depended upon his knowledge of the minutiae of valleys, streams, mountains, lowlands, deserts, rock outcrops, and trails. Biachi Bruno had asked to go with Robinson to gain such navigational knowledge of the varied Ethiopian landscape from the man he considered the master pilot of Ethiopia. Such knowledge can still mean life or death to pilots navigating through the Simien, Chercher, or Aranna Mountains in the Western Highlands, the Rift Valley, or the Ahmar or Mendebo Mountains of the Eastern Highlands. In the event of a crash, survivors can die of thirst or starvation before they can walk out or be found and rescued.

The two men reached their destination and landed safely on a short, flat, slightly uphill strip of dirt road. They handed the medical supplies to a waiting barefoot runner from the local village. Leaving a trail of dust behind its bone-jarring takeoff roll down the stone-strewn road, the little plane lifted into the air. After he turned on course for home, the colonel wiggled the control stick and lifted both hands into the air, a signal for Bruno to take over. The Italian was delighted. He put his right hand on the rear stick and rested his left on the throttle. Occasionally he peeked around one side or the other of the colonel sitting in front to check the instrument panel for airspeed, altitude, compass heading, and oil pressure.

Robinson relaxed, his gaze sweeping the horizon from right to left. *I never tire of the view from up here.* Mile by mile, the terrain slipped beneath them. *How good this rugged, savage, beautiful country has been to me.* Flying had been his life. He had read somewhere that flight was perhaps mankind's greatest technical achievement—"*the dream of countless millions of man's ancestors who for eons could only stare at the sky and wish.*" Even so, John knew the plane was but a tiny, fragile, man-made toy winging above the awesome, God-made Ethiopian expanse of jagged, mountainous, plateaus, lush jungles, and deserts of volcanic sand. Here and there, the terrain was ribboned with silver streams that tumbled into wild rivers coursing through falls and rapids eventually to calm and spill out onto valleys, nourishing the fertile plateaus, seeping into desert sands and simply disappearing. Three of the rivers—the Lesser Abay, the Reb, and the Gumara—feed Lake Tana, source of the Blue Nile. Robinson had flown over it all.

"Colonel," Biachi Bruno asked, "when did you first know you wanted to fly?"

The question interrupted Robinson's reverie and propelled him through time to a sliver of beach where the Gulf of Mexico lapped onto the shore of Mississippi.

***

The year was 1910. An airplane with a wooden float in place of landing gear, circled over the town of Gulfport, touched down in the shallow water of the Mississippi Sound, and taxied to the beach at the foot of Twenty-Third Avenue. The pilot, John Moisant, usually flew his Blériot monoplane with which he had recently won an air race in Paris. He had shipped it to New Orleans to race the Blériot against a Packard automobile. But he borrowed the float-equipped biplane to visit the young Mississippi town of Gulfport, developed twelve years earlier by Captain Joseph T. Jones, a former Yankee soldier turned oilman from Pennsylvania. Moisant's interest lay not with the town, but rather with Captain Jones's daughter, Grace, whom he had met at a gala in New Orleans some seventy-five miles to the west.

It had not taken long for a large crowd of townsfolk to gather in a semicircle around the flying contraption. John had borrowed the latest model of a Curtiss pusher biplane. It was a strange-looking contrivance composed of a fragile, wire-braced, wood-and-bamboo frame with wings and control surfaces covered in varnished linen, and it was powered by a rear-facing engine mounted behind the pilot's seat. The wheels had been removed and a wooden float attached to the fuselage. Two smaller floats, one mounted under each lower wing, kept the wingtips from dipping into the water.

Two young women, late arrivals, pushed their way through the crowd and approached the intrepid flyer. He was standing by his machine answering questions from the curious crowd.

"Hello again, John," Grace Jones said, and without giving Moisant time to answer continued, "I want you to meet my friend, Elsie Gary . . . and we have come to take a ride in your flying machine."

Nodding to Elsie, Moisant replied, "I don't know about that, Miss Jones. What would your father say?"

"Come on, John, take us flying." Grace smiled. "Please."

Elsie agreed. "My daddy might kill me, but I want to go, too."

"Listen, you two," Moisant said, "Captain Jones will hang me for sure if I do."

"You promised, John," Grace said, and she touched John's arm. She had the kind of eyes that could turn men into putty.

"All right, Grace, but I can't take but one of you at a time. Who goes first?"

The toss of a coin decided Elsie Gary would become the first known air passenger in the state of Mississippi. (There is a photograph to prove it.) Elsie climbed up on the plane and sat on little more than a board fastened next to the pilot's seat on top of the lower wing.

Among the growing number of excited spectators, there was a seven-year-old black boy standing at the back of the crowd clutching his mother's hand. From her vantage point, the small, stout woman could see only the aircraft's upper wing above the heads of the crowd. The little boy stood on his tiptoes but could only see the backs of the people in front of him. He squatted down and tried to look between their legs to no avail.

At Moisant's direction, a half-dozen excited volunteers took off their shoes, rolled up the legs of their pants, pushed the plane into water just deep enough for the craft to float freely, and swung it around to face away from the beach. John instructed them to hold tightly to the wing struts and warned them not to let go until he gave the signal. He switched on the magneto, set the throttle, waded around behind the wing, ducked under a tail boom, and hand-cranked the wooden propeller. The warm engine roared to life with a burst of black smoke from the exhaust.

The startled little boy jumped behind his mother and peeked around her skirt. He was not alone in retreat. A great many adults had quickly backed away. Moisant calmly sloshed through the shallow water around the lower wing and climbed into the pilot's seat.

Satisfied all was well, John checked to see if his passenger was ready. "Miss Gary, are you all set?" he yelled. Sitting on the quivering machine, holding on for dear life, too scared to speak, she bravely nodded her head. With a crowd-startling roar, Moisant throttled up the engine. The pickup ground crew struggled to hold the plane while spectators on the beach scattered from the blast of the propeller. John signaled the men to let go.

Blowing swirls of spray in its wake, the plane waddled away from the beach. Gaining speed across water rippled by a gentle southeast breeze, the fragile craft at last lifted into the air. Looking more graceful in the sky than it had on the ground, it circled over the harbor and turned back toward the crowd waiting on the beach.

Down it came, only fifty feet above the sand. Those in the crowd gaped open-mouthed up at the fantastic machine as it flashed over them at the incredible speed of forty-five miles an hour. The wide-eyed little boy stared up in awe. He broke from his mother's grip and ran down the beach with hands stretched high toward the flying machine. There was joy in his heart, wonder in his eyes, and laughter on his lips. The black child had found his impossible dream. His name was John Charles Robinson.

***

Returning from his reverie the colonel answered Bruno's question: "I made up my mind that I was going to fly when I was seven years old." He paused, then added, "But for a black child in Mississippi, it wasn't an easy dream to follow."

Robinson's attention quickly focused on the present. What had broken his thoughts? He wasn't sure, but his sharply honed pilot's senses were registering mild alarm. Vibrations in the cockpit were vaguely different from what they had been moments before. He scanned the engine instruments for clues.

Bruno, concentrating on flying to impress his old instructor, had yet to notice anything unusual. They had just cleared the last high ridge and started the long decent toward the high plateau. Addis Ababa was barely visible in the distance.

The engine noise changed faintly. The tachometer needle began to wiggle slightly. Now Bruno took notice. He opened his mouth to speak, but the engine spoke first. A loud metal-to-metal pounding sent both pilots to red alert.

Robinson reached for the fuel selector and switched tanks, checked both magnetos and the fuel mixture setting, and pulled the throttle back to reduce stress on the engine. The pounding, like a trip hammer on boiler-plate, could be felt through the control stick, rudder petals, and airframe. The shock-mounted instrument panel was vibrating violently.

John yelled, "I've got it," and took control, got on the radio, called Addis Ababa, declared an emergency, and gave their position.

Bruno tried to sound calm, but there was fear in his voice. "What now, my friend?"

The colonel turned the plane in a gentle bank to the right and then left, searching the ground below, behind, and ahead for a place to land—any place free of boulders, jagged rocks, and steeply sloped terrain.

"We can try to put it down now, but we don't stand a chance in hell of doing it in one piece. With a little luck, the engine will hold together for a few more minutes and we'll make it."

"And if we're not so lucky?" Bruno asked.

The colonel answered, "Well then, my little momma might turn out to be right after all these years."

"Your mother?"

"Yeah," Robinson replied. "She told me a black man had no business fooling around with airplanes."

Chapter 2

Mississippi, 1910

THE SEVEN-YEAR-OLD BLACK CHILD WAS ALMOST UNCONTROLLABLE as he and his mother walked west on 13th Street, crossed the Gulf & Ship Island (G&SI) railroad tracks, and turned north toward the Big Quarter, the segregated neighborhood where many black families lived. He jumped and skipped and made engine noises with his arms outstretched like wings, mimicking the airplane he had just seen.

"Johnny! You calm down! You're gonna embarrass your momma right out here on the street."

His mother's appeals went unheeded. The child was too excited to calm down. "Wait till I tell Daddy I seen a real airplane fly!"

Later that afternoon, Johnny sat on the front steps of his house waiting for his father to get home. The dirt road soon filled with men returning from their day's work. John could always pick his stepfather out of the crowd. Charles Cobb walked with a pronounced limp, the result of an accident at the G&SI locomotive shop where he worked. Johnny spotted him and ran to tell him, with wide-eyed excitement, about the flying machine he had seen that day.

When the two reached the house, Johnny's sister, Bertha, was playing in the front yard. Mr. Cobb picked her up and carried her into the house to join Celeste in the kitchen for supper. Charles Cobb listened to Johnny talk about the airplane and how it had carried people up in the sky.

"That thing flew out over the water and come back right over my head. It scared the devil out of a bunch of seagulls. Scared me too when it first started. Near 'bout blew down some peoples standing behind it. I bet most nobody in Mississippi seen anything like that. I'm gonna fly in one of those things some day, Daddy."

Charles Cobb listened to the excited little boy and wondered if one day he would have to try and explain to the child that a black man had about as much chance of flying as he himself had of being an engineer for the railroad. He tried to remember the moment he had finally accepted the fact that he would never drive a steam locomotive on the main line. Even today the dream haunted him. That's why he had become a railroad mechanic, working his way up from laborer and gandy dancer. If he couldn't drive, one he would keep them running. They still thrilled him. He must have been about Johnny's age when he saw a steam locomotive come thundering by for the first time. He had been sitting on his daddy's wagon when the huge puffing monster with its big driving wheels roared past the crossing, scaring his daddy's mule nearly out of its hide. The engineer had waved and Charles Cobb knew that somehow steam locomotives would be a part of his life. He knew everything there was to know about them, every part. To him, a locomotive with steam up was like a giant, live, breathing thing, powerful and mighty and thrilling to the bone.

When there was some unusual problem with an engine at the shop, his boss would come to him to fix it. Mr. Cobb knew how to drive a steam locomotive; he drove them out of the shop, across the roundtable, and down the siding to wait for an engineer to come along to put it in service and make up a train, but that was not the same as climbing up into a cab, opening the throttle, and highballing down the main line pulling a string of cars toward some destination miles away. Now he was worried, saddened really, that his boy might be haunted by a dream that would remain a dream.

John Robinson was born in Carrabelle, Florida, in 1903, coincidentally the same year the Wright brothers made the world's first powered airplane flight. Following the accidental death of his father, his mother, Celeste Robinson, moved to Gulfport, Mississippi, with her baby boy, John, and his four-year-old sister, Bertha, to live with her father. At the African Methodist Episcopal (AME) Church, Celeste met Charles Cobb. It was not long before they were married. Mr. Cobb was employed in a good paying job at the G&SI engine shop and roundhouse at Gulfport, the southern terminus of the line that hauled Mississippi timber and cotton to the port. He was a gentle man that had taken to the baby boy and little girl as if they were his own. He was rewarded with the love of the little children who worshiped the man who would be the only father they would ever know. Although Charles Cobb wanted to adopt the children and give them his name, Celeste insisted that they keep their real father's name. In Johnny's case, whenever someone asked about his name Celeste would answer that Robinson was his dead father's name, then smile and say, "but Charles was for his stepfather, Mr. Charles Cobb." No one ever knew if that was true, but the name by which the world would know him was John Charles Robinson.

***

Gulfport was founded in 1898 on the foundation of the man-made port, railroad, and timber industries. The virgin, long-leaf, yellow-pine forests of south Mississippi were being cut, shipped by rail to the port and by ship to the world. By 1910 Gulfport was the second largest timber exporting port in the world. It boasted a population of ten thousand and had an electric company, streetcars, waterworks, and many brick-paved streets downtown. Between the north/south G&SI and the east/west L&N railroads, eighteen trains arrived and departed daily. Some would think that a town with a constant flow of lumberjacks, sailors, railroad men, construction workers, and fishermen, and with more bars than churches, would be a rough place—and it was. But it was also a town of law and order with a thriving middle class. Many blacks owned their own homes at a time when that was uncommon in the South. This was largely due to the relatively good wages that the railroad paid and the black stevedores, who had formed a union at the busy port, earned.

The Cobbs built a white, two-story wood frame house at 1905 Thirty-First Avenue in the middle of the Big Quarter. It had half brick and half wooden columns across the front porch and was large enough for Celeste Cobb to rent several rooms to boarders. There were two bedrooms downstairs and five bedrooms upstairs. The Cobbs took the front bedroom downstairs and the babies at first were in the downstairs back bedroom. As Bertha grew older, she got a front bedroom upstairs.

As the years passed, there was very little doubt about John Charles Robinson's continued interest in all things mechanical—especially airplanes. By the time he was twelve, the Great War burst across Europe, and stories about airplanes and the daring pilots who flew them and fought high in the sky covered the pages of newspapers and magazines. When there was time between school and chores at home, John would whittle out model planes and build kites and fly them on the beachfront.

In an interview in 1974, Mr. Harvey Todd recalled, "Designing and building kites and fighting them was big sport to all us black kids. To kite fight, the boys would fasten razor blades or broken glass to the tails of their kites to try to cut their opponents' kite strings. Johnny designed a kite with wings like a bird and could make it dip and then go straight up. He was considered the best, the best at everything he tried. He could sit backwards on the handlebars of his bicycle and pedal as fast facing backwards as we could forwards."

Sightings of planes were rare, but while flying his kite one day in 1916, Johnny saw a Navy flying boat making its way along the shore. It had come from the Navy's new flying school, established in 1914 in Pensacola, and was headed in the direction of New Orleans. Johnny talked about it for days.

One clear March afternoon just at sunset, Celeste stepped off the streetcar that ran along the beach between Biloxi and Pass Christian. She noticed a boy flying a kite and recognized it was her son, Johnny. *That boy and his kites.* Celeste was about to call Johnny when the kite caught her eye. It was made from white butcher paper. The reflection of the sun, now a great orange ball touching the far western horizon, flashed for just a moment on the white kite fluttering down on a dying breeze. For just an instant, the kite appeared to burst into orange flame as it fell rapidly to earth.

Celeste felt a cold shiver of fear and called to him, "Johnny Robinson! You get yourself home! You got more to do than sit down here playing with a kite and dreaming 'bout airplanes and such foolishness."

Johnny gathered his kite and string and approached his mother.

"You get your mind off all that and put it on your schoolwork and making something of yourself. Daddy Cobb is working extra to put up money for college for you and your sister, and so am I. You're nearly fourteen, old enough to get your attention on important things."

Caught by surprise and hurt by the scolding, Johnny was confused. "Why you so mad at me, Momma? What did I do?"

Celeste couldn't answer. Her anger had covered the unexplained feeling of fear she had felt watching the kite fall against the flaming orange sun sinking into the Gulf of Mexico. She put her arm around John. "I'm just tired, I guess, and I'm gonna be late with your Daddy's supper if we don't get on home. Here, you carry the groceries and I'll carry the kite."

"Momma, I'm workin' hard at school."

"I know you are, son. Your daddy and me are gonna do everything we can to help get you to Tuskegee Institute, but you got to help, too. You old enough to get a little work on your own.

"And you gonna have to put away all that dreaming 'bout flying. The truth is, no black man got any business fooling 'round with airplanes."

Johnny took the bag of groceries and walked silently beside his mother across the streetcar tracks and shell road and on north past the neatly painted frame houses of the white middle class that lived south of the L&N Railroad tracks. Presently they crossed the tracks into the Big Quarter with its mixture of small frame structures, some painted, some with bare weathered siding, and some with tar paper nailed to their sides. Few had grass lawns in front, though nearly every one had a small garden and a chicken pen out back. Here and there along the way there was an occasional small enterprise: a corner grocery, a used clothing shop, maybe a barber or beauty shop, a small general store, a café, a bar or two. In a converted frame house across the street from the Cobb home was the J. T. Hall Undertaking Company, which had just opened.

As they neared the corner, a boy about ten came by rolling a tireless bicycle wheel down the street with a stick. "Hey Teddy, Teddy Collins!" Johnny called to him. "Come here! I got something for you."

Teddy controlled the wheel with his stick so that it made a perfect turn over to where Johnny was standing. "Hey, Johnny. What you got?"

"How do you like this kite I made?"

"You make the best kites 'round here."

Johnny took the kite and string from his mother and handed it to Teddy. "Here. You take it. And don't you let it get hung up on no trees."

Teddy carefully took the kite with one hand, put the ball of string under his arm, and held the rusty bicycle wheel with the other. "Man, thank you, Johnny." He smiled and started across the street, yelling to a friend half a block away, "Hey! Osborne Barabino! Look what Johnny give me. Look at this, man!"

Celeste said, "You didn't have to do that, son."

It was dusk when Celeste and Johnny reached home. Charles Cobb was sitting on the porch.

"Where ya'll been? I was starting to worry, not to mention get hungry." He laughed. "Bertha and me even got the stove hot."

"I'm sorry, honey. I'll warm up some gumbo and some hot French bread." Celeste took the bag of groceries from Johnny and walked to the kitchen.

From a small cloth bag, Charles Cobb shook a little tobacco onto a cigarette paper, curled the paper around the tobacco with his free hand, lifted it to his lips, licked one edge of the paper, and pressed the edges together to make a cigarette tapered at both ends. Holding the cigarette in one hand, he lifted the little tobacco bag to his lips with his other, grabbed the drawstring in his teeth, pulled it tight, and stuffed the bag into the top pocket of his bib overalls. Charles took a lucifer match from his pocket, lit it off with his thumbnail, and took a satisfying drag.

"Nothing better than your momma's gumbo. What you got to say for yourself, Johnny?"

"Nothing, Daddy, except I'm gonna look for work to help with my school money. I figure I can keep up with my chores 'round here and still shine shoes at Union Station."

Charles eyed Johnny. "You and Momma must a been talking mighty serious like."

"Naw, Daddy. I just figured it's time I did something on my own. And I'd like to go with you to the shop, too, learn more 'bout machinery and things. Maybe I could help sweep up."

Charles stood up and put his arm around the stepson he loved as his own. "That would be fine, son. Now let's go in and light a fire. I think it's gonna be right chilly tonight. Maybe after supper you can read me the paper 'bout the war and how our boys are doing over there. Might be a story 'bout those airplanes fighting in the sky. This world's in a real mess, but some mighty interesting things happening. You keep up with things, Johnny. This old world's changing, changing for colored folks too. Yes sir, you keep up with it boy. Now let's go see 'bout supper."

Every morning Johnny walked the short distance to the three-room school he attended on Thirty-Second Avenue where grades seven through ten were taught. High school only went to the tenth grade. It was a wood frame building in need of paint. Inside it was clean, the bare wood floors smelled of linseed oil. In the center room there stood a large potbellied stove. On the coldest days, the center room was always too warm and the two rooms on either side too chilly. There were black boards, worn thin, on the walls of all three rooms. The schoolbooks were dog-eared hand-me-downs discarded by the white schools. A one-room building next door, called The Annex, served as the elementary school for grades one through six.

After school all the next week, Johnny looked for a spot with busy foot traffic where he could shine shoes. What he found was that all the best spots at Union Station were already spoken for by a healthy number of shoeshine boys, most of who were older than John. Then he discovered that his friend Collins was shining shoes at the OK Shoeshine Parlor on Fourteenth Street downtown. John applied to the owner, Mr. Sam Alexander. The small shop was a five-seat shine parlor and newsstand, and Mr. Alexander cleaned and blocked men's hats. John got the job and Collins showed him how a "professional" shined shoes. The shoeshine men weren't paid by the customers. The shine men would give the customer a token in a color assigned to them. The customer turned in the token and paid for the shine at the store register. The shine men were paid a percentage in salary for each of their tokens turned in. John figured the small salary plus tips was better than nothing.

Robinson was always interested in machinery and spent any time he wasn't shining shoes helping a mechanic who had a shop in his neighborhood. The man taught John to drive when he was fourteen. It was a task for which he quickly developed both skill and judgment.

In 1918 John turned fifteen. He was tall, carried himself well, and was a good student. One spring morning, he wore his Sunday suit to school.

In the school yard a young girl named Miomi Godine ran up to Johnny. "You're sure dressed up, Johnny Robinson, just like when you walk me to Sunday School. What you dressed up for?

They were joined by a boy Johnny's age wearing bib overalls, but no shirt or shoes. "Yeah, John, you gonna shine up to the teacher, or you been struck by love or something? You sure ain't gonna play no baseball after school in that getup."

"Now don't you go messing with me, Ross. I'm dressed up 'cause I'm going to town after school to look for me a summer job, something better than shining shoes. School gonna be out soon." Johnny turned to the girl. "Miomi Godine, you get yourself over to The Annex where you belong and don't make nothing out of me walking you to Sunday School. The only reason I do it is 'cause my momma and your momma are friends and ask me to look after you. Now you get! I don't want no smart mouth from you either, Ross."

"Aw man, I don't mean nothing. How come you always gotta be so serious?"

"I just got things I gotta do, and getting me a summer job is one of 'em."

Two weeks passed before John got what he considered a real job. He had impressed Mr. C. A. Simpson who owned a ship chandler business. When school let out for the summer, Johnny was first assigned to the warehouse where he did anything from sweeping to unloading and loading trucks. Mr. Simpson learned John could drive. He had just lost a driver to the army.

"You think you can handle that?" Simpson pointed to his 1917 REO stake bed truck.

"Yes sir, I can."

Simpson told John to get up in the truck, got up beside him, and ordered, "Let me see you drive around town and then down to the port and bring me back here."

John did and got the job driving the truck all that summer and every summer until he finished college. He was responsible for loading the truck with ship orders for parts, marine hardware, and groceries, delivering them dockside, and taking new orders while he was at the port. It was a job that required driving skill, accountability, and dependability. John excelled at it.

Halfway around the world, another young black man was busy at his first job. The young man was twenty-six-year-old Ras Tafari Makonnen, second cousin to Zaudith, the daughter of the late Menelik II and empress of Ethiopia. Ras Tafari had been appointed by the ailing Zaudith to be the ruling regent of Ethiopia, still known in much of the world as Abyssinia and before 1000 BC as Aksum. Fate would one day place the two black men together, the first to serve the second, the second to place his life in the hands of the first.

Chapter 3

Northbound

BY THE SUMMER OF 1920, THE GREAT WAR WAS A BAD MEMORY. Johnny had come marching home victorious. America was settling in to a joyous peace, gleefully entering the prosperous, anything goes Roaring Twenties—the age of short-skirted flappers, jazz, prohibition, bootleg whiskey, speakeasies, automobiles, and barnstorming pilots.

At seventeen, John Charles Robinson carried himself confidently with a warmth about him that made him immediately likeable. In 1974, looking back some fifty years, different contemporaries, including Miomi Godine, Osborne Barabino, and Teddy Collins, described him in these terms:

"Kind, good at sports. He played on our baseball team."

"Johnny was the best at everything he did."

"I wanted to be just like hm."

"He was dependable, always there to help others, an all-around guy."

"Johnny was serious sometimes, but when he laughed, there was honest joy in it shared by all around him."

"He never started trouble, got along with everybody. He was a leader."

Most Sundays, Johnny attended the African Methodist Episcopal Church, a small building at the corner of Thirty-Second Avenue and Twenty-First Street. The minister of the AME church, Pastor Lanoa, was also John's school principal. He recognized Johnny as an exceptional student and encouraged him to follow his parents' desire for him to attend Tuskegee Institute in Alabama.

On a Sunday afternoon in late August of 1921, Johnny walked aimlessly down Thirty-First Avenue all the way to the beach road. The Gulf waters sparkled under a blue sky laced with fair weather clouds. The breeze filled his lungs with the clean, salty scent of the sea. Thoughts about leaving home for the first time weighed heavy. *I'm gonna miss that water and the fishin' and swimmin' out there. Ain't nothin' like it up in north Alabama.*

Johnny turned east toward town, paying attention to the surroundings as if seeing them for the first time . . . or the last. *Leavin' a place you know and love is harder than I reckoned now that it's almost time to go.* He passed the electric power plant at the foot of Thirtieth Avenue. Heavy black smoke billowed from the towering chimney. Behind the plant was the car barn where the town's streetcars were maintained. To the south he could see the harbor filled with steamships and tall-masted sailing ships, most taking on loads of lumber, some loading cotton bales. Since the Great War, steamships were beginning to outnumber the graceful, tall-masted barks, brigantines, and schooners that called at the port. Streetcars were running back and forth out to the grand pavilion at the end of the East Pier. Sunday strollers dressed in their best moved along the boardwalk parallel to the streetcar and railroad tracks. Men wore hats and ladies carried parasols for protection from the sun. John passed the ice plant where blocks of ice were being loaded into insulated boxcars that would transport vegetables and oranges, gathered from the outlying farms, all the way to Chicago. Johnny picked up a chip of ice and chewed it as he walked east across the front lawn of the Great Southern Hotel that faced the Gulf.

At Twenty-Fifth Avenue, he turned north to the center of town. On Sunday afternoons he had always liked to go downtown to watch the increasing number of automobiles. They were beginning to replace horse-drawn buggies and wagons just as steamships were replacing those powered by sail. Miller Tire and Gasoline Store stood not far from Alexander Livery, Harness and Vehicle Company. There were even two motorcycles in town.

Johnny turned off Twenty-Fifth Avenue at the Parlor Drugstore and walked west on Fourteenth Street past a restaurant. Black people were not allowed in the dining room, but they could buy a meal if they went down the alley to the back door. He walked on past the Hewes Brothers Building, turned on Twenty-Seventh Avenue at the Inn Hotel and crossed over to Union Station where signs lettered "White Only" and "Colored Only" marked separate waiting rooms. The station was always a center of activity—locomotives moving through, wagons and trucks loading or unloading, people coming and going, some being picked up or let out by the station taxi that ran between the station and the Great Southern Hotel as well as to businesses downtown. Between the G&SI and the L&N railroads, some twenty-two trains a day now stopped at Gulfport, passenger trains at the station and freight trains that rumbled onto sidings alongside loading docks. The air was heavy with the mingled odors of steam, burning coal, and heavily oiled machinery.

Soon it's gonna be my turn to get on one of those trains and leave this town. It's a good town with mostly good folks. Ain't been no trouble like I hear there's been in the Delta.

Johnny knew that he would have to leave the comfort of the familiar behind, and the thought troubled him. He had never been further out of Gulfport than Biloxi to the east and Pass Christian to the west. He was tall, black, leaving home, and a little afraid.

The September day he left for Tuskegee, Celeste Cobb packed Johnny's freshly washed and pressed clothes into a small worn trunk, the same one she had used when she traveled from Carrabelle, Florida, to Gulfport so many years ago. Just before closing the trunk, she tucked in a small Bible and a little extra house money she had been saving. Then she went to the kitchen and put sandwiches, cookies, a polished red apple, and a Mason jar, filled with iced sweet tea and wrapped in newspaper for insulation, into a brown paper bag.

"Charles," she called. "We better go. He can't miss his train."

Celeste and Charles Cobb, Pastor Lanoa, and many of Johnny's friends walked to Union Station with him. For all of them, this was a big occasion. He was one of only two young black men in town leaving for college.

Celeste hugged him. "I'm gonna miss you, baby. You be good and write to us, you hear?"

His father shook his hand. "Do the best you can, son. I know we'll be proud of you."

John, dressed in a new suit, shirt, and tie, pushed his trunk up onto the landing and climbed the iron steps of the coach, the one marked RESERVED FOR COLORED ONLY. He waved from an open window as the train pulled out of the station.

"You can cry now, Momma," Charles Cobb said as he wiped the corners of his eyes. He offered his arm to Celeste. The two of them turned to walk home.

"Our boy is leaving, but I'm so proud we're sending him to college. You a good man, Charles Cobb."

They crossed the tracks silently, arm and arm, Charles limping on his bad leg, Celeste in her best go-to-meeting dress.

John Robinson watched the countryside slide by as he gazed out the open train window. The Colored Only coach was at the front of the train just behind the baggage and mail cars. A little more soot and smoke from the engine filtered through the open windows into the front car set aside for blacks, but John didn't think much about the dirt and grime collecting on the window sill. He liked being up front where he could hear a great, rumbling symphony—the rhythmic puffing of steam driving the piston rods, the great steel driving wheels click-clacking over rail joints, the whistle sounding at crossings. It was fire and steam, steel and motion, and it took his mind off leaving home and the anxiety of what lay ahead.

John had read about Tuskegee. He knew the school was founded by a man born a slave in Virginia, a man who at age sixteen walked almost five hundred miles to get an education at Hampton Institute in 1872. The man was Booker Taliaferro Washington. In 1881 he opened a school with thirty pupils in a church. Because of him, Johnny was on his way to that school that had grown into Tuskegee Normal and Industrial Institute. Booker T. Washington died in 1915, but an equally famous man was a resident professor there. His name was George Washington Carver whose research in agricultural chemistry resulted in his election as a fellow in the Royal Society of Arts in London, an honor only a handful of Americans had earned at the time.

Watching the scenery slide past his open window, John saw an automobile turn off a rutted farm road onto the clay-gravel highway running parallel to the railroad tracks. It was a cut-down Model T. The auto had no top and the windscreen was folded down flat. The goggled driver, bent low over the steering wheel, tore off down the road to race the highballing locomotive. He was giving it all he had, kicking up a swirling trail of dust and scattering chickens along the way. Ever so slowly the train pulled away.

Won't be long before automobiles be outrunning this train. Robinson leaned out the window and waved.

Johnny's daddy had told him that now that the war was over, the automobile was the coming thing. John believed him. And though he did not mention it, he believed something else was coming too. Airplanes! Yes! He had seen more than a few flying down the coast the last two or three years.

At Tuskegee, John paid his entrance fee of two hundred dollars plus eighteen dollars for the first month's fee for room and board due the first of every month during the school year. At the time, these fees represented about thirty percent of the yearly average income (twelve hundred dollars) for a steadily employed, skilled male worker.

John's dormitory roommate was Joseph Flowers. In an interview in 1974, Mr. Flowers stated that John was a top student. "We had fun at the occasional social activities at the college." When asked if John partied at school, Mr. Flowers said, "John was a dancer, liked the girls, but I never saw him drink or smoke." He also said there was a very short Christmas break at Tuskegee and that most students remained on campus. "We didn't have the money to pay for travel home. We hardly had money to give each other presents. I think I spent a dollar and ninety-five cents on a book to give Johnny. When either of us got a package from home, cookies and things, we shared them. Money was tight but Tuskegee was a wonderful place. Everyone was friendly, and there was never any trouble. I think everyone loved it."

John chose to study a new technology: automotive mechanical science. After the Great War, automobiles were all the rage. Only the wealthy were able to afford the expensive, powerful, handmade brands, but Henry Ford, with his revolutionary assembly line and Model T, made the automobile available to the average working middle class. In a relatively short time, the automobile industry had become the largest in the United States. By 1921 there were well over seven million automobiles registered in the United States with the largest concentration in the big cities.

John traveled to his college by steam engine and, for the last several miles, by a mule-drawn wagon. By the time he graduated, three years later, he and his classmates had studied mechanical theory, internal combustion engines, automotive electrics, mechanical drawing, and they had assembled a real automobile, rebuilding the engine, chassis, transmission, drive-train, suspension, and electrics. In addition to their chosen trade, all students studied mathematics, English literature, composition, and history.

An average student in English, Robinson had a natural mechanical ability that distinguished him from most of the other students. Although he finished near the top of his class in mechanical science, he was so quiet and serious at school that years later some of his classmates had a hard time remembering John C. Robinson until they saw his picture in the newspapers. It can be said that young ladies didn't have as hard a time remembering John. Most took note of the tall, quiet student from Gulfport. His shy but self-confident manner and winning smile would not only serve him well in business, but would also charm the ladies, young and old alike.

During the summers, John worked for Mr. Simpson at the ship chandlery and saved his pay to help his parents with his next year's school expenses. Still, he wasn't all work. There were social activities and dances where the young people got together. One girl in particular caught Johnny's eye. Her name was Janette Sullivan. She was a pretty Creole young lady from Pass Christian. Janette played jazz piano so well she became a member of the Tuxedo Band, which performed along the coast and even in New Orleans. She and John would remain friends throughout his life. On his occasional trips home, she always brought him a chocolate cake, his favorite.

On a wonderful day in 1924, a proud Celeste and Charles Cobb sat in the audience to watch their boy graduate from Tuskegee. They had worked hard for this day and John knew it. His mother cried happy tears. His daddy felt a little taller and limped a little less when he walked up to John, put his arm around him, and said, "Son, no man has ever been more proud of his boy than I am of you today." His parents had every reason to be proud. What they didn't know was that there were very few men, young or old, white or black, who knew more about the workings and intricacies of automobiles and internal combustion engines than their son.

They all returned to Gulfport that summer of 1924. John was glad to be home. His mother's gumbo, pies, collard greens, and ham tasted even better than he remembered. It was good to see his friends, including Janette, but the longer he stayed, the more restless he became. He would leave the house in the morning, come home for lunch, and leave again in the afternoon. Charles Cobb could see that something was troubling him; John talked less and less.

One day Charles asked his son to sit with him out on the porch. Celeste brought out two big glasses of sweet iced tea and then returned to her kitchen. Charles took a sip of tea and opened the conversation. "You did so fine at school and now you're sitting in the right seat. The streets are beginning to fill up with automobiles, especially those Model T Fords. There's gonna be plenty of work for an automobile mechanic."

"That's right, Daddy, but not for me, not here in Mississippi."

Charles glanced up quickly. "Why, son, there's more than three garages here in town."

"And I've talked to every one of 'em and to the ones in Biloxi, too. That's what I've been doing all day every day: going up and down the whole coast looking for a job. They'll give me a job sweeping, filling gas tanks, changing tires, or washing, but I'm an engine man. All the automobiles belong to white folks. When I talk to the garage owners about automotive science they smile, look at each other, and then look at me like I belong behind a mule with a plow. The last thing they want is a black man knowing more 'bout automobiles than they do. I just don't think I'm gonna get the chance here at home to do what I know I can do." He spoke quietly, telling the facts as he saw them, the truth as he understood it. "I could work full time for Mr. Simpson, but that's not what I went to school for."

"Son," Charles replied, "me and you are colored, can't change that, but there are some good white folks here that will give you a chance if you'll just give 'em a little time to recognize what you know, what you can do. I don't exactly sweep floors over at the railroad shop. You know that. And your Momma and I haven't done too bad. We own this house, don't owe but a little on it. We educated you and your sister."

John's sister was now a well-regarded teacher.

"I know, Daddy. I'm grateful to you, and more proud of you and Momma than you can ever know. But I want my own business one day, and I can't do it down here. How many blacks here have cars? How long would it take for whites to take their business to a black man, leave a white business for a black man's garage?" There was no answer from his father. "I'm going to Detroit, Daddy. That's the center of automobile science. There's a friend from school I can stay with till I get started."

John reached over and laid his hand on his father's knee. "You gonna help me tell Momma?"

Charles Cobb stood up. "I been helping you tell your Momma things for a long time, son. I guess we better go on in and tell her together."

Chapter 4

Taste the Wind

AFTER ARRIVING IN DETROIT AND SETTLING IN WITH HIS FRIEND from Tuskegee, his first priority was to get a job. He didn't anticipate what a difficult task this would be. Although there were scores of small automobile manufacturers scattered around the country (there was even an attempt to start one in Gulfport), Detroit was the center of the growing automotive industry. As a result, job-seekers, white and black, were pouring into town.

By 1924 Detroit had a large black population. Most were migrating from the rural South and were unskilled. John discovered that blacks in the North were expected to "know their place" pretty much the same as in the South. There weren't "colored only" and "white only" signs posted, but there were restaurants and hotels that simply turned away black customers. He had grown up around that sort of thing. He hadn't let it bother him much at home so he determined to ignore it "up North."

John spent every day looking for a mechanic's job. Many of the places where he applied had openings, just not for him, or at least not jobs where he could use his skills. Johnny was determined to get a job as a mechanic and turned down offers for work as a "sweeper" or "errand boy" or "clean-up man." But he found himself a minority within a minority: a black man college-trained in automotive technology. Try as he might, he could not convince garage bosses that a young black man from Mississippi had arrived in Detroit already highly trained in the field of automotive mechanics. He wasn't arrogant or uppity when he applied for a job, but the fact that he had a diploma proving that he had learned his trade in college was often resented by white men who had learned the trade in the school of "skint knuckles" or spent long hours with little pay as apprentices. The truth was that Robinson was more knowledgeable than many of the people to whom he applied for work. He knew and understood internal combustion engines backwards and forwards—engine blocks, cylinders, pistons, valves, rods, crankshafts, carburetors, magnetos, generators, oil and water pumps, clutches, gears, axles, radiators, gages, electrics, etc. He could read engineering drawings and diagrams.

Finally, even with free room and board at his friend's house, what little money he had ran out. He took the best offer he was given, that of mechanic's helper.

There were three mechanics and a manager who doubled as a tire and parts salesman. There was also another young black man that pumped gas, swept floors, emptied trash cans, and washed cars—the kind of job John had often been offered. Robinson found that of the three regular mechanics—all white—one was friendly, one ignored him, and one was openly hostile toward him. He also discovered that the new "mechanic's helper" got to do a lot of tire changing and was mostly called upon to do work on the automobiles of occasional black customers, members of the small but growing black middle class. He spent most of his time as a "pair of extra hands" and "tool fetcher" for the other mechanics.

After several months on the job, the mechanics in the shop began to admit two things about John Robinson. The first was that he was good at what he did. The second was that they were learning more than a few things from him. There was never a complaint about his work. Customers, including a growing number of whites, began to ask specifically for him to work on their cars. Eight months after he started work, the word "helper" was dropped from his job title and he discovered more money in his pay envelope.

Things were looking up for John C. Robinson. He now owned a car, or rather a lot of parts he had bought from wrecking yards, repaired, and assembled into a car. He moved from his friend's house, thanking the family for putting up with him and offering them money, which they refused. He took up residence at a boarding house, which cost four dollars a week and included breakfast.

One day, a man stopped by the garage and asked to speak to the black mechanic.

John walked out front, wiping his hands on a rag. "I'm Robinson."

The man was dressed in work clothes, wore a leather coat, and looked to John a little on the rough side. "I'm told there's nothing you don't know about engines."

John stood quiet for a moment. He wasn't sure the man wasn't being sarcastic. "I'm a good mechanic."

The man handed him a slip of paper. "Here's an address. My boss has heard about you, been looking for somebody that can keep his taxis and trucks running. Stop by after work and talk to him. You get the job . . . it'll pay a lot more than you make here."

Robinson thanked the man. After work, he looked up the address he had been given. It was an old, brick building in the warehouse district. Centered in the front was a vehicle entrance with tall, wide double doors. Loading docks ran along the street on both sides of the entrance. Except for the street number, there was no sign on the building. Johnny walked inside and saw a few taxis and two large delivery trucks.

"Hey! Hold it, buddy! What you doing here?"

John saw a heavyset man wearing dusty wool pants, a dark sweater, and a grease-soiled driving cap. He had a thick neck, a big nose, and bushy eyebrows.

"I was told to stop by here to see about a mechanic's job. My name is Robinson, John Robinson."

"Oh, yeah. The boss is expecting you." He didn't offer his name.

John followed the heavyset man through the cavernous building into an office with glass windows overlooking the garage floor.

"Boss, this here is the mechanic you sent for."

The boss sat behind a large oak desk. He had gray hair, was overweight, and wore wire-frame glasses, a white dress shirt, a tie, loose at the neck, and suspenders. A suit coat matching his trousers and a felt hat were hung on a clothes rack in a corner. There was an electric fan mounted on the wall to the left with a calendar hanging below it. A large blackboard showing some sort of scheduling was on the wall to the right. A gas heater was against one wall. Robinson stood before the desk. The boss remained seated. Papers were scattered over the desk and there were several cigar stubs in a large ashtray.

"A couple of people I know say you're not a bad mechanic, better than average. That's saying something in Detroit, especially you being black."

"Yes, sir. Thank you, sir."

"I could use somebody like you."

John remained silent.

"How much they pay you over where you work?"

John told him.

"That's an honest answer. I already knew what you make. You told me something different trying to jack me up, you'd be outta here."

"Yes, sir."

"I need a mechanic that really knows what he's doing. I got one good mechanic with a helper, but they can't keep up with the work no more. Business growing, see? I got three trucks and eight taxis. I plan to add on another truck and four more taxis. When they need fixing, they need fixing right and fast. Trucks and taxis don't make me a dime sitting in this garage, see?"

"No, sir. I reckon not."

"I tell you what. I'll pay you twice what you been making. You keep 'em running and you got a solid job, provided you show up on time and do the work eight till five, six days a week, and maybe nights sometimes if I need you. You want the job?"

"I'll take it, Mr. . . . " John paused.

"You just call me Boss."

"Yes, sir. Boss. I should give my old boss two weeks notice."

"I like that. Loyalty. But if you want the job, you start next Monday. One more thing. I don't like my business getting out on the street. My people keep their mouths shut. You understand what I'm saying?"

"Yes, sir."

John's old boss said he would be sorry to see him go, but that he could not compete with the pay. Then he said something John thought was a little peculiar.

"Johnny, I know the money's good, but don't do nothing for Fitzgerald other than keeping his taxis and trucks rolling. Don't drive for him, don't poke around in his business, and don't ask questions. Just keep a tight lip and do your job."

John had not known that his new boss's name was Fitzgerald, but he was quick to understand the advice. After he went to work, he learned that Mr. Fitzgerald's trucks worked mostly at night. The drivers that brought them in for work or picked them up didn't have much to say. It was pretty easy for John to figure things out. Prohibition had been passed in 1919. Whiskey was illegal in the United States but not next door in Canada. He knew that bootleg whiskey flowed south across the Canadian border through Detroit—boat and truckloads of it. Around the garage no one gave him any trouble. He did his job, got along, rarely spoke. That earned him the sobriquet "tight-lipped Johnny." It also kept him out of trouble.

John put most of his pay in the bank. He moved into a three-room, cold water flat that had a bedroom, a tiny kitchen with a sink and an icebox, and a small sitting room. It was equipped with electric lights and had an oil stove for cooking and heating. There was a bathroom in the hall that he shared with the flat next door.

Robinson was not all work and no play. The girls knew Johnny was in town. On Saturday nights, in certain quarters of the town, John gained a reputation as a smooth dancer. In the flashy age of flappers, jazz, and speakeasies, the ladies were not slow to notice the tall, quiet, confident man who had nice manners, dressed well, and could make a girl look good on the dance floor.

For those who knew him, there was a certain restlessness about Johnny, a restlessness that seemed more than just the desire to succeed in his trade. He continued to learn and study. He built a bookcase in his flat and filled it with books and manuals on mechanics and those he could find about managing a business. A few books and magazines on aviation began to appear. John knew what was eating at him. During his years of school, he had put away what his mother had referred to as "that foolishness," but there was little he could do to keep his heart from jumping whenever he heard the sound of an engine overhead. He would look upward with the anticipation of a child at Christmas in the hope of catching a glimpse of an airplane winging its way across the sky. Now there were more airplanes and frequent news about aviation records being made—planes flying higher, further, and faster. John knew what was driving his restlessness. He just didn't know what he could do about it.

From what he read in the newspapers, only army-trained, barnstorming air-gypsies from the Great War, a handful of government and business leaders, and wealthy white playboys actually worked or played with aircraft. How could he learn to fly? He had asked around. Word was there were no black men even working on airplanes, much less flying them. There were plenty of people, black as well as white, who would tell you a black man wasn't capable of adjusting to the unnatural environment of flight or acquiring aviator skills—meaning they weren't smart enough to learn.

John first took his money out to Detroit City Airport where he was told "not a chance." The next weekend he drove out to the corner of Oakwood and Village Road where Ford Field was located. He couldn't get in the big hangar where they were assembling Ford tri-motor planes. He went down the line of private planes and begged to be taken for a ride, said he would pay, wash the plane, anything. He found that his daddy had been right when he said that the South was not the only place where a black man's money wouldn't buy the same things as a white man's money. It looked to John that what his momma had said years ago, what he had refused to believe, was true: Aviation was closed to blacks. All his life, ever since he could remember, Johnny Robinson longed to experience the joy and excitement and freedom he was sure was part of flight. He could not, would not, go all his life without somehow getting up there to find out for himself. *Somehow, I'm gonna fly.*

Despondent, John was walking past the Ford hangar when a man called to him, "Hey, boy." The man was wearing a pair of white, grease-stained overalls.

John didn't much like the term "boy," but he stopped. "You calling me?"

The man walked up to John. "I overheard you asking for a ride out on the line," the man said. "You're not likely to get a ride around here, but you might have a chance at one of the small fields out in the country. That's where barnstormers operate, away from government rules and regulations. Maybe you'll catch a fellow short of cash—most of 'em are. A guy like that might look more at a man's money than the color of his skin."

"Why you telling me this?"

"Because I used to be one of 'em, and because maybe I can still remember how I used to ache to get up in the sky."

"Couldn't you give me a ride?"

"I could, but I'd take a lot of flack around here for doing it. Sorry, but that's just the way it is."

"Well I ain't gonna give up," John replied.

The man smiled. "I wish you luck." He turned and walked off toward a Model-T roadster.

John asked around. One of Fitzgerald's truck drivers mentioned that he had seen a sign about flying on the road out past Willow Run or Ypsilanti, but he couldn't remember which.

Early on a Sunday morning in April, John dressed in work pants, a sweater, and jacket—spring was laboring to push winter's chill from northern Michigan. He drove out of Detroit toward Ypsilanti on a clay-gravel highway. Out past Willow Run, he found what he was looking for: a sign pointing down a farm road that said "Airplane Rides." He turned off the main road and after traveling a mile or so came to an open field where a faded red, white, and blue banner strung on a drooping, barbed-wire fence invited one to "Take an Airplane Ride with an Ace." He pulled off the road, parked by the fence, and got out. A motorbike was parked under a tree but he didn't see anyone around. John followed a well-worn path leading through a gate and around to the front of a large, weathered barn that had been converted into a hangar. The roof sagged a bit. He could see three airplanes inside, or rather two and a half since the one on the right, shoved toward the back, was disassembled. The fuselage was standing alone, missing its engine. Its wings were propped on edge against the back wall. John recognized that one and the one nearest him, which had all its parts but didn't look much better. They were both Curtiss JN-4Ds, better known as Jennies.

It was the third plane, bright red and clean as a whistle, that caught his eye. It was the most beautiful thing John had ever seen. He called out and got no answer. Nobody was around so he walked into the hangar to get a closer look. John moved carefully around the wing tip and stood by the rear cockpit of the red plane to look inside. He surveyed the instruments, the rudder bar, control stick, seat belt, everything so different from an automobile. The name WACO was painted on the vertical part of the tail. He walked back to the front of the plane. From pictures in one of his books, he figured the engine as an OX5 water-cooled model, the same engine that powered the Jenny beside it only this one was mostly hidden by a streamlined cowling. *Well, at least airplane engines are not so different from automotive engines I've worked on.* While he was admiring the plane, he heard a car drive up and two car doors open and shut.

"Hey! You, boy! What the hell you doing fooling around that plane?"

Startled, John swung around to face a short, heavily built, redheaded man with grease stains on his face. He was dressed in soiled khaki pants and a leather jacket. Walking up behind him was a younger man, cleanly dressed in polished riding boots, riding britches, and a blue sweater over a white shirt and tie. He was holding a jacket slung over one shoulder. The young man had a smile on his face. The redheaded man did not.

"Well, boy?" The redheaded man spoke with an Irish brogue.

"I came out here to get a ride. I didn't see anyone around. I was just looking. I didn't touch anything."

"A ride, eh? You come all the way out here to get a ride did you, boy? Would that be because they don't give rides to niggers at big city airports?"

The fact that what the man said was true hurt John as much as the grossly offensive word "nigger." John, outwardly quiet, had never been one to look for trouble (friends later couldn't remember a single fight he had been in except when in the boxing ring at school), but he did have a temper once provoked. He struggled to hold it now. "Look here, mister. I just came out here to pay for an airplane ride. I got the money same as anyone else. I want to see what it's like, that's all."

"Aw, come on, Percy. What the hell you being so grumpy for?" the young man asked. Looking at John, he said, "Percy here has had a bad week. His engine is down." Turning back to the redheaded Irishman, he offered, "Come on, Percy, drop the whole thing. This fellow didn't mean anything. Follow me back into town for a beer."

"Why not? I won't be making a dime standing here." He turned to follow the younger man, then turned back to Johnny. "The field's closed. You came for nothing. Don't you be messing with anything, boy. Time you be going back where you came from." He once more turned and walked away, following his friend.

"Hey! Wait a minute!" John called after them. "What's the trouble with the engine? Maybe I can fix it. I'll do it for a ride."

The two men turned to face Robinson. The one named Percy asked, "Now what would you be knowing about an airplane, boy, seeing as how you never been around one before?"

"I got a name and it ain't 'boy.' I'm John Robinson, and I don't know anything about flying, but I know something about engines. I'm a trained mechanic."

"Sure you be." Percy started walking again and rounded the corner of the hangar.

"Percy," the younger man said with a laugh. "My father's opinion of all Irishmen is that they are butt-headed, rude, and think with their fists instead of their brains. You trying to prove him right?"

"I'll tell you what, sonny. I'll be buying me own beer and you can take your new toy and shove it in someone else's hangar."

John hadn't moved. He could hear them talking though they had disappeared around the corner of the barn.

"Come on, Percy. You can't afford to buy a beer or anything else. You're down to one worn-out Jenny with an engine problem. You're too Irish proud to let me help you out. You can't get a flying job around here because you got drunk and took your boss's daughter flying . . . under a bridge for Christ's sake. And now you won't even find out if maybe this guy is telling the truth and can put you back in business in time to make a few bucks this afternoon."

Percy stopped, looked at his companion. Without a word, he turned and walked back around in front of the hangar. "All right, Robinson. Tell me what kind of mechanic work you do."

"Automotive," John replied.

"And just how did you get to be a mechanic?"

"Three years of college. I been working nearly two years in Detroit. I put together that car parked out there by the fence, rebuilt the engine."

"Have you done any brazing work and can you get an outfit?"

Johnny nodded 'yes' and answered, "I can borrow an outfit from the shop in town."

Percy picked up a stepladder leaning against the wall, walked over to the engine of his Jenny, and set the ladder up. "Climb up there and look real close at the neck of the radiator under the filler cap." Johnny climbed up as he was told. "You see that hairline crack right there near the top?" Percy pointed at the spot.

Johnny nodded. "Looks more like a scratch than a crack."

"That's why it took me so long to find it. You start it up and everything works fine. You taxi out, take off. About ten or fifteen minutes into the flight, the engine runs rough and then quits. You glide down and land somewhere, get out, and look it over and find nothing. You prop the engine, it starts right up like nothing's wrong. I found I had to add a little water the next day. That made no sense. Next day it quit in the air. It was a real thrill for the passenger, I tell you. I could start the engine again, takeoff, and ten minutes later it would quit again. I couldn't get out of gliding distance from this cow pasture. Finally, I tied the tail to the fence, cranked the engine, set the throttle at about eight hundred revolutions per minute, and let her sit there and run. That's when I saw the trouble. As soon as this thing gets good and hot, that tiny crack opens up and water spews out of it in a fine spray that blows over the engine from the prop wash. It shorts out the spark plugs, and then the engine starts missing and quits. When it did that while I was flying, by the time I got it down the water had evaporated, the engine had cooled, and that hairline crack was closed up. That's why I couldn't find the trouble. Anyway, boy, you get that brazing outfit out here and fix this thing and I'll give you the ride you want. But you mess up, burn a hole in the radiator, I'll put more than a hairline crack in your water jacket. You understand me? You better know what you're doing or don't fool with it."

John didn't care much for the ill-tempered Percy, but he figured he had a chance to do two things. One was to fly for the first time. The other was to show the redheaded bastard that a black mechanic could put him back in business. He looked at Percy.

"It's a deal. It will take me a while to get to town and back, but I'll fix it for a chance to fly."

It was three-thirty in the afternoon when they rolled the faded yellow Jenny out of the hangar.

"Well Robinson, your work is pretty enough. Now we'll see if it holds. You stand there while Robert gives the prop a twist. You'll do that for me, will you, Robert?"

While working on the radiator, John had learned that Percy's friend, Robert Williamson, was fresh out of Harvard and had returned to Detroit to work for his father. Percy had taught him how to fly, a fact Robert's father still did not know. Robert had paid for his flying lessons and bought the red WACO-9 with money his grandfather had left him, also without his father's knowledge.

Robert walked up to the prop. "This is your first lesson, John. This is the end that will bite you if you're not careful. Watch and learn."

He called out, "Switch off! Throttle closed!"

Percy called back, "Off and closed."

Although the Jenny's tail skid would generally hold the plane in place while the engine idled, the plane had no brakes. Should the throttle be inadvertently left open while cranking, the plane, even with a wheel chocked, could easily run down anyone standing in front of it. The results would not be pleasant.

Robert pulled the propeller through several times. "Switch on! Contact!"

Percy cracked the throttle open a little and repeated, "Contact!"

Robert put both hands on the big wooden propeller, swung his right leg up toward the plane, and, in one fluid motion, swung the leg back as he sharply pulled the prop blade down. The momentum of his right leg swinging out behind him twisted him around and carried him away from the propeller. From there, a couple of steps and he was safely to the side. After three attempts, the engine coughed, burped, and roared alive with a belch of blue smoke, then settled down to a more or less smooth rumble, idling at around 450 revolutions a minute.

Robert pulled the chock from in front of the left wheel and grabbed hold of the outer wing strut. He motioned for John to do the same on the right wing. Percy, after checking to see that his "anchor" men were all set, advanced the throttle. The engine roared, the grass behind flattened in the prop wash, dust and loose leaves swirled behind while the plane shook from wing tip to tail. Robert and John had to dig their heels in to keep the plane from dragging them forward. After what seemed to the two "anchor" men a lot longer than ten minutes, Percy closed the throttle, pulled the fuel mixture control to the Off position, and switched off the magneto. The field was suddenly quiet. Percy jumped down, grabbed the ladder, and ran around front to check the radiator.

"Dry as a bone. 'Tis a good job, Robinson."

John hardly had a chance to break into a grin before two carloads of chattering young people drove up.

"Hey, Percy! Quit fooling around over there. I've brought my Sunday School class out to take a ride with you."

The voice belonged to a young lady waving from the running board of a shiny touring car that had parked by the fence.

"Come on, Percy dear, all six of us want a ride." She stepped down from the car and came through the gate followed by three other girls and two young men.

"Sue said you shot down a German in 1918. Is that true, Mr. Percy?"

Percy tried to not look embarrassed. The more he tried, the closer his face came to matching his flaming red hair. He took a handkerchief from his back pocket and wiped at the oil stains on his face and hands.

"Young lady, 'tis too pretty an afternoon to talk about such things. Sue, why don't the lot of you draw straws to see in what order you'll be flying while we get some fuel." Percy motioned to Robert and Johnny to follow him over to where two metal barrels were lying on a wooden rack. He picked up a five-gallon can equipped with a spout and began filling it from the petcock of one of the barrels.

"Come on," Johnny said. "I mean, what about our deal? I've done my part."

"So you have," replied Percy. "And I'll take you up, but I can't do it right now. Can't you see the situation here? I mean, I can't take you for a ride and make them sit over there and wait. Can't you understand what I'm saying?"

"I understand what you're saying. You're telling me you can't make that nice white Sunday School class wait around while you take a nigger for a ride."

Percy turned blood red in the face, and Robert stepped between the two men.

Percy hissed, "Damn you, boy. Can't you understand anything? If I hadn't given you my word on this deal, I'd split your head wide open for a crack like that. Look at 'em. Six people over there, each one with five dollars for a ride. That's thirty dollars! I can buy a brand new surplus OX5 engine for fifty dollars. Hell, there are more people waiting over there than I flew all last week because of that damn radiator."

Johnny looked past Robert straight at Percy.

"Look," said Percy, "I got six dollars in my pocket. You take all six dollars for fixing the engine or you come back when I ain't got a line of paying passengers waiting."

Johnny looked more humble than angry. "I don't want your money. I want to fly. I want to fly more than all those people over there. I been waiting to fly all my life."

"And I need that thirty dollars to stay in business."

"Okay. Both of you listen," Robert J. Williamson III broke in. "Percy, you go fly the Sunday School, and I'll take our friend John here up in my plane in exchange for two hours of lessons in stunt flying from you." He turned to John. "Robinson, will you settle for thirty minutes or so with me for free instead of ten minutes with him even though I'm too young to have any Germans to my credit?"

All three men exchanged glances. Robert was the first to smile. Percy looked quizzically at Johnny, who was looking over his shoulder at the red biplane waiting in the hangar.

In spite of the hurt and anger he had felt moments ago, he broke into a wide grin and laughed out loud. "You white boys just made yourselves a deal."

Robert and John helped Percy top off the Jenny and strap his first passenger into the front cockpit. The warm engine caught on the first swing of the prop. To a round of applause, the Jenny waddled off over the grass, bumping and bouncing as it gained speed. After only a few hundred feet it lifted into the air, labored to clear the trees at the end of the field, and turned gracefully away, free and clear.

"All right, John, help me roll out the WACO." Robert motioned for John to move behind the right wing and push on the outer wing strut while he did the same on the left. Compared to the maze of bracing wires and multiple inter-plane struts that braced the wings of the Jenny, the WACO-9 was a sleek, uncluttered design. As did many such post-war designs, the WACO used the same Army surplus, ninety horsepower, Curtiss OX5 engine as the Jenny. The reason was simple. Although it was heavy, 390 pounds not including the radiator, it was both plentiful and cheap. Compared to the Jenny, the WACO-9 was smaller, lighter, and had a strong steel-tube fuselage, all of which gave it far better performance. With its glossy new crimson paint, it was beautiful. Robert Williamson had used $2,475.50 of the rather sizable sum his grandfather left him to pay for it. Of the ninety-one hours of flying time to his credit, the last forty-seven had been logged in the WACO.

"John, walk around her with me and I'll explain anything you want to know while I check things out. I haven't had one problem with her yet. I had six forced landings in that damn Jenny, four of them with Percy and two by myself. That taught me to always keep an eye out for a clear place to land." He pointed to the radiator. Unlike the Jenny that had the radiator attached to the front of the engine, the WACO's radiator was mounted just under the center of the upper wing. "Hasn't leaked a drop yet. Of course if it does, hot water will blow back on the passenger and pilot, but mounted up there it likely won't short out the ignition. It does interfere with forward visibility, you have to look under it and over the nose, but you get used to it. "

Robinson asked so many questions that Robert finally protested, "If we don't get going, Percy will have us fueling up the Jenny again and acting as ticket takers. Besides, for a fellow who's never flown, you seem to know a lot about planes."

"I guess I been reading 'bout airplanes as long as I can remember, but this is as close to one I've ever been. Now it's really gonna happen. I'm gonna fly."

Robert grinned at him. "Not if you don't get up in that front cockpit. Step up on that black step pad there on the wing and swing your legs on in. Put on that pair of goggles hanging on the throttle. I don't have an extra helmet. Here, I'll give you a hand with your seat belt."

When Robert was satisfied that John wouldn't fall out, he instructed him on what to touch and what not to touch and explained the flight controls. Then he reached in the rear cockpit to make sure the magneto switch was off and the throttle closed. He walked around front, turned the propeller through eight blades, walked back around, climbed up on the wing, reached in the cockpit, cracked the throttle open a bit, and switched on the single magneto.

"John, remember, when she catches you close the throttle like I showed you and hold the stick all the way back. Otherwise this thing might run over me and take you God knows where. Now, you got it?"

"I got it!" John was more excited than he had ever been in his life. He was also a little afraid, but he managed to look calm. At least he thought so.

"Relax, John. If you don't loosen your grip on that stick, your hand is going to turn as white as mine." With that, Robert jumped off the wing and walked around front.

"Here goes." Robert grabbed the propeller blade with the fingers of both hands, called, "Contact!" and gave the blade a hefty swing, careful to stay clear of its arc. The plane rocked slightly but nothing else happened. The second attempt woke up the OX5. It spit, belched a little smoke, and settled down to behave itself with a smooth, rhythmic 450 revolutions a minute.

Robert climbed back up on the wing and leaned over Robinson. "While we're up I'm going to let you try your hand. If I wiggle the stick like this," he moved the stick quickly side to side several times, "it means you can take over and fly. If I wiggle it while you have it, you let go so I can take it back. When that happens I want to see both your hands held high to let me know you understand. I don't want you freezing up with a death grip on the controls. That could kill us both. Understand?"

John nodded that he did.

Robert continued. "I won't be able to hear you, so if everything is all right after we do a maneuver, put your thumb up like this. If you don't like it, shake your head from side to side. If you want to come down, point down and I'll bring us back and land. You got it?"

John started to answer, then grinned and held his thumb up. Robert slapped him on his shoulder, climbed into the rear cockpit, fastened his seat belt, buckled on his flying helmet, and pulled his goggles over his eyes. He checked the oil pressure instrument. Satisfied, Robert taxied the plane toward the downwind end of the field. There he stopped and tested the controls. (A magneto check was not needed. Unlike modern aircraft, the OX5 did not have dual ignition. If it was running smoothly, then the single ignition was working. You didn't make a static power run-up check either—there were no brakes on the WACO. Instead of a tail wheel it had a tail skid, the only thing to slow it down on the ground.) Robert twisted his neck around to check the sky for traffic. He saw Percy lined up on final approach for a landing. The Jenny floated over them, settled to the ground, and taxied toward the eager group of waiting passengers.

Robert shouted, "You ready?"

John nodded his head and held up a thumb. He whispered to the breeze, "I been ready for this all my life." His senses were more alive than they had ever been. He felt the gentle rocking of the plane, the vibrations of the engine, the smell of hot oil wafting in the propeller wash—and the beating of his own heart.

Robert smoothly pushed the throttle all the way forward, feeding in right rudder to counteract the torque of the engine and the twisting flow of the propeller wash. It was the only way to hold a straight takeoff run. The wooden propeller bit into the air, washing the myriad odors of the roaring engine back over John as they rushed at the wind.

John tightly griped the sides of the cockpit, his view restricted by the plane's long nose still angled skyward. As the WACO accelerated, Robert eased the stick slightly forward to lift the tail. Looking forward between the high-mounted radiator and the top of the engine cowl, Johnny could now see ahead, see the grass turn into a green blur as it rushed ever faster beneath the plane carrying them ever closer to the trees bordering the field, trees scantily dressed in their new leaves of spring. The wheels now bumped and bounced along on the unimproved pasture. Robert eased back on the stick. The bouncing ceased as the WACO, its red wings turning golden in the haze of the late afternoon sun, climbed into the sky. The ride through the still air was as smooth as a mouse's belly.

John watched the field and forest drop away. Everything below, the hangar, the cars, the people, appeared miniature while the Earth itself expanded in every direction. He had never forgotten the excitement and joy of the child he had been that day long ago when he ran down the beach after the first airplane he had ever seen. That same childlike wonder and excitement rushed over him, filling him, fulfilling him.

They climbed 3,500 feet. John was glad he had worn a sweater and jacket. The crisp air was much cooler than it had been on the ground. Below he could see newly plowed fields, small lakes, and forest. To the northeast was the haze and industrial smoke of Detroit. On the far horizon, John could just make out Lake Erie.

The smoothness of the flight was interrupted by the rocking of the wings from side to side followed by smoothness followed again by the rocking of the wings. Johnny glanced down in the cockpit to see the stick wiggling from side to side. He tried to look back at Robert but his seat belt was too tight for him to twist around enough to see him. The stick wiggled again, this time with more authority. It finally dawned on Johnny, *He wants me to take it!*

John relaxed his grip on the sides of the cockpit and placed his right hand on the unfamiliar control stick. He wiggled it side to side. Instantly the smooth sure path of flight changed to a weaving, dipping track like that of a gentle roller coaster ride. The WACO was in unsteady, unsure, but willing hands. John Robinson felt clumsy and embarrassed by his awkward attempt to hold the craft steady. He could keep the wings fairly level but he could not keep the nose from climbing and dropping. He always seemed to be behind the plane, catching up only to over-control.

Then realization struck him. *I'm flying this thing! God Almighty! I'm flying!* He tried a turn using just the stick to bank the wings. The plane seemed to slide a little sideways. Then he remembered the rudder and put his feet on the bar and tried again using stick and rudder. He got a pretty good turn except he did not hold a steady altitude. When he turned one way the plane climbed and when he turned the other way he lost altitude. The path was still that of a gentle roller coaster, up a little, down a little, but he was flying. *Not too smooth but it's not falling out of the sky.*

The stick wiggled in his hand. John let go and held both hands up in the slipstream before taking hold of the sides of the cockpit once again. The flight steadied into a graceful, sure path as Robert took control.

The nose dropped smoothly. Wind began to whistle past the bracing wires between the wings as speed increased in a dive. Johnny's eyes widened at the sight of the earth coming up toward him. He tightened his grip on the sides of the cockpit. A few moments later, he was pressed deep into his seat as Robert pulled back on the stick bringing the plane's nose sharply up. As the horizon again came into view, John, still pressed firmly into his seat, felt and heard the engine roar to full throttle. The nose rose steeply past the horizon, past the vertical. The world was upside down. John was momentarily light in his seat as Robert relaxed a little back pressure over the top of a graceful loop. *Oh! Lord Jesus!* As the plane screamed down the back side of the loop he shouted into the wind, "God Almighty!" Once again he was pressed into his seat and felt his cheeks sag a little as Robert pulled out of the back side of the loop to level flight.

"Yeah! *Oh yeah*!" John hollered. He held up both hands with his thumbs straight up. Robert laughed and performed another loop followed by a sweeping barrel roll.

After nearly an hour, the sun was low on the horizon when they entered the landing pattern and flew downwind parallel to the field. John looked down to see the Jenny taxiing toward the hangar as the last of Percy's passengers moved along the fence toward their car. Robert gently banked the WACO, first turning base and spilling altitude, then turning upwind to line up on final for the landing. With the engine throttled back to idle, Robert brought the WACO over the fence. Easing the stick back, he held the plane just off the ground. As speed bled off, the WACO settled gently onto the grass, the main wheels and tail skid touching simultaneously in a perfect three-point landing. After a short roll, Robert taxied to the hangar, swinging around in one last blast of the propeller so that the tail faced the opening as he shut down the engine. The propeller ticked over a last few revolutions. Then silence, sudden and complete.

John sat in the cockpit almost afraid to move least he lose the moment and awake from a dream. His ears rang from the engine's roar. His body relaxed in the absence of movement and vibration. His goggles now felt uncomfortably tight and his bare head tingled from the wind buffet. His nostrils filled with odors emanating from the hot engine, dormant except for an occasional "tick" common to the cooling of a hot engine pot.

"Robinson? Robinson, are you all right?"

"What? Oh! Yes, sir!" Johnny replied. "I don't think I'm ever gonna get this smile off my face. I mean, there's nothing like it, is there? Nothing as free."

Robert grinned. "Now get down from there and help put this thing in the hangar."

Together they pushed the WACO tail first into the hangar and walked around the corner of the building in time to see Percy driving off with the young Sunday School teacher. Robert walked toward the motorbike parked near John's car.

"Hold on, Mr. Robert." Out of gratitude and respect for the man who had taken him on his first flight, John had reverted to his Southern roots and the way he would have addressed a white man back home. "Do you think I could learn to fly? I mean, well, I know I can learn, but can I get someone to teach me?"

"Sure. Why not?" Robert looked back at John. "Oh, I see." Robert paused. "You learned to be a mechanic."

"Yeah, but that was at a Negro college. Do you know any Negroes enrolled in flying school? Any being taught by private lessons?"

"Can't say I've heard of any. That doesn't mean there aren't any. I have a feeling that if you want to learn badly enough, you'll somehow find a way. I did even though my father tried every way he could to stop me. He owns a factory that makes coffins. He thinks I should, in his words, 'make the damn things, not fly one.' Every flying school in Detroit owes money to one bank or another. Dad happens to be on the board of the largest bank in the city. He and friends at the other banks made it clear to the established flying schools that they were not to teach me if they wanted to keep a line of credit. Airplanes are expensive. None of the schools would even talk to me. I did just what you did today. I came out to the country and found Percy. He didn't owe any bank because no bank would lend him money on that old wreck of his. I had a little money my grandfather left me so he taught me to fly."

"Trouble for you is Percy is leaving. The Jenny is outdated. Rumor has it that new government regulations are going to bar Jennies from any commercial use. They say the old Jenny won't pass the new government design and licensing criteria. All the schools are getting newer planes. Percy can't compete and he's broke. He's taken a job flying the mail out of New York. I think he's crazy. About twenty mail pilots were killed this past winter. Percy says he has to do that or give up flying and get a real job. I don't know what to tell you."

"Well, what about you? I can pay you. Would you teach me?"

"Me? I'm afraid I can't do that, John."

"Sure. I understand. Wouldn't look good to your flying buddies and society friends." Johnny turned to open the door of his car.

"Now you hold on. If you're thinking I'm handing you the nigger boy bit, you're out of line. I'll tell you something else. If every time you don't get the chance to do something, you think it's because you're colored, you're going to wind up using that as a crutch not to try. Sure, some people won't give you a chance, but some will. You'll just have to find them. As for me, there are two reasons I can't teach you. One, I don't have an instructor's ticket. Even if I could give you flying lessons, they wouldn't mean anything to the government and they wouldn't give you a license. Two, my WACO and I are leaving for Texas. I've got a job with a college buddy who's drilling for oil down there. That sounds better to me than making coffins. I think you owe me an apology, John. I'm the one that just took you flying, remember?"

Chastised, Johnny said, "I'm sorry. It's just that I been dreaming 'bout flying since I was a kid. I heard plenty of those 'Willie, get away from that wheelbarrow, you don't know nothing 'bout machinery" kind of jokes when I first started work as a mechanic. I took it cause I had to if I wanted to work. I guess I proved them wrong. I got white folks come to me now. I just don't like facing the fact that I gotta go through all that again with airplanes. I gotta fly. I'll do anything. I'll knock on hangar doors till my fists bleed."

"Look," Robert said. "You got a good paying job in Detroit. Do you think you could get one in Chicago?"

"Maybe. There are plenty automobiles there need fixing, I reckon. But why? Things are going good for me here."

"I was just thinking along your line, John. If you're going to get turned down by a lot of flying schools, you might as well start with one of the best. That's the Curtiss-Wright School of Aeronautics in Chicago. I think they teach aviation mechanics there, too. Maybe you could work days and go to their night ground school. There's a lot to learn before you ever get in an airplane. If you can get through a school like that, you'll be more likely to get some kind of aircraft mechanic or maybe flying job. That's an idea you can chew on, anyway."

Robert put his weight down on the foot crank of his motorbike. After a couple of attempts, it fired up. He put on a pair of goggles. Before leaving, he turned back to Robinson. "I think you have what it takes, Robinson. I really do."

John nodded his head in thanks. "I don't think you know what flying with you has meant to me. Just saying thank you is nowhere near enough, but I don't know how else to say it."

Robert grinned. "Oh I know what it meant. There's not a pilot alive who doesn't remember his first flight." He switched on his bike's headlight, nodded a smile, and disappeared down the dirt road into the falling darkness.

John sat alone on the running board of his car. In the stillness of the early evening he could hear all the sounds of the country, so different from the noise of the city. Away from the lights, he could see stars popping out as darkness descended. It was spring and awakening insects chirped their mating calls. A cow bellowed somewhere in the distance. Nearby, a sudden whirring announced some winged night fowl was on the hunt. It was a peaceful place to get his thoughts together. There was no way to justify, much less explain to anyone, why he would even think of giving up his job to go to Chicago on the chance he might somehow get into not just a flying school, but the best in the Midwest. His friends would think him a fool.

Sitting there he came to two conclusions. The first was that his Momma was right a long time ago when she had said that it was foolish for a black man to think about flying. The second was that as soon as his boss could find a replacement, he was going to take his foolish self to Chicago. He shook his head, laughed, and climbed into his car to drive back to Detroit.

***

Back at the shop on Monday, he was taking a break out front when a shiny new Pierce-Arrow sedan stalled on the street right in front of him. The driver tried several times to restart the car without success. The back seat passenger and driver, both black men, got out and walked to the front of the car. The driver opened the hood and both driver and passenger stood in the street pondering the situation. John walked out to them, introduced himself as a mechanic, and asked if he could help.

The passenger turned out to be a doctor and the owner of the car. The three men pushed the car to the side of the street, and then the doctor, without so much as a thank-you, told John, "No one is to touch this car until I can get my mechanic here. Is there a telephone nearby? I need a taxi."

Although not the least bit pleased at being dismissed in favor of some mechanic from clear across town, Robinson told the doctor his boss had a taxi company and there was one ready to leave the shop. The doctor returned to his car, told his chauffeur to wait for the mechanic, and, glancing at Robinson, repeated his instructions that no one was to touch a thing on his car. A few minutes later he left in the taxi

After nearly an hour, the doctor's mechanic arrived. John walked out to see the mechanic the doctor had prescribed to fix his new car. The mechanic's name, John learned, was Cornelius Coffey. The introduction led to a discussion between a rather sarcastic Robinson and a somewhat indifferent Coffey who made it clear he did not need any help. Things could have gone downhill from there except by chance aviation was mentioned.

As the conversation progressed, Coffey told John how he became interested in flying. "One day in Newport, Arkansas, where I was raised, I toted a five-gallon bucket of gasoline all day long between a barnstormer's Jenny in a pasture and a country store half a mile away. White folks paid the barnstormer for rides in the Jenny. Just before dark, when everybody else had left, the barnstormer paid me with the ride of a lifetime. He let me take the controls a little bit. I could barely see out the cockpit but I made up my mind I would fly some day. That day ain't come yet, but somehow it's gonna."

The two men discovered they shared a dream so far denied them. That led to both men working together to troubleshoot and fix the problem with the doctor's car. It was the beginning of a lifelong friendship.

Chapter 5

Chicago, 1927

ONE OF JOHN ROBINSON'S TRAITS WAS DEPENDABILITY. HE remained at his job until a satisfactory replacement could be found, which took almost a month. Before he left, Mr. Fitzgerald called him into the office. "You do good work, Robinson, and you know how to keep your mouth shut, you know what I mean? I got contacts in Chicago that could use a guy like you. Money would be good. What do you say?"

Johnny had to admit the money had been good, but he had been bothered by the fact that he was working for an outfit that, besides running taxis, transported bootleg whiskey after it had been smuggled across the Canadian border. *What would my Momma and Daddy think if they knew that?* He hadn't done anything illegal exactly, but he thought it would be better not to have his name going to any of Mr. Fitzgerald's contacts in Chicago. He had read about the bootlegger wars in the Windy City.

"I thank you, Boss, but I've saved my money and believe I can start my own small shop there. That's what I'd like to do."

Those friends of John's who knew the real reason for his move to Chicago thought it was a crazy notion. Giving up a good job and moving to a new city on the chance you can get into a flying school? They thought it was plain nuts. Perhaps among the most disappointed at his departure were several young ladies who had set their sights on Johnny.

John Robinson was never foolish about anything. Determined, independent, smart, often stubborn, he was also possessed with enough common sense to temper his dreams with sensible priorities. In Chicago he took a room on the south side and transferred his savings to a local bank.

After two weeks of looking, he found a small vacant building that had at one time been a combination livery stable and blacksmith shop. It needed work but was suitable for conversion into a small mechanics garage and the rent was right. John set to work. He modified the rear blacksmith shop area that faced an alley with a door large enough to drive a car through and fitted a wide double door onto the front of the building with a window on one side. He purchased a professional mechanics tool set for twenty-five dollars, a welding/cutting set for ninety-five dollars, and a bench vice and electric grinder for four dollars total. He used wire fencing to enclose a storage area for parts and built a long workbench along one wall. The last item he purchased was a sign that said Robinson's Auto Garage. With pride, he hung it on the front of the building. He was nearly broke, but for the first time he had his own business.

John slept on an old army cot on the second floor, really an attic that had been used for storage. Working nights after closing, he converted the area into living quarters. He gradually furnished the big room with a bed, table, chair, and couch, all bought second hand. He built bookshelves across one end. At the other end he installed a sink, an oil stove, water heater, and icebox. In one corner he walled in a small bathroom with a bathtub and a sink that he had to bend over to use because of the slant of the roof. He did all the work himself using materials bought from a wrecking yard. John knew he would need better quarters come deep winter, but it would do till it got so cold he couldn't stand it.

At first things were more than a little slow, but with the help of a few friends from Tuskegee and others he had met in the neighborhood, a little business began to trickle in. Most of the customers returned. It was evident to them that the quiet young man from Mississippi knew what he was doing. In the beginning, all his customers were black. Many of them could only afford to purchase used, run-down cars that needed a lot of work. By word of mouth, news got around that the work was good and the price was right. After a few months, white automobile owners began coming to his shop. Robinson's Garage was going to make it.

John hired an assistant named Jules Tuggle. As chance would have it, Tuggle had moved to Chicago from Mississippi. He was a self-taught mechanic, but John found him competent. Most important to John was having a trustworthy helper. It would give him a chance to get away for a couple of hours now and then.

Robinson splurged and spent twenty dollars on a new suit and pair of shoes. He wore the outfit the first time he applied to the Curtiss-Wright School of Aviation located on South Michigan Avenue. His application was turned down. Not easily deterred, he kept applying. But each time his application was turned down. They never said being black had anything to do with it, and they had various excuses: "The classes are filled up"; "You just missed the beginning of a new class"; "Try us next spring."

John had heard it all before. He was angry but he could hold his temper when he tried. The rejections made him all the more determined. He discovered that Curtiss-Wright was starting a Saturday night ground school. He had left his home in Mississippi because, as he told his daddy, the only work he was likely to get at an automobile garage there was a sweeping job. Now he applied for and got a sweeping job Saturday nights at the Curtiss-Wright school. It wasn't easy. Curtiss-Wright had a janitorial staff that worked during the week. John convinced them they needed one man part-time to clean up evenings on the weekend because they were starting Saturday classes and would need clean rooms to begin regular school on Mondays. He told the building manager he needed the job for extra money and would do it for whatever pay was offered to him. The building manager was impressed. John got the job and was paid twenty-five cents an hour for four hours work Saturday nights. On the way home, after his first night shift, Johnny laughed at himself. *What would Daddy think if he knew I begged for a sweeping job in Chicago?*

There was method to his madness. He would close his shop late Saturday afternoon and rush out to Curtiss-Wright and tidy up all but the room designated for the ground school. Just before class John would enter the classroom and quietly do a little dusting and sweeping at the back. No one paid him any mind. The small class filled less than half the rows at the front of the room.

John listened to every word of instruction. After the class was dismissed, he copied the notes, drawings, and figures that had been left on the blackboards before finishing up the cleaning, emptying the waste baskets, and sweeping the hall before heading home. The class members rarely took notice of him at the back of the room, but the instructor could see him. John approached him the first night and explained why that particular classroom was the last on his cleaning list. He was fortunate that the instructor had a sense of humor. Without his cooperation, John would have very likely been dismissed from his job.

Sometimes the instructor would note John's presence during class. He might look to the back of the room and say, "You got that, Johnny, or are we moving too fast for you?"

The students would look back with amusement to hear John's reply. "No, sir. I'm ambidextrous. I can move this dust cloth and my mind at the same time."

With friends who shared his interest in aviation, John established the Aero Study Group. On Sunday afternoons the group would meet and he would pass on the knowledge he gained while sweeping the back of the Curtiss-Wright classroom the previous Saturday. The field of aviation was growing daily, but was virtually closed to blacks. Nevertheless, John Robinson was determined not only to find a way to enter the field but help others do the same. He would share his knowledge and skills with others for the rest of his life.

John's friend from Detroit, Cornelius Coffey, would often commute to Chicago to meet with the study group on weekends and talk about the possibilities of learning to fly. One day Coffey suggested that the study group needed a project. Why couldn't they build an airplane? It seemed a wild idea at first, but the more the group talked about it, the more they convinced themselves they could do it. There were advertisements in aviation magazines for plans for home-built airplanes. John and Cornelius pooled their money and ordered a set of plans for five dollars from the Heath Airplane Company. They also bought a twenty-seven horsepower motorcycle engine off a wrecked bike and rebuilt it themselves. The Aero Study Group now had a real aviation project.

Chapter 6

But Will It Fly?

"YOU BEEN ACTING NERVOUS AS A CAT, JOHNNY. WHAT YOU SO UPTIGHT about? We almost have our plane ready to assemble and give a try."

"Cornelius, between you and me, that's exactly what I'm worried about. I agreed the project was a good way for all of us to learn more about aviation, but I didn't think about what we would do if we actually finished this thing. That's what's worrying me. You think about it. Everyone in the group has worked hard. They all studied, learned how to make the patterns, jigs and parts, covered the wings, rib-stitched the fabric, coated it with dope, and painted it. Now we're assembling the whole thing. After all the hard work, they gonna want to see it tried out. None of us can fly it. How we gonna find someone qualified and willing to fly it? Even if we do find someone crazy enough to try, I don't think we should let 'em. I mean, we don't even know if this thing will fly, do we? It could kill somebody."

"Well, we've been doing things right, following the plans, haven't we? Our figures check out on dimensions and weight and balance. The workmanship looks good, don't it?"

"Yeah, I believe all that. I'm proud of the job everyone's done. But trying to fly it? I got to tell you that scares the hell out of me."

"You and I rebuilt the engine. We know that's right."

"It runs all right, but I think it might not be big enough."

"Well all I know is everybody's excited about this thing. They've put in a lot of time and sweat. You know that. Some have worked every weekend and all their other spare time and chipped in money when they had it. I bet no other group like ours has ever built an airplane. It don't have to fly far—just get off the ground, you know, like the Wrights did. They didn't fly but about a hundred feet or so the first time but it counted. What you gonna tell 'em?"

"I don't know. Hand me that torque wrench. These propeller attachment bolts have to be tightened exactly right."

A few weeks later, John told the whole story to Bill Henderson, the night school instructor at Curtiss-Wright who had not only allowed him in the classroom, but also often stayed after class to answer his questions.

"Johnny, are you pulling my leg, or have you really built a plane?"

"Mr. Henderson, the group has built every part according to the plans we bought. Now they have it all ready to take out to a field this Sunday and assemble it. They expect me to find them a flyer to try the thing out."

"Now wait a minute, John. I think I can guess what you have in mind and the answer is not just *no*, but *hell, no!*"

"I'm not asking you to fly it, Mr. Henderson. I just thought maybe you could come out and see the thing. You know, look it over, inspect it, and tell 'em what a good job they've done. Then you could tell them there are a few things that won't pass inspection, maybe not their fault but something about the design, or the engine we're using, any excuse to postpone a real flight. They might be disappointed, but you'd encourage them to keep their interest up. Maybe if you told the school we built an airplane it'd help me at least get accepted into aviation mechanics school. Besides, if someone like you don't come out to see it, who at the school will believe a group of Negroes can build an airplane. "

"John, you're determined, if a little crazy. I give you that. Damn if I don't believe you."

John couldn't help but smile. "Does that mean you'll come out next Sunday?"

"It means I'll come out and look at the contraption, play your game, try to save your reputation with the group. I'll inspect the workmanship and make some comments. I'm going out there to satisfy my curiosity, that's all."

That next Sunday, the group carefully loaded the disassembled aircraft onto a stake bed truck to transport it out to the pasture they had rented for the day. John's entire study group gathered at the field. Cornelius Coffey, who usually rode the train, had driven the 260 miles from Detroit to be there. It was a clear day with fair weather clouds lazing against a blue sky. The fuselage, sitting on its main wheels and tail skid, complete with tail empennage, engine, and propeller was secured to the bed of the truck. The wings, carefully padded with quilts, were tied to the stake sides of the truck. They had one five-gallon can of gasoline. Once they were at the field, the group unloaded the fuselage and wings. Supervised by John and Coffey, they carefully attached the wings and bracing wires. With string, plumb bob, and tape measure, they rigged the wings and bracing wires as they had done on the first assembly back at the shop, and checked everything else at least five times. When they had finished, they put five gallons of fuel in the tank, all it would hold, and tied the tail to the fence. Several members of the group took hold of the plane while John hand-propped the propeller. After several attempts, the engine sputtered to life, scattering dust and loose grass and startling several of the members who had never actually been around an aircraft when the engine started. John squeezed into the tight cockpit—not an easy task—and checked to see that the controls responded freely and correctly. Then he advanced the throttle to full power. The plane, vibrating from wingtip to tail, tugged at the tether rope. Satisfied, John shut the engine down and climbed out. In spite of himself, he could not hold back a smile.

They had worked hard since morning. On the outside of the fence, more cars arrived as friends and relations came out for the big day. John paid no attention to them. He turned to the study group. "I want everything checked out one more time. Mr. Henderson said he would be here at three o'clock and it's almost two now."

There were no complaints. Every member of the group had done some work on the plane. They had cleaned, sanded, filed, drilled, sawed, sewed, glued, primed, painted, and assembled all the pieces into a slab-sided little monoplane made almost completely of wood except for the welded steel tube fuselage. During the weekends and evenings they had spent building their flying machine, each had taken a turn sitting in the cockpit even before the fuselage had been covered. Now they checked their work one last time. The plane was as good as they could make it.

John watched them, listened to their excited chatter. He was proud of the group and proud of their workmanship. He was also weighed down with worry. He and Coffey had conceived the project and paid for most of the materials. He had talked the group into studying aviation and building a plane. They had all worked hard and learned much. Now he worried about the outcome. Would the members ever be able to put their skills to use? His most pressing worry at that moment was knowing they all longed to see the plane given the ultimate test: to see if it would fly. He felt guilty for the deal he had made with Bill Henderson, a deal that would ultimately disappoint his group by telling them the plane showed good work but not quite good enough to actually fly. He never thought the whole thing would get this far. He felt terrible at the deception he was committing, but he sure didn't want the project to end with someone getting killed trying to fly the thing. He didn't think the small engine, all they could afford, was powerful enough to lift the weight of the plane and pilot into the air. Yet he knew he wanted to see the plane fly more than anyone there. He looked at his watch. *Well, it's quarter past three. Maybe Mr. Henderson isn't coming.*

A few minutes later someone shouted, "Here he comes! Here comes Mr. Henderson."

John saw a white man in a top-down Ford roadster kicking up a trail of dust on the main road. The car slowed, turned in the gate, and headed for the plane. *Well, God help us.*

They all escorted Mr. Henderson to their pride and joy, the culmination of over a thousand hours of volunteer labor. Henderson nodded to Robinson and began his inspection with a walk around the little craft. He stopped here and there to check a control surface, smooth his hand over the wings and tail, inspect a fastener, check a control wire tension, look carefully at attachments, inspect the firewall and engine mount, check the bracing wires and struts and their connections, examine the landing gear, look into the cockpit, move the control stick, and check the glued, wooden joints of the ribs and the welds of fuselage he could see through the inspection plates. Then he studied the engine installation, particularly the fuel and oil lines, magneto, and wiring. He asked to see the weight and balance calculations and looked at the mail-order plans.

After about an hour of inspection, he turned to Johnny. "This is the group you shared all you learned from sweeping up the back of my classes at night?"

John nodded his head. "Yes, sir."

"And this project was your idea and you oversaw all the work on this bird?"

The group that had been silent except when answering occasional questions from Henderson now gathered around to listen.

"Coffey and I did, yes, sir," John answered. "He and I did some of the work, but these people here did a lot of it."

"Well, to be honest," Henderson said, looking around at the group, "when you told me about this project, I really had my doubts. I expected to come out here and see some sort of crude kite thrown together with more enthusiasm than mechanical skill. Now I find the workmanship, in fact, the whole plane, is not bad at all. I have to tell you, I'm surprised. It's not a bad looking little plane, all things considered. Would you mind if I got in and taxied it around the field?"

In unison, the group answered for John. "No, sir! We knew you would like it."

John laughed and motioned to Henderson. "Help yourself."

Henderson was helped into the cockpit. He fastened the seat belt and familiarized himself with the simple controls. "Anyone have a pair of goggles?"

One of the group ran to his motorcycle, retrieved a pair of goggles, and brought them to Henderson. Henderson turned his Irish tweed driving hat around, put on the goggles, and called for a start.

"Switch off, throttled closed," called Johnny.

"Off and closed," replied Henderson.

John pulled the propeller through several times to prime the engine just as Robert Williamson had taught him that day at Willow Run. "Contact!" he called.

Henderson switched on the single ignition. "Contact!" he repeated.

John pulled the wooden prop down, stepping quickly away. The warm engine caught first try and settled down to a rhythmic putter. Bill Henderson motioned for the tail to be freed. The tether rope was untied. Johnny moved around to the cockpit and spoke into Henderson's ear.

"I don't know about this, Mr. Henderson. I thought you were going to find something wrong and this would be over."

"So did I, but I haven't found anything really wrong. Besides, I'm just going to make some taxi tests. I don't think this little engine will get this thing off the ground with me in it. Looks like a motorcycle engine."

"It is a motorcycle engine," John said.

"How much fuel do I have?"

"There's a little less than five gallons in the tank. Please don't do anything foolish, Mr. Henderson. And remember, this thing don't have brakes. All you got to slow you down is a tail skid."

"Look," Henderson said. "I'm supposed to be the expert here, remember? I'd be in a hell of a fix if I got hurt flying a contraption built by a bunch of African engineers, none of who can fly an airplane."

Henderson studied the few instruments in front of him: a tachometer, an oil pressure gage, an altimeter, a crude airspeed indicator, all of them old, used types from the Great War. A marine compass was fixed to the floor in front of the stick. Henderson motioned the group to get out of the way. Those holding the tail released their grip. Bill Henderson eased the throttle forward and the little plane began to move off down the field. He taxied off down the field, bumping along, kicking up meadow larks and flushing a covey of quail. He gave a little blast of power while feeding in a little right rudder and then a little left, turning down the field in an "S" to test the effectiveness of the rudder. When he reached the end of the field, he turned around and taxied upwind toward the group, increasing speed until he had enough to lift the tail off the ground. As he neared the little group he slowed down, waved as he turned around, and started down the field again, this time at a good clip. As he reached the end of the field, he once more turned upwind, facing the group at the far end.

John realized the engine noise had changed to a new level. It was making a high whining sound as it spun the flashing propeller at full power. He stared down the field as the small plane came toward them, growing nearer by the second. *Oh, Jesus! Don't do it, Mr. Henderson!*

Still some distance away, the plane lifted momentarily into the air. Henderson gently banked the plane from side to side testing the controls. The needle of the airspeed indicator passed fifty miles an hour. As he reached the middle of the field, Henderson made his decision.

"There he goes!" someone in the group shouted. "Hot damn! He's flying!"

"God Almighty, Johnny, we made an airplane!"

And then it was there, flashing over them. It wasn't exactly clawing its way into the sky, but it was flying. For the group, it was an emotional moment. Some of them had tears in their eyes.

John Robinson, his heart in his throat, was the most amazed of all. He was also scared to death.

Henderson made a shallow bank and flew completely around the field, staying within gliding distance of the grassy meadow. He waved as he once again came over the group. Carefully he turned downwind and eased the throttle back. Too far! The plane exhibited a high sink rate. It was close to a stall. Henderson quickly fed in more throttle. It took nearly full throttle to maintain level flight. Very carefully, using a shallow bank, he turned 180 degrees and lined up for the landing. He didn't trust the crude airspeed indicator and held a little extra speed. As the plane crossed the fence at the far end of the field, he was careful to correct a slight left wing drop with rudder only. He didn't want to risk stalling the wing with too much aileron drag. He eased back the stick for the flare and then pulled the throttle back to idle. The little plane dropped about a foot to the ground, bounced once, and rolled out across the grass with Henderson working the rudder to hold it straight. Once slowed to taxi speed, he continued on to the end of the field where a jubilant group of airplane builders waited. Upon shutting down the engine, he sustained cheers and slaps on the back wildly given by the excited crowd. They helped—practically jerked—him out of the cockpit. Every last member of the group pumped Henderson's hand vigorously, each asking more questions about the flight than he could possibly answer. Everyone was talking and shouting at the same time.

Finally, in desperation to get away from the crowd, Henderson frantically looked for Johnny.

Robinson was leaning against a fence post, his arms folded across his chest, a big grin on his face. Their eyes met. Henderson grinned and John laughed, his head shaking from side to side in mock disbelief.

Henderson walked over to him. Robinson reached into his back pocket and pulled out a pint of bonded bourbon, a rare commodity during Prohibition. "I thought maybe you would deserve a reward for coming all the way out here. I'd have gotten you a bigger bottle if I'd known you were gonna fly." He held the bottle out to Henderson. "You said I was crazy when I told you we had built a flying machine, but you must be just as crazy 'cause you just flew the thing."

Henderson opened the bottle and took a sip of the bourbon. He offered it to John who declined. "Thank you, but I don't much like the stuff."

Henderson took another sip. "Well, John, if a nigger can build an airplane," (Johnny's head snapped up in hurtful surprise) "then I guess I'll have to go back to Curtiss-Wright and somehow convince them that a nigger can fly one." He grinned, took another sip. "This is the real thing, Johnny. Where you get it?"

John shook his head. "Just don't tell anybody I gave it to you. They'll think I'm a bootlegger. You really think you can get me in the school?"

"If I do, John, you can expect to hear some of that kind of talk. Some will try their best to wash you out, or bait you enough to make you lose your temper and do something to get yourself kicked out."

"Won't be the first time. I can handle it. I've had plenty of practice with that kind of thing."

Other bottles began to appear among the crowd. From the trunks and rumble seats of the assembled automobiles, baskets of fried chicken, potato salad, boiled eggs, ham, cake, and other goodies emerged. It was a wonderful, happy afternoon.

A few days later, John learned there was one more hurdle he had to make before he could join a flying class.

Henderson told him, "John, I've got to tell you that in spite of my report and recommendation, there is still more than a little opposition and skepticism among the powers that be at the school. The class beginning flight school next week has finished ground school and their exams. The administration has agreed that if you can pass the written exam before next Monday, you will be allowed to join the flying class. No one in the administration thinks you will pass, and a lot of people here hope you don't. Can you do it?"

"I reckon I don't have much choice, now do I? But you know I haven't been hanging around nights sweeping up the back of your classroom for the money. I got lots of notes, the book you gave me, and a little time to study. I think I can do it."

"I think you can, too. One thing I didn't mentioned to the administration was that you have been doing more than cleaning up the classrooms. I think we should keep that to ourselves. Now if you do qualify, there will be people here that are going to be surprised and not very happy about it. You're going to get a rough introduction to flying by some guys who think they can give you more in the air than you can take. They plan to blame your quitting on you being colored. Do you get what I'm saying?"

"I been getting it all my life, but I ain't quit nothin' yet. When I was a boy in Mississippi, I was told that things were a lot different in the North, and I guess there are better job opportunities up here, but when it comes to relations with white folks, well I find the North and South aren't so different, 'cept maybe the South is more honest about it. I know you have stuck your neck out for me. I'm gonna do my best not to let either one of us down."

"Okay, Johnny. I guess that covers it." Henderson turned to leave.

"Not quite, Mr. Henderson."

Henderson looked back.

Johnny said, "I want to thank you, sir, for all you have done."

Henderson nodded and walked toward his car.

The following Thursday, John passed the examination with a good score. He paid in advance for his first few lessons and was scheduled for flying instruction two afternoons a week. He also enrolled in the aircraft mechanics course. His garage business was making enough to pay his flying fees, pay Tuggle, and keep the bill collectors from his door provided he didn't tire of canned beans, a little bacon, potatoes, and once in a great while a pork chop.

Chapter 7

A Twenty-Dollar Bet

JOHN ROBINSON REPORTED EARLY FOR HIS FIRST FLYING LESSON. He sat on a bench facing the flight line watching students practicing takeoffs and landings. Bill Henderson, walking toward the flight shack, saw him.

"It's a good day for flying."

John stood when he heard the familiar voice.

"The air is smooth, but remember what I told you, John. Your first lesson won't be. You're the first colored person ever accepted here and some of the guys don't like it. I won't be your instructor. We're given a list of students and you weren't on mine. I expect whoever draws you will try to shake you up, wring you out. Most think you'll quit after that. Don't. Just hang in there. If you get sick, get sick. Plenty have before you. But if you really want to fly, take whatever they dish out and you'll get through."

"I won't let you down, Mr. Henderson."

Bill nodded and continued toward the line shack to pick up his second student of the day.

John knew his passing the written exam had come as a surprise to the school's staff. He could tell by the grudging way he was informed he had passed. There had been no congratulations, no welcome to the school. "I don't know how, but it says here you passed the written. Pay your fees up at the front office. When you bring me the receipt, I'll give you a training schedule."

Johnny heard a voice behind him. "You have to be Robinson. I don't see any other nigger around here."

Robinson jumped to his feet, hurt, trying to hide anger, afraid to lose his chance to fly. He took a deep breath and turned around to face a tall, sandy-haired man he judged to be in his thirties. "Yes, sir, I'm Robinson."

"My name is Snyder. I want you to know I didn't volunteer to teach the first black at Curtiss-Wright. Your name turned up on my list. Some guys think it's going to be a big joke, and that the joke's on me. They're wrong. I'm not a very funny guy. If business was slow, I might put up with a poor student, nurse him along. But business is good. I don't turn out fly-babies like a factory. In the war, I saw more so-called pilots killed by lack of flying ability than by the enemy. My students learn to be good pilots or I don't pass them. I don't like clowns, Robinson, and I won't be made a fool by one. If you really want to be a pilot, I'll know soon enough, but if you're out here just to make yourself a big nigger with the girls on Saturday night, you better quit now and save your money. In the meantime, you'll call me Mr. Snyder. If you have anything to say, let's hear it now."

John shook his head from side to side and remained silent.

"What's that?"

"No, sir, Mr. Snyder."

"That's better. Follow me."

"Yes, sir."

Jack Snyder carried a paper sack. John followed him toward a biplane parked on the grass. After John conducted a pre-flight inspection of the plane and answered questions to Snyder's satisfaction, the instructor reached in the sack and pulled out a flying helmet and goggles. "This is yours. You'll be charged for it. Every student has his own. You'll notice it has nipple fittings on the ear cups connected to rubber tubes leading to a 'Y' fitting. When you get in the cockpit, you'll see a rubber tube leading from the front cockpit. Hook the tube to your 'Y' fitting. It's called a Gosport tube. Normally, each pilot has a speaking horn connected to the other pilot's helmet for communication. Notice that in this case, you do not have a speaking horn. I can speak to you, give you instructions during the flight. You cannot speak to me as I won't need your advice. If I tell you to take the controls, you do so and let me know you have them by wiggling the stick. At that time I'll tell you what I want you to do. If at any time while you have the controls I wiggle the stick, you will immediately release the controls to me. Is everything clear up to now?"

"Yes, sir, Mr. Snyder."

"It better be. I had a student freeze up on the controls once. He damn near killed us both. You've passed the ground school so I'm told. I assume you know something about what makes a plane fly and what the controls are for. You're going to take off, climb to thirty-five hundred feet, do some turns, some straight and level, climbs and descents, and some stalls in order to give you a feel for the aircraft, introduce you to all the maneuvers you studied in the book. Remember, if I wiggle the stick or you feel me on the controls, let me take over. Any questions?"

"No, sir."

"Then crawl into the rear cockpit. A lineman will give us a prop. I assume you know the drill."

Before getting into the front cockpit, Snyder checked to be sure John's safety harness was securely fastened. He motioned over a lineman, got in the front cockpit, and fastened his own seat belt.

The lineman called out, "Off and closed."

Snyder spoke into the Gosport tube, "Answer him, Robinson!"

John went through the starting procedure. "Off and closed."

The lineman called, "Brakes and contact!"

This training plane had a tail wheel and small heel brake petals on the floor beneath the rudder controls. John pushed the brake petals, cracked the throttle opened, switched on the magnetos and repeated, "Brakes and contact."

The lineman swung the prop. The air-cooled, radial engine caught after one or two smoky burps and settled down to a throaty, syncopated rhythm, giving off the peculiar hot oil smell John had noticed in Robert Williamson's WACO.

The faraway sound of Snyder's voice coming through the speaking tube instructed John to stay lightly on the controls through the taxi and takeoff.

Snyder began to taxi the plane in a snake-like "S" course down the field. "Notice with the tail on the ground you can see nothing directly ahead because the plane's nose blocks your vision. That's why we 'S' taxi so you can see ahead a few degrees off each side of the nose as we work our way forward. On the takeoff roll, as we gain speed, you push the stick a little forward to lift the tail. Stay off the brakes! Once the tail comes up you can see straight ahead over the nose. The same holds true for landing. Once you flare for landing, you won't be able to see a thing ahead. You'll have to use your peripheral vision to keep the plane rolling straight with rudder until it has slowed enough to taxi 'S' turns safely." Snyder's voice sounded funny coming through the Gosport tube as he continued to shout commands

Snyder let John try his hand at taxiing. The voice again, "Even out your 'S' turns, Robinson! You're all over the place!" Jack Snyder took back the controls. At the far end of the field he turned the plane completely around to check the sky for landing traffic. Satisfied, Snyder turned the plane upwind. "Stay lightly on the controls during the takeoff, get the feel of them," the Gosport voice ordered. Snyder advanced the throttle. The plane had hardly lifted into the air when John felt the stick shake. The voice from the little tube, shouting over the engine and wind noise, commanded, "You have the airplane. Climb to four hundred feet and turn to the left ninety degrees. Then climb to eight hundred feet and turn forty-five degrees to the right and climb straight ahead to thirty-five hundred feet. Don't let the nose get above the horizon and keep an eye out for other planes!"

John put his left hand on the throttle, his right on the stick, his feet on the rudder petals, and began a timid turn to the left.

"Use your rudder, damnit!" shouted the voice in his ears. "Watch the nose! You're letting it drop." A moment later, "Now the nose is too high."

Each comment was followed by an unmistakable firm corrective movement of the controls momentarily over-riding John's stiff, clumsy attempts to perform the maneuvers. After a period of too much up followed by too much down, John began to settle the plane into a more or less steady climb.

"Robinson," the little voice returned. "Don't you think we could stop climbing now? We're at four thousand feet. I told you to level off at thirty-five hundred feet. Ease off that throttle and get back down to thirty-five hundred." There was a pause, then, "Don't dive it, damnit!" It was followed by, "Now you're climbing again. Get this thing in a glide and hold it with a steady airspeed! Show me you know the difference between a glide and a dive."

With much effort at changing altitude while watching for traffic and checking the altimeter and airspeed every few seconds, John found himself proudly flying straight and level at thirty-five hundred feet. The feeling was short-lived.

The commands came fast and often. "Turn to the right. Rudder, damnit! Use the rudder! You have to use the rudder and the stick together. Now turn left. Watch the nose! Use the stick! Get this thing back to level! Look at your airspeed, for Christ's sake! You're supposed to be at thirty-five hundred feet, so get the hell back up there!"

John was sweating and doing his own share of swearing, more at himself than at the voice that constantly assaulted his ears over the roar of the engine.

"All right, Robinson, let's try a few stalls. You studied about stalls in the book? Too little airspeed and/or too great an angle of attack and the wings

stall. Remember? You now have the opportunity to study them up close."
Johnny felt the stick move back. The plane changed from level flight to a
nose-high attitude. "Okay, you take it and hold it there." The stick wiggled.
John grasped it and put his feet back on the rudder pedals. "When you feel
the plane buffet and the nose begin to drop, remember to move the stick
forward, get the nose down, add power, and get the wings flying again.
You've got the airplane."

John felt it was the other way around. The plane began to buffet and
suddenly the nose fell out from under him. At the same time, the left wing
dropped and was followed by a sickening descent that left John's stomach
somewhere above. His eyes wildly stared over the nose straight down at the
earth.

His first reactions were all wrong. He jerked back on the stick, forgot to
push in the throttle, and tried to pick up the low wing with aileron instead
of rudder. He felt a great desire to wet his pants.

The voice again, "Get that nose down! Give it full throttle! Get this
thing flying again! Use a little rudder. I said a little! Get off the ailerons!
You put in too much rudder or aileron in a stall and you'll wind up in a
spin, maybe on your back."

John pushed the stick forward. With the earth rising rapidly toward
him, it seemed an unnatural thing to do, but he did it and held the stick
there. He got off the aileron and remembered to use a little opposite
rudder to get the low wing level. The airspeed began to build and he was
flying again but in a dive. He eased the throttle back a little.

"All right. Now ease the stick back and get us level again."

With the ground still rushing up at him, John pulled the stick back too
rapidly and too far. The G-force of the pullout pushed him down in his
seat; his cheeks began to sag.

"Ease it, damnit! You jerk back on the stick like that in a high speed
dive and you'll get a secondary stall or pull the wings off this thing."

John eased the stick pressure and found himself in straight and level
flight. He was much relieved—for the moment. For the first time he looked

out at the beautiful sky and the green fields below. The tension in is mind and body began to fade. He was flying!

Then the voice came at him again. "Okay. Now let's try a power-on stall from a climbing turn, shall we?"

Robinson's stomach, which had only just caught up with him, tightened in a knot as he reluctantly eased the plane back to altitude. Following instructions, he found himself at full power in a steep climbing turn to the left. When the buffet began and the nose dropped, John thought he would be ready—terrified but ready—and he was. He got the stick forward, left the power at full, and managed to catch a wing drop, bringing the plane back to normal straight and level flight. *Oh! Please let's go home now.* He was worn-out.

"That was better," the voice said. "Now let's try one to the right."

John groaned and felt his stomach do a flip. As instructed, he pushed the throttle full forward and began a steep climbing turn to the right. This time, just as the plane began to buffet, Snyder slammed the right rudder pedal full forward. The plane whipped viciously over on its back. The nose dropped straight toward the earth, which began spinning rapidly before the wide-eyed stare of the panic-stricken Robinson.

John couldn't help but cry out, his shout torn away into the screaming wind. He felt himself pressed down into his seat. He could barely hear the amazingly calm voice from the tube. "Rudder, damnit! Left rudder! We're in a spin to the right. Neutralize the stick! Pull the throttle back! Do it now! You hear me, boy?"

The "boy" got through to him. John shouted in his mind, *I'm not a nigger, you hear me?* Anger overcame fear and John's mind began to work again. He pushed in full left rudder, relaxed back pressure on the stick, and pulled the throttle off. At first nothing happed. The plane continued its sickening rotation as it spun toward the earth. Panic clawed at him but he held opposite rudder and neutral stick. It's what the book said to do. The rotation began to slow. Another turn and the plane stopped spinning, airspeed increased, and with shaking knees and hands, John eased the plane back to level flight.

"All right," the voice said. "There's the field over there to the left. I'll take it now. You follow me through on the controls and pay attention to the landing pattern, left downwind at eight hundred feet, turn left base down to four hundred feet, turn final for the last four hundred feet. You got that? And don't forget to look for traffic. I don't care to die in a midair collision. And keep your feet off the brakes."

John released what had been a death grip on the stick. He was covered in sweat. His mouth was dry as cotton. He could feel the convulsions rising up from his stomach. He leaned over the edge of the cockpit and vomited in mixed agony and relief. The spittle was sucked from his lips by the slipstream rushing past. The contents of his stomach flowed back down the fuselage. Spittle spread over his chin, cheeks, and nose like rain over a windshield. He wiped his mouth with his sleeve and wiggled the stick to let Snyder know he was still willing to fly. Surprisingly, Snyder let him fly down to landing pattern altitude before taking over. Robinson kept his hands and feet on the controls to get the feel of landing.

John hardly remembered the touchdown and taxi to the flight line. The sudden silence after the engine stopped snapped him back to time and place. The flight was over. He was relieved, but his arms and legs felt so heavy, he wasn't sure he could pull himself out of the cockpit. He unfastened his seat belt and removed his helmet. He struggled out of the plane and climbed down from the wing, his clothes stained with sweat and vomit.

Snyder stood before him, calm, neat, dressed in immaculate khaki jodhpurs, white shirt, black tie, leather jacket, and polished brown boots.

"Same time day after tomorrow, Robinson. That is, unless you decide to quit."

John looked at the instructor. "I been wantin' to fly all my life, and if I can't learn to fly because of you, Mr. Snyder, then I'm gonna learn to fly in spite of you and all them that thinks I'm a joke."

To John's surprise, he thought he detected a slight smile on Snyder's face.

"You just might do that. Now go get that bucket and rag over there by the hangar and clean off the side of this airplane. You're pretty much a mess, too. If you want to leave by the gate, I'll log you in, save you a little embarrassment. Next time, bring a paper bag with you."

"Thank you, Mr. Snyder. I won't need no paper bag. I'm gonna be a pilot."

"Day after tomorrow, Robinson."

Snyder turned and left John alone with a very messy airplane. It didn't matter. John felt a little shaky but determined to have his dream. He filled the bucket with water, picked up the rag, and began to clean the airplane.

John had intended to catch up on work at his garage after his flying lesson, but he was worn out and still felt a bit queasy. To avoid any friends who might be hanging around to hear about his first flying lesson, he took the back stairs to his room and crawled onto his cot. Staring up at the unpainted ceiling, he couldn't shut down the voices arguing in his mind. One kept telling him that flying wasn't worth feeling so bad, that he couldn't go up again and go through that spinning misery. Somewhere a voice echoed in his mind. *Look at you! You can't even make your supper, much less eat it. They ain't gonna let a nigger learn to fly. Whoever heard of such a thing?* But another voice cried out, *You gonna stick it out! You gonna fly, damn it!* Finally the voices stopped. John drifted off to sleep.

There were other voices that afternoon, voices at the flight line shack. A group of instructors and a few students were sitting around, some filling out log books, others drinking coffee.

"Did you see that nigger cleaning off the side of the plane? Snyder must have put him through the wringer."

"Hell, that must've been them I saw spinning. I thought they were out of control and might go in."

"If Snyder put him through it, I don't think we'll see any more nigger students out here. Snyder wasn't too happy when he drew him, you know."

"I got twenty dollars says the nigger never shows up for another lesson. Anyone want to cover that?"

From a chair over in the corner, Bill Henderson said, "I'll take ten dollars of that bet."

"Hell, Henderson, from what I hear, it's your fault he made it this far. Anyone want to put another ten bucks on the nigger?"

From the doorway someone replied, "Yeah. I'll cover the other ten."

Everyone in the room looked toward the door to see Snyder reaching into his hip pocket.

"Here's my ten, Smitty." He handed the bill to one of the men up front. "Pass it back to him." Snyder turned to the blackboard to check the day's schedule, then walked out the door toward the flight line for his last student of the day.

Robinson did show up for his next lesson and for every one that followed. Snyder dropped his sarcasm, never used the word "nigger" again, but never let up on the instruction. He continued to shout through the Gosport tube, hammering out the rudiments of airmanship to the intensely determined Robinson. Snyder was hard on his students because he knew flying was no game. It was a serious endeavor that could kill you quick if you got sloppy.

Near the end of the eighth flight hour, an hour that had been spent practicing endless circuits of touch-and-go landings, Snyder wiggled the stick and took over the controls. He landed the plane, turned it around, taxied back to the end of the field, and brought it to a stop just clear of the touchdown area.

The engine was ticking over at idle. John watched Snyder get out of the front cockpit and step down from the plane. *Something must be wrong. What did I do?* John checked the engine instruments. They all looked normal. *It must be something I did. Lord, don't let him ground me.*

He was looking down at the controls, trying to hear or feel what was amiss, when he heard the impatient voice of his instructor.

"Well Robinson, what are you waiting for?"

John looked at him with a blank expression on his face.

"You going to sit there all day confusing everyone who wants to land sometime this afternoon, or are you going to fly this thing?"

John's expression changed from blank to startled and comprehending.

"Now remember," Snyder continued, "do just what you've been doing all day. I want you to take off, come around for one touch-and-go, then on the next circuit make a full-stop landing and taxi back here to pick me up. Don't forget to look for other traffic in the pattern. You got that?"

"Yes, sir."

"We'll see." Snyder turned and walked away.

John stared at him for a second and then looked up front at the empty cockpit. His palms were sweaty. Sitting in the airplane alone, he had a flash of self-doubt. He heard the faint echo of his mother's voice, *You got no business fooling 'round with no flying machine.* He thought he heard a voice say, *The white boss man leaving you, boy. This here machine gonna bite you.*

Johnny wiped his hands on the knees of his britches and carefully went though the simple checkout of the engine and controls that had been pounded into habit. Then he craned his head around to check for any landing traffic. There was none. He looked in Snyder's direction, seeking a last official "go ahead." His instructor was standing near the fence, legs apart, his back to Johnny, relieving himself.

Well, hell then! John eased the throttle full forward. All his thoughts were now concentrated on making a smooth takeoff. The propeller clawed at the air. The plane rushed at the wind. John had hardly gotten the tail up when the wheels stopped bouncing and the turf quickly dropped away. Without Snyder's weight in the front cockpit, the takeoff roll was much shorter and the plane climbed faster.

For the first time there was no distant voice from the little tube. *God Almighty! You flying this thing Johnny Robinson!* John whooped and shouted, reached out into the slipstream, and beat his hand on the side of the plane as if to urge his winged steed onward. His senses filled with the moment—the sounds, the smells, the rush of air, the beauty of the earth spreading out below him. It was a moment of exhilaration that would stay in his memory forever: his first solo flight.

His landing was not too good but it didn't matter. He had flown solo. Self-confidence is born from such acts. He would work harder now to smooth out his novice technique. He would be a pilot.

John taxied to the corner of the field where Snyder was waiting.

"All right, Robinson, now that we've got that over with, maybe you can settle down and learn how to fly an airplane. If you think the undercarriage won't collapse on us after that last landing, taxi back to the ramp and I'll buy you a cup of coffee."

"Yes, sir!" John tried to look serious, but he couldn't get the grin off his face. There was something else that happened that day. Back at the line shack, he got more than coffee. He got handshakes and was congratulated all around. The other students no longer made it a point to shun him, always stand apart from him. He was accepted as a fellow student, a fellow flyer.

The days at Curtiss-Wright were wonderful beyond Robinson's fondest dreams. He not only qualified as a licensed pilot, but he continued his training, learning aerobatics and qualifying in all the types of planes including multi-engine craft such as the big Ford Tri-motor, the most popular plane among commercial airlines at the time.

He so impressed the school with his mechanical knowledge and ability that he was offered an instructor's job with the Curtiss-Wright School of Aviation Mechanics upon graduation.

These were no small accomplishments for any young man, but especially for a black man from a small town in Mississippi. Yet Robinson retained his modest demeanor. Instead of using his accomplishments to set himself apart, Robinson convinced the school to allow him to recruit a class in aviation mechanics from interested members of the study group that had built the little Heath Parasol. The first all-black aviation mechanics class pioneered in another way as well: There were women in the class.

He did not forget his friend Coffey. Cornelius Coffey moved to Chicago and enrolled in John's first class in aviation mechanics. From there,

John arranged for him to be accepted into the flying school. Robinson received his pilot's license in 1927. Coffey got his in 1928.

Robinson's energy and enthusiasm were limitless. He continued to teach mechanics at Curtiss-Wright while pursuing the advancement of his flying career. He earned a commercial, multi-engine, and air transport pilot rating, the first black in the United States to do so.

Because the Curtiss-Wright flying school was still not "generally available" to black students, Robinson called upon the leaders of Robbins, Illinois, an all-Negro town on the outskirts of Chicago. With their cooperation, Robinson led the group to establish Robbins Airport, America's first airfield completely owned and operated by blacks.

Robinson with Coffey founded the Challenger Air Pilots Association for blacks interested in flying. The board of advisors was made up of John Robinson, president, Cornelius Coffee, Albert Crosby, Janet Waterford Bragg, Ben Hall, and George W. Mitchell. It cost three dollars to join. Members got a discount on flying lessons. One of the members, aviatrix Willow Brown, began taking lessons from Coffey in 1934, got her license in 1937, and became the first black pilot and one of the first women to be accepted by the Civil Air Patrol during World War II. The club grew in membership and adopted uniforms and wings for its members. The little Heath Parasol plane was put to use as a static display at dances and other social functions to help raise funds to benefit Robbins Airport and the Challenger Air Pilots Association.

Chapter 8

Hummingbird

Both Robinson and Coffey knew there were many black Americans who wanted to learn to fly and that the field of aviation was all but closed to them. They decided they should provide a school for black pilots. The question was how. You could not start a flying school without a plane. True, they both had paying jobs, but all of Robinson's and Coffey's savings had gone to pay for advanced flying lessons. They were living paycheck to paycheck.

Fortune helped solve the problem. John read a newspaper advertisement by a car salesman named Abbott. The ad stated, "Airplane taken in on trade for sale." John Robinson knew a thing or two about trading automobiles.

Abbott, a pilot himself, did not expect a black man to reply to his ad and at first did not take Robinson seriously. As with everything else concerning aviation, John was persistent. He had a Hudson sedan that he had completely rebuilt. John took Coffey with him to see Abbott. The car salesman inspected the Hudson, raised the hood, started the engine, and drove the car around the block.

"It's a nice car," he told them, "but I can't trade even for the airplane."

Robinson asked, "What kind of plane is it?"

Abbott answered, "It's a White Hummingbird."

"I've never heard of such a plane. Let's go out and see it."

The three of them climbed in the Hudson and drove out to the Chicago Airpark (later called Chicago Metropolitan Airport, and, later still, Midway Airport) where the plane was kept. They found it in the back of a hangar, rolled it out, and inspected it. They started the engine and ran it for a few minutes. It had a surplus OX5 engine from the Great War just like the one Robinson had fixed for the barnstormer's Jenny and the one in Robert Williamson's WACO-9 at Willow Run.

John asked, "The Hudson and how much more?"

Abbott replied, "How much you boys have?"

John, who had the car but no cash, looked at Coffey. Coffey said he had two hundred dollars. Robinson turned to Abbott. "The car and two hundred dollars, and you give each of us a one-hour checkout in the plane. Take it or leave it."

Abbott scratched his head. "I don't know . . ."

"Hell," Robinson interrupted, "who else would buy an off-brand airplane as ugly as that one?"

Abbott walked up and down, looking first at the Hudson, then at the plane. Finally he walked back to them. "Okay, boys. Give me the keys to the Hudson and the two hundred bucks."

Ironically, the White Hummingbird, a biplane that seated two in the front cockpit, was painted black. It was slow, a handful to recover from a spin, which it was prone to do if handled sloppily, but it flew. Robinson and Coffey had their first plane and their first partnership together. The John Robinson School of Aviation[1] was soon to follow. One of the first students to apply to the school was a nineteen-year-old named Harold Hurd, who, it turned out, already had experienced basic training. Hurd, exhibiting some of the same persistence as Robinson, had talked a white

---

1 Coffey was often overheard calling it the Coffey School of Aviation. Though he later had a school of his own, some modern articles list Coffey's name erroneously as Cornelius Robinson Coffey

instructor at the Chicago Air Park into giving him a few flying lessons at a price twice what he charged white students. It seems the only time available for Hurd's lessons was in the morning at first light. It was obvious that the instructor picked that time of day so no one would likely discover that he was giving lessons to a black man. The instructor took Hurd's money for lessons, but refused to solo him, arguing, "it would be bad for business."

When John met Harold Hurd, he took an immediate liking to him. In turn, Hurd grew to look upon Robinson almost as a big brother. Robinson allowed Hurd to tag along with him in the air if he had an extra seat, as well as on the ground. Hurd once heard one of Johnny's girlfriends complain, "Why do you always have to bring that kid along?"

Hurd recalls one incident that well illustrates the problems facing black pilots and students of aviation during the twenties and thirties: "On one occasion, Robinson agreed to check me out in an International OX5 biplane. When we took off, the International had less than a third of a tank of fuel. At the time, the Robbins Airport did not have aviation fuel facilities. Although the International had enough fuel for a checkout flight in the area of Robbins Airfield, John decided to let me fly to Ashburn Field so they could fill up the tank before returning to Robbins. (Ashburn was the oldest airfield in Chicago. It was often visited by Lindbergh and other great aviators of the day.) After landing at Ashburn, we taxied up to the fuel pump. When the attendant came out and discovered that the flyers were black, he informed us in no uncertain terms that Ashburn Field was closed to coloreds. He flat refused to sell us any gasoline. We were low on fuel, but had little choice but to take off since the ground crew and a couple of pilots hanging around were openly hostile toward us. We barely managed to reach Chicago Airpark. They allowed us to buy fuel."

But despite the refusals he received and racism he faced, by persevering and pursuing his aviation dreams John Robinson was helping to break down barriers and to establish a legacy that would eventually open the way for black flyers to enter service in the Army Air Corps.

Chapter 9

Tall Tree, Short Cotton

Robinson became a professional pilot during the Golden Age of Aviation during the 1920s and 30s. Lindbergh soloed the Atlantic in 1927, the year Robinson earned his pilot's license. New aviation records were being made almost daily. Air races, stunt flying, and the rapid advance of aircraft design were all making headlines. Jimmy Doolittle, using Sperry's new gyro-stabilized instruments and newly developed radio aids to navigation, successfully took off in a plane with a hood blocking his vision to the outside world, flew a predetermined course, and referring only to the aircraft's instruments found the field and landed blind. Air travel was becoming more acceptable to the public.

John believed there was a place for Negro youth in aviation. He searched for better facilities and tools with which to teach them. He also believed that the best way to lead was by example and hard work, traits he had been taught at Tuskegee.

The Roaring Twenties rushed full throttle to their disastrous end, plunging the world's economies into depression. Aviation suffered serious setbacks, but the strongest companies held on. One of those was

Curtiss-Wright that retained, among its best employees, a black commercial pilot and aviation mechanic named John Robinson. And while the Robinson School of Aviation he and Coffey had established was hurt, it was not wiped completely out.

Determined to keep alive his own aviation career, Robinson was driven toward two unselfish dreams: One was to find a better way to open the field of aviation to black men and women; the other was to find an opportunity to prove to the world beyond doubt that Negroes could not only handle the mental, physical, and technological demands of flight, but could also excel in them. The timing of world events would offer him one or the other, but not both.

Unknown to John Robinson, there were two other men who had dreams, conflicting dreams, that would draw John Robinson into harm's way.

One was named Ras Tafari and served as regent to Empress Zauditu, ruler of an ancient, unconquered Christian nation. His dream was to bring his people into the modern world. In 1930, upon the death of Empress Zauditu, her cousin and regent, Ras Tafari, became emperor of Ethiopia, formerly called Abyssinia. As was the custom, Ras Tafari took a new name, Haile Selassie, which translates as "Power of the Trinity." Besides the title of Emperor he was also given the traditional titles Neguse Negest (King of Kings), Seyoume Igziabeher (Elect of God), and Moa Anbessa Ze Imnegede Yehuda (Conquering Lion of the Tribe of Judah).

After his coronation, Emperor Selassie opened the doors of his country to Western influence. His nation had chosen Christianity in the fourth century AD and had been isolated by the rise of Islam in Africa in the seventh century AD. Ethiopia was the only nation in Africa not to fall before Islamic swords or Western imperial powers. When Haile Selassie was made head of Ethiopia, it was comprised of five different peoples and numerous tribes. Four major languages were spoken. There were few schools. The country had never been fully mapped, never had a nationwide census. Slavery was common; the highland Ethiopians often raided the Negroid Abigars and Annuaks of the Sudan area for manpower.

As regent, he had guided Ethiopia to membership in the League of Nations in 1923. As emperor, he implemented a new constitution that set up two houses of parliament. He appointed the members of the senate, not unlike the House of Lords in England, while the provincial leaders chose the members of the chamber of deputies. One of the many difficult changes in rule and policies assigned to the new parliament was the abolishment of slavery. He knew that to obtain respect and true recognition among the member states of the League, he would have to abolish slavery. The new government and its ambitious programs were not always well received by some of the tribal leaders. Nonetheless, Haile Selassie was determined to bring his nation into the twentieth century. This dignified African leader, small in physical stature, was growing tall in terms of world respect.

The second of the two men with a dream that would affect John Robinson was a school dropout, an atheist, and a former Italian corporal during the Great War. His name was Benito Amilcare Andrea Mussolini. Fancying himself a modern Caesar, his dream was to restore the "Glories of Rome" to Italy. Dubbed Il Duce (the leader) by his followers, he invented a new dictatorial form of government called Fascismo and seized power over Italy in 1922 using the brutal force of his black-shirt Fascist thugs to intimidate opposition. For a while it looked as though he might have his dream of a new Roman Empire. With the total power of a dictator, he did much to modernize Italy beginning with war machinery. By 1930 Italy was a leader in terms of modern tanks, planes, and guns. Mussolini built roads and bridges. He decreed that the trains would run on time. They did. He strutted out on balconies to tell his people what a great man he was. The problem was his spending. Italy was already under great stress when world depression threatened to collapse its economy altogether and Mussolini with it. He had promised a new Italian Empire. At great expense, he had built a war machine. His only choice now was to use it. But where?

Back in Chicago, John Robinson was too busy chasing his own dreams to pay attention to world affairs. In his quest to open the field of aviation to America's black youth, he hit upon an idea. Why couldn't his old school, Tuskegee Institute, create a school of aviation? His inquiry to Tuskegee's officials raised interest. He received an invitation to visit the school for the tenth reunion of his graduation class. It was 1934. John accepted.

What better way to present Tuskegee with his idea for a school of aviation than to arrive by air? John invited his partner, Cornelius Coffey, and Grover C. Nash, a black pilot Robinson had taught to fly, to make the flight with him.

The immediate problem was what plane to use. The Robinson School plane was heavily scheduled by student pilots. Considering the times, it would not be prudent to turn away paying customers. Nash owned a small Buhl Pup monoplane with a forty-five horsepower, three-cylinder Szekely radial engine, but it had only one seat. What John needed was a two-place plane to fly himself and Cornelius to Tuskegee. John turned to Janet Waterford Bragg, a former flying student of his and member of the Chicago Challenger Air Pilots Association. It was no secret that John Robinson had a certain attraction to the ladies. Janet Waterford Bragg could not only fly, she was the proud owner of an OX5 biplane. In 1934 that was extraordinary. Bragg was a registered nurse with a steady job that paid well by Depression standards.

It took all of John's considerable charms to persuade Bragg to lend him her plane to fly all the way to Tuskegee, Alabama, and back. She was not enthusiastic, but finally agreed with the stern warning, "I paid all my savings, $600, for that plane. Don't you put a scratch on it!" (As a registered nurse she made, on average, $936 a year at a time when an average doctor's income was $3,382.)

The flight took careful planning. Gordon Nash's Buhl Pup carried only ten gallons of fuel and burned a little over three gallons per hour at a cruise speed of seventy miles per hour. Some of the planned legs of the flight would stretch the little Buhl's range to the maximum. The ninety horsepower OX5 in the International biplane burned nine gallons per hour, but had considerably more range with its fifty-gallon tank. Although the biplane could cruise at eighty-five miles an hour, they would fly at the Buhl's slower speed to keep Nash in sight.

The flight went well until they left Tennessee heading toward Birmingham, Alabama. On this leg of the flight they encountered twenty mile per hour headwinds. Checking his progress over the ground and watching his fuel indicator, Nash began to doubt he could reach Birmingham. An hour later, he was sure of it. He was running out of fuel.

Nash looked back at the trailing biplane, waggled his wings, and pointed at his gas tank. Coffey nodded acknowledgment. While Robinson flew the plane, Coffey got out a chart to search for the nearest airfield. Trying to unfold a map and read it in an open cockpit biplane takes concentration. When unfolding it to the section needed, one slip and the whole thing will blow out of the cockpit. Coffee held onto the chart, but couldn't find a nearby airfield marked on it. They remained on course toward Birmingham while looking for a field, any field suitable for a safe landing. Twenty minutes later, Nash waggled his wings again and began pointing with more gusto at his nearly empty fuel tank.

Not quite to Decatur, Alabama, where there was an airport, Nash signaled that he had to land, airport or not. He turned and began to descend toward the only available landing area he could see, the Decatur Country Club, about two miles to the west of their course. The nearest suitable fairway was smooth and straight but pretty short. Nash landed with only a few drops of fuel left in his tank. Robinson, who had circled above while Nash landed, now brought Janet Bragg's biplane around and slipped it nicely onto the short, smooth fairway.

To say that the few golfers out that day were surprised is hardly adequate. Not one, but "two airplanes landed right there on number six fairway!" If the golfers were startled at seeing the two planes land, they were utterly astonished when three black pilots climbed down from the cockpits. No less awed were their Negro caddies who couldn't have stared more wide-eyed if some ghostly apparition had suddenly appeared.

Only one of the golfers recovered sufficiently to draw attention to his game. "By God! I should be allowed a free shot. That damn airplane nearly took my head off!" There was some merit to his argument. He had been engaged in putting just as Nash flew close overhead for a landing. The golfer's ball shot clear off the green to the next fairway.

It was such an amazing event that once things calmed down, the foursome and their caddies led the intrepid pilots to the clubhouse, but stopped short of inviting them into the all-white establishment. They did have a colored locker room attendant bring them glasses of ice water on a silver tray while one of the members volunteered to go in and call for a gas truck.

He returned to say that he had the gas supplier on the line and he wanted to know how much fuel was needed.

John knew the fairway offered only minimum takeoff distance. On the other side of a fence at the far end there was a row of sharecroppers' cabins and beyond them a cotton field. John decided he didn't need any extra weight in getting the biplane out of the short field. They would refuel only the little Buhl Pup. The OX5 had enough fuel to reach Birmingham.

"Tell him we need ten gallons."

The man disappeared into the clubhouse only to return again.

"The fuel man says he can't afford to drive all the way out here from town for less than the price of twenty-five gallons plus two dollars each way to make the trip. What do you want me to tell him?"

It was 1934, the depth of the Depression. Money was not wasted by anyone, certainly not by a struggling black flying partnership. Still, John had little choice.

"Tell him okay."

The fuel truck arrived some forty-five minutes later but wasn't allowed to drive onto the fairway. John had to pay cash for twenty-five gallons at ten cents per gallon plus four dollars for "hauling the truck clear out here"—a total of six dollars and fifty cents—before they could have any fuel. They had to carry fuel from the truck using a five-gallon bucket and

and a funnel to fill Nash's plane. When they had finished filling the Buhl Pup, it took a little over nine and one-half gallons, the fuel deliveryman asked what he was to do with the remaining fifteen and one-half gallons they had paid for.

John thought a moment. "Let's go ahead and put it in the OX5."

Coffey spoke up. "John, that will add almost a hundred pounds to our takeoff weight. Let's think about that a minute. That field looks mighty short to me and we got to clear those cabins."

It would be tight, but John was confident he could clear the fence and cabins with room to spare. "We'll make it," John said. "We'll push it as far back as we can to use every bit of the fairway."

Coffey usually went along with John's decisions, but on this occasion, he disagreed. "We don't need to be adding a hundred pounds on this short field."

"Well." John said, "You can stay here and take a bus to Tuskegee. That will more than make up for the extra fuel weight."

"Like hell, I will." Coffey replied. "But this is how we'll do it." He walked off the fairway into the rough, found a suitable stick, came back to the plane and paced off down the field to a point where he figured a take-off run could be aborted and still have enough room to stop before they reached the fence. He tied his handkerchief to the stick and stuck it in the ground at the side of the fairway. Satisfied, Coffee walked back to where Robinson was finishing a pre-flight check of the biplane. This included oiling and greasing the valve rocker arms and springs by hand since the OX5 engine had no other means of lubricating these parts. This hand oiling and greasing had to be done prior to every flight. They paid four caddies fifteen cents apiece to help turn the biplane around and push it back to the base of the fairway tee. They did the same for the Buhl Pup. A small crowd of club members and caddies gathered to watch the intrepid airman. One was heard to say, "I ain't never seen no airplane crash before."

Grover Nash got in the Buhl. John propped his engine. Nash gave the Pup full throttle. It rapidly gained speed down the smooth fairway. Robinson and Coffey watched as the small plane lifted off. It cleared the fence and cabins with no problem. Nash put the Pup in a climbing turn to circle above until John and Coffey could takeoff and join up with him.

John got in the rear cockpit. Coffey said, "Remember, if we aren't off by the time we reach my marker yonder, you cut the throttle and stop this thing." He walked around front and propped off the engine, climbed into the front cockpit, fastened his seat belt, and signaled with a thumb up that he was ready.

John gave it full throttle. Coffey leaned his head out the left side of the front cockpit to look for the marker he had placed down the fairway. The plane quickly gained enough speed for John to lift the tail. Now he could see ahead and concentrated on keeping the roll straight. The plane was accelerating nicely on the smooth turf. The controls came alive in John's hand. *No sweat,* he thought. *She's going to fly us out of here with room to spare.* John began to ease back on the stick. The plane was on the verge of lifting into the air.

Just at that moment, Coffey saw his marker fly past. He reached for the throttle and closed it just after the plane lifted into the air.

Startled, John immediately rammed the throttle all the way forward, wondering how in the hell the thing had slipped back to idle. The plane momentarily lost altitude, bounced on the turf, and struggled into the air again as full power was restored. They crossed the fence at the end of the fairway. Directly in front was one of the sharecropper cabins with its little brick chimney sticking about three feet higher than the roof.

John was careful to maintain best angle of climb airspeed. He was sure the wheels had cleared the roof of the cabin when there was a sharp bump. Immediately, John could feel a terrific vibration through the control stick. Cornelius, whose vision was blocked by the lower wing, thought the main gear must have struck the cabin. He turned around to see John's reaction. That's when he stared past John at the tail empennage. It was missing most of the right horizontal stabilizer and elevator, torn off when they struck the brick chimney. He motioned wildly at John, pointing toward the tail.

John snapped his head around and saw what Cornelius was pointing at. He very gently eased back on the stick, testing to see if the plane would respond to what was left of the elevator. It did so, but very sluggishly. This time it was John who closed the throttle, anxious to get the plane down before they lost what was left of the tail. He hoped there was enough of it left to flare the plane for a landing. The biplane began to settle toward earth. From the back cockpit, when a pilot eases the stick back to flare for landing, he can see very little of what lies directly ahead. John was not too concerned since they would be landing parallel to the cotton rows. The plane, shaking from nose to tail, was about twenty feet off the ground when the very top branches of a tree climbed into Coffey's view from the front cockpit. Startled, he shoved the throttle forward and grabbed the control stick in an effort to bank the plane to avoid the tree. By this time, John could see the top of the tree and was already taking evasive action.

They almost made it. Only a few feet off the dry, sun-baked cotton field, the right upper wingtip brushed tree branches. There was a sickening crack as the wingtip and aileron were torn off.

Nash, circling above waiting for the two pilots to take off and join him, watched in horror as the biplane spun around and crashed tail first onto the field. A huge grey explosion grew into a cloud obscuring the plane and its crew from his view. Flying above the frightening scene, Nash thought the plane had exploded and surely killed his two friends. A few minutes later, he was astonished to see both Robinson and Coffey walk out of the grey cloud and wave up at him.

As he continued to circle, Nash realized there had not been an explosion. The frightening cloud had been an enormous swirl of dust thrown up by the plane whirling onto the dust-choked cotton field. As the dust drifted off downwind, Nash was sure he had witnessed a miracle. His two friends had walked away from all that was left of Janet Bragg's 1928 OX5 biplane: a fuselage bereft of the better parts of its wings and tail. At least there had been no fire.

As he continued to circle above, Nash could see his two friends engaged in a lot of gesturing, stomping, and walking around one another. John took his flying helmet off, threw it on the ground, and kicked it toward Coffey. Gordon Nash decided he better land. A storm was raging below.

Robinson and Coffey were furious with one another.

"It's your fault, Coffey, for chopping the power on takeoff."

"Well it's your fault, Robinson, for cutting the power for the emergency landing without clearing the area in front of us. You should have 'S' turned to see what was ahead."

"I didn't dare do that. What was left of the elevator may have torn away. I didn't know how much longer the control cable would hold. If either had failed, we would've nosed down and gone straight in. Who the hell would leave a tree in the middle of a cotton field anyway? You ever seen a cotton field with a tree in the middle of it? Damnit! If you hadn't put that stupid flag out there and cut the power as we lifted off, we would have made it with altitude to spare."

"Well, we didn't make it, did we?"

By the time Nash once again landed on Fairway Six, a crowd of golfers and their caddies had climbed over the fence to see the crash.

With a crowd gathered, Robinson and Coffey calmed down and decided not to kill each other. They had both made mistakes, but by some miracle they were alive and unhurt. That was enough, they decided, until a new, more pressing argument arose between them. As Nash walked up the two were going at it again.

"You call her! You're the one who sweet-talked her into loaning us the plane. Maybe you can sweet-talk her into not killing us."

"Not me, Coffey. You call her. You're the one who pulled the throttle on takeoff and caused us to hit the chimney."

"I ain't gonna."

"The hell you ain't."

Just who was to call Janet to inform her that her airplane was scattered all over a cotton field in Alabama was a serious matter, not to mention the cost of buying her another airplane.

It was Gordon Nash that negotiated a truce. He reminded them of the purpose of the trip. The most important thing was for John to continue the trip in pursuit of their goal: establishing a school of aviation at Tuskegee. To prevent bloodshed, Nash took on the fearful task of informing Janet Waterford of what had happened to her pride and joy. "She can't yell at me too much. I didn't have anything to do with borrowing her plane." He was wrong, of course. She was not amused. She entered into what is referred to in the South as a genuine hissy fit.

"What did she say?"

"She's gonna kill all three of us just as soon as we get back to Chicago."

The trio calmed down enough to agree that John would continue on to the reunion celebration at Tuskegee in Nash's Buhl Pup. That was the moment another problem, in the form of an irate cotton farmer, showed up. He was not amused either. He insisted that his crop had been damaged to the tune of one hundred and twenty-five dollars, including the cleanup of "all them pieces of airplane scattered out yonder." He further indicated that if they didn't like the price, or couldn't pay, they could take up the matter with the sheriff.

Coffey had been raised in Arkansas, Robinson in Mississippi. They definitely did not want to settle things with a white Alabama sheriff.

"All right. John, you go on right now. Get in the Buhl and fly out of here," Coffey said.

"We don't have a hundred and twenty-five dollars between the three of us," Robinson replied.

"I'll call some of the Air Challenger members. They'll get up the money and wire it to us at Western Union. In the meantime, Nash and I will salvage the engine and whatever else we can from the wreck. Now you go on to Tuskegee."

It was a beautiful afternoon when the sound of an aircraft circling in the blue sky overhead caused eyes to look skyward from the campus of Tuskegee Normal and Industrial Institute. John had called from Birmingham to ask Captain A. J. Neeley, the registrar of the college, for permission to land on one of the Institute's farm fields adjacent to the campus. Now, as he made several low passes over the campus, students and faculty poured out of the buildings and rushed to the field to witness the very first visit to Tuskegee by an aircraft, and not just any aircraft, but one flown by a graduate of the institution. John brought the plane down smoothly to settle on the pasture and taxi over to the gathered crowd. When the flight-helmeted and parachute-attired Robinson climbed from the open cockpit, he was somewhat embarrassed by the cheers that rang from the crowd. The welcome given was that for a returning hero: He was Tuskegee's own intrepid aviator.

Robinson enjoyed the festivities but wasted no time in discussing the possibilities a school of aviation with Tuskegee's president, Dr. Robert R. Moton, and his visitor, Dr. Frederic D. Patterson. John told them about the first all-Negro airfield he had helped establish at Robbins, Illinois, and the flying and aviation mechanics school he had established with his partner Cornelius Coffey, and the organization of the Challenger Air Pilots Association. He pointed out the prestige such a school would give to the Institute, and how it could be the first college to exclusively and formally open the field of aviation to black youth. He went on to lay out the details of how all of it could be accomplished and what they would need: a classroom, a grass landing strip, a plane, a hangar, an instructor, a mechanic's shop, and tools. His arguments in support of establishing a school of aviation at Tuskegee were enthusiastically received.

Before he left to return to Chicago, Dr. Moton assured Robinson that Tuskegee would establish a department of aviation as soon as necessary funds could be obtained, hopefully within the next two to three years. They also stated that they would engage him to head the department. Feeling a sense of accomplishment, he found the sky brighter and the earth greener as he flew northward toward Chicago. With an occasional roll or loop, he danced with the clouds. It was his sky that day.

Upon his return to Chicago, he sent the news to his parents and his sister. He informed Coffey and Curtiss-Wright of Tuskegee's plans. News got around and the local press began to seek him out for interviews. All seemed right with his part of the world. Unfortunately, it was not with the rest of the world.

Chapter 10

A World Away

PILOTS WILL AGREE THAT AN AIRCRAFT WILL ALMOST ALWAYS GIVE indications of oncoming problems—increased oil consumption, low compression, subtle noises, vibrations—in time to allow the prudent pilot to avoid catastrophe. Unlike well-trained aviators, those in high places who pilot nations almost always seem unable or unwilling to recognize signs of serious trouble and take corrective action in time to prevent disaster.

Far from the shores of America, dogs of war were howling to be let loose. The scent of blood was in their nostrils. Their master in Rome would soon unleash them to tear apart the flesh of an ancient Christian people on the high plateaus of Ethiopia.

What better place to begin Mussolini's conquest for a new Roman empire than an African nation assumed to contain rich farmland and great, unexploited natural resources? It was true that Ethiopia was the only African nation that had never been conquered by colonial powers or its Muslim neighbors. Italy knew that firsthand. In 1896 Ethiopia, then called Abyssinia, had given the Italians an embarrassing defeat at Adowa, but that was well over a quarter century ago. Italy now had modern industries that turned out tanks, guns, and aircraft. Ethiopia had no such capacity. Il Duce bragged that he would avenge the defeat of 1896 and bring glorious new empire to Italy. The new colony of Italian Ethiopia would, he said, provide land for the crowded Italian citizenry and greatly benefit Italy's faltering economy.

Few in the world paid attention. That would prove to be a very bad mistake. Mussolini, you see, a former corporal during the Great War, invented Fascism in 1922. That most in the Western world chose to ignore Mussolini and his new form of government would prove terribly costly in terms of human life, not to mention treasure. The one man who did pay close attention, who took notice not only of Mussolini's Fascist form of government but of the way he had used his Black Shirt thugs to gain power, had also been a corporal in the Great War, a German corporal. This ex-corporal's name was Adolf Hitler. American newspapers did carry a little news about Mussolini and "incidents" along the border between Italian Somaliland and Ethiopia, but such reports were mostly on the back pages.

Haile Selassie appealed, as leader of a member nation, to the League of Nations, asking for them to send neutral observers to the area to arbitrate any border disputes or incidents. The League refused. France and England saw no reason to antagonize Fascist Italy bulging with Mussolini's arms, or, for that matter, Mussolini's good friend Adolf Hitler and his Fascist thugs in Germany who had come to power in 1933. After all, what interest did England and France have in an obscure African country?

Encouraged, Mussolini sent large numbers of troops and arms to Africa, stating in the world press that Italy had "a civilizing mission" in "backward Ethiopia." He declared that he would avenge the atrocity committed by Ethiopia in 1896 against Italy at Adowa, never mind that Adowa, an Ethiopian town, had first been attacked by Italy.

In his appearance before the League of Nations in Geneva, Switzerland, Haile Selassie made an impassioned plea before its assembly. He asked for peace, saying he had withdrawn his troops from the disputed borders to prevent any further incidents. England, though sympathetic, refused to pledge support to Ethiopia in the event of war. France's response was cold. The Italian delegation arrogantly walked out of the assembly during Selassie's speech. The League of Nations did nothing.

The United States had refused to join the League of Nations following the end of the Great War. America was in the grip of the Depression and officially wanted nothing to do with another conflict abroad, although many Americans, especially black American citizens, formed societies to send aid to Ethiopia.

John Robinson was aware of Haile Selassie's struggle. Like many in the world, he viewed Selassie with admiration, but on the American side of the Atlantic, John's life seemed very much in order. His attention was focused upon the challenge he would eventually face heading up a new department of aviation at Tuskegee. Not only did he believe the school was needed, but he also knew that for the students to be accepted as pilots and aircraft mechanics, there needed to be an opportunity to prove beyond doubt that black students of aviation could excel in the field.

There had been a few news stories about another black pilot, but in John's opinion, the stories were not the kind that were needed. The subject was Hubert Julian who, in the mid-1920s had billed himself as the first black parachutist and first black licensed pilot, not in the United States but in Canada. Julian claimed to have been born in Trinidad, and he said he had learned to fly in Canada and was licensed there. John considered him more of a self-promoter of moneymaking scams than a serious aviator. Julian parachuted into Harlem as a publicity stunt. He promoted himself as the Black Eagle and collected funds, mostly from black citizens, for a proposed solo flight in a single-engine floatplane to Ethiopia. He had concocted similar scams before, taking the money and then finding an excuse not to carry out the project. For the Ethiopia flight, when few backers appeared, Julian appealed to the public through advertising and direct mail. Because of his previous actions, both the FBI and the United States Postal Service (USPS) had taken an interest in him. He was informed by an agent from the US government that he had better make the flight because there was a law against collecting funds through the mail with intent to defraud.

With much fanfare and publicity, Julian took off from the Harlem River on his great African flight. The flight ended five minutes after takeoff in a crash in Flushing Bay. Julian must have miscalculated his "forced river landing," for he wound up in hospital where he was visited by a USPS inspector. Considering the seriousness of his injuries, the inspector decided the attempt might meet the criteria for collecting money via the mail and decided not to put Julian in jail.

John Robinson despised Julian for pulling such stunts. He knew Julian set the sort of examples that would hold back black aviation, make it a laughing stock. Nonetheless, by 1929 news of the attempt had somehow reached the then regent of Ethiopia, Ras Tafari, soon to be coronated emperor. He was interested in the idea of black pilots. At the time, Ethiopia had just three large transport planes, two German-made single-engine Junkers W33c monoplanes, a Fokker VII3/b tri-motor, several single-engine types including a handful of French Potez biplanes, and a few other single-engine planes such as a Farman F-192, a Breda BA 15, and Breguet XIX. Most of Ethiopia's pilots were white Frenchmen. Ras Tafari wanted to prove to his people that black men could indeed learn to fly, an idea that was not encouraged by his French pilots.

Julian, the self-proclaimed Black Eagle, happily accepted an invitation to travel to Ethiopia to demonstrate his flying ability. He was promised all expenses and a salary of a thousand dollars a month, a huge amount at the time. Upon his arrival he was given rank, a uniform, living quarters, and much attention. He did demonstrate, to the emperor's pleasure, and to the consternation of the French pilots, that a black man could fly. But then Julian overdid things a bit.

Selfridges department store in London, which received the majority of Ethiopia's royal mail-order trade, presented, as a gift to the emperor-to-be, a new, white, sporty little two-place de Havilland Gypsy Moth biplane. It became a much-prized possession, even more so than his royal automobile, a Rolls Royce touring car painted deep maroon. Ras Tafari had a hangar built to shelter the little plane and keep it from public view. He gave orders that no one was to fly his Gypsy Moth until his coronation as emperor, at which time it would be unveiled and flown with himself as passenger before the coronation crowd.

Part of the celebration was held at the racetrack, which at the time doubled as a landing field. Julian gave a special public aerial demonstration for Ras Tafari featuring aerobatics in an old Potez 15 biplane and a parachute jump. Tafari was very pleased by the show. He awarded a medal to Julian, gave him a raise in pay, granted him the rank of colonel, and offered him Ethiopian citizenship. Julian, immensely pleased with himself, thanked the emperor-to-be and walked away from the viewing stand. Shortly afterward, a member of the royal staff, somewhat astonished, directed the regent's attention toward the landing field. Tafari, to his surprise and shock, saw his white de Havilland biplane accelerating across the grass to lift into the air just in front of the royal tent. Julian had been asking to fly the little plane since he first laid eyes on it. Now, full of the accolades he'd received from Tafari, the cheers from the crowd echoing in his ears, Julian had taken it upon himself to try out the plane, even though he was perfectly aware that it was not to fly until the coronation. Perhaps he thought Tafari would be pleased to see what his Gypsy Moth was capable of doing in the air.

The future emperor was not in the least pleased. No one had ever disobeyed his direct orders. What's more, the unveiling of the little plane and his courageous flight was to be the highlight of his coronation celebration. Now that surprise for his subjects was ruined.

Things got even worse. Julian, who had never flown a Gypsy Moth, came over the field and performed several steep turns at low altitude. With Tafari looking on in anger, Julian attempted a maneuver that ended in the branches of a eucalyptus tree, destroying the regent's favorite mechanical possession before he had a chance to fly in it.

On the emperor's direct order, Hubert Fauntleroy Julian was immediately banished. He was put on the next train to Djibouti. Some said he was lucky not to have been fed to the pair of royal lions, which were always kept chained to either side of the entrance to the royal palace.

Arriving by ship back in the United States, Julian found himself once again ridiculed for his antics. The news media carried stories reminding the public of Julian's failed attempt to fly to Africa and with gleeful sarcasm announced, "American Negro Pilot Lands in Eucalyptus Tree."

John Robinson was convinced that Julian was undoing everything that he, Coffey, his classes at Curtiss-Wright, and the Air Challenger Pilots Association were doing to promote black aviation.

All that happened in 1930, the year Ras Tafari became Emperor Haile Selassie. In 1934 Robinson continued working with Coffey at their flying school while Tuskegee sought funding for a school of aviation. John's quiet manner and his demonstrated abilities and steady progress in the field of aviation stirred the interest of the local press. He found himself giving interviews and receiving invitations to speak before leaders of business and education.

It was at one such meeting sponsored by the Associated Negro Press (ANP) that John stated that he knew firsthand that airlines refused to hire black pilots qualified with commercial and transport ratings. He voiced, for the first time publicly, that what might most suitably support black Americans entering the field of aviation would be the opportunity to prove, beyond doubt, a black aviator's professional ability. He said that such an opportunity had so far been unavailable, but that he would gladly accept such a challenge.

Claude Barnett, founder of the ANP, was present. As fate would have it, Barnett had a rather special friend, Dr. Halaku Bayen, nephew of Emperor Haile Selassie. Halaku was in the United States at the time. Following Robinson's speech, Barnett traveled to Washington, DC, for a conference with the Ethiopian prince to tell him about John Robinson's talk. Consequently, Bayen traveled to Chicago to meet with Robinson.

At the meeting, Bayen said that perhaps he could provide what Robinson stated he desired: "an opportunity to prove beyond doubt black aviators' professional ability." Bayen told John that his country, Ethiopia, in spite of the emperor's appeal to the League of Nations, was facing an invasion by Fascist Italy and that Ethiopia desperately needed pilots. He asked, "Mr. Robinson, would you consider serving in the Imperial Ethiopian Air Corps?" Robinson accepted without reservation, saying it would be a chance to prove that black American pilots were fit for any challenge in aviation.

Bayen had not made the offer without first confirming Robinson's professional flying qualifications. He then had to determine if Robinson was sincere in his offer to serve in Ethiopia. Satisfied, Bayen forwarded a report of his findings to Addis Ababa.

In spite of Ethiopia's urgent need for skilled technical personnel, the emperor, remembering the embarrassment and loss of his prized de Havilland Gypsy Moth caused by Julian, received the report about another black American pilot with serious reservations. But he and his staff made a careful review of Robinson's aviation records and references and found them impeccable. John received a cable from Selassie inviting him to Ethiopia, offering a generous salary and all transportation and living expenses. It was not an invitation to be taken lightly. John's parents, sister, and many friends pleaded with him not to go. They did not match his conviction that going halfway round the world to risk his life in an African country headed for war would advance the opportunities for black Americans. They argued that he could do more by teaching aviation at Tuskegee. John reminded them Tuskegee still did not have the funds to establish a school of aviation, that the endeavor may take years.

In the end, John Robinson chose to accept the offer. He would go, he said, because it provided the best opportunity to prove by example that black pilots were capable of performing professionally. It was a heavy burden, one he was determined to carry.

John turned the aviation school over to Coffey, tidied up his affairs, packed, and said goodbye to his family and friends.

Chapter 11

Lonely Voyage

Dr. Bayen made all the arrangements for Robinson's trip, helping him secure a passport and visa. The passport had presented a challenge. Robinson certainly could not say the reason for the trip was to become a member of the Imperial Ethiopian Air Force. It was and is against US law for an American citizen to serve in the armed forces of another country, particularly one at war, which worried Robinson. He did not want to lose his citizenship. On his application, John had to fib a little. He stated the reason for his travel to Ethiopia was business. He claimed he was going abroad to sell unarmed, civilian aircraft to the Ethiopian government, aircraft manufactured by a new, small company named Beechcraft (which would turn out not to be a complete lie).

As for war, John still hoped that the League of Nations would somehow prevent it. After all, wasn't that the main purpose for which it had been established after the Great War—the war to end all wars?

The United States, which had refused to join the League of Nations, decided to remain neutral and follow the initiative of the League to put an embargo on the sale of military arms to either Italy or Ethiopia. This diplomatic gesture of neutrality by the League of Nations and the United States hurt only Ethiopia; Italy had the ability to manufacture all the guns, bombs, ammunition, artillery, planes, and tanks it needed, whereas Ethiopia had no means whatsoever to manufacture modern weapons.

Bayen met John in New York and assured him that all the tasks that needed to be accomplished before he could go had been completed, right down to the delivery of his steamer trunk to his cabin. Bayen provided Robinson with a first-class ticket for the Atlantic crossing and beyond, checked his papers a final time, handed him an envelope containing cash for expenses, and accompanied him to Pier 57 in New York, used by both Grace Lines and French Lines. The French liner's officer receiving passengers aboard seemed a little taken aback; he checked John's papers twice to be sure the black man was indeed booked first class on the luxury liner outward bound for Marseille via the Strait of Gibraltar.

On that late afternoon in May 1935, passengers lining the rail of the French ship watched the skyline of New York slowly descend toward the western horizon. Among them, standing alone, was a slim, brown-skinned young man.

The chilled evening breeze smelled of the sea, taking Robinson back to his childhood in Gulfport on the Mississippi shore of the Gulf of Mexico. He thought of his mother's seafood gumbo, flying kites, and fishing with his father. How far away those days now seemed. When his mother learned her only son was headed halfway round the world to an African country threatened by war, she had cried and begged him not to go. He had asked himself a dozen times, was he choosing or being chosen? Had he deliberately set a course, or was he being swept along by Fate's troubled times and tides?

The glow from the bright lights of New York followed the sun beyond the horizon, leaving the ship in darkness to slice its way cleanly through the ocean. John left the liner's rail and walked to his cabin.

Dressed formally in black tie, John Robinson garnered curious glances as he followed a waiter across the lavishly decorated dining salon to his assigned table. Conversation paused as he was seated. He smiled and nodded to those at the table. A few nodded in return, but when conversation resumed, he was ignored. Nervous about proper dining etiquette, he carefully spread his napkin in his lap and followed the silverware selections and manners of his fellow diners as he ate his meal in silence. It was the first five-course dinner he had ever experienced. He spoke only once, excusing himself from the table.

By lunch the next day, some at his table were more friendly, intrigued by rumors that originated, it was said, with the ship's purser, and before him the equally curious black baggage handlers in New York. Who was the mysterious black passenger in first class? Word spread that he was a pilot and soldier of fortune. To his embarrassment, John became somewhat of a celebrity to many fellow passengers. There were also some aboard who made no secret of their disgust at booking expensive first-class passage only to find "a damn Chicago nigger" enjoying the same privileges. A group of German businessmen did not miss the opportunity to discuss the Nazi theory of a superior race when they were sure Robinson could not help but overhear.

Most of the first-class passengers were American vacationers of old money, the class that is usually hurt least by monetary Depression, and which generally is the last to change lifestyles. Among them was a former pilot who had flown with the 94th Aero Squadron in the Great War. He approached John on the second afternoon of the crossing.

"Robinson, I hear you've done a little flying. Is that true?"

"That's right. I've done a little."

"Heard you're from Chicago, but you don't sound like a native of the Windy City."

"I was raised on the Mississippi coast. You don't sound like a Northerner yourself, if you don't mind me saying so."

"No. I'm from the Carolina coast. Charleston. Is it true you are headed for Ethiopia and the mess that's fixin' to happen over there?"

"I've accepted their invitation. I still hope the mess, as you put it, can be avoided."

"I made the same mistake in 1917. I suppose you've been told you're crazy enough times already. Why don't you and I go to the bar and talk about flying. I'm already damn tired of bridge, my children are driving me crazy, and my wife stays seasick in her cabin, or so she tells me. I haven't done any flying for a while. I'm forty-one and am constantly reminded that I should be wiser at my age, but I miss it."

The two men spent much of the remainder of the cruise walking the decks or sharing a table at the bar while exchanging flying stories. To most passengers, especially Northern Americans, their apparent ease with one another seemed ironic, a white Southerner and a Negro. It was not strange to either man. In the segregated society in which they both grew up, such relationships were often black employee to white employer, the former subservient, the latter patronizing. Nonetheless, both John and the Carolinian were at ease with one another in a way peculiar to the South, a way John had not found prevalent in the Northern urban centers of Detroit and Chicago.

The Carolinian said he had first been assigned to fly a slow, lumbering observation plane that seemed to be the prey of every German flyer.

"I spent most of the war running like crazy. I learned to love the clouds. If you get in trouble in Ethiopia, clouds may be your best bet. If I found myself with Germans all around, I flew flat-out crazy, tried everything I knew, made up stuff, all the time running for the clouds if there were any. Once inside a cloud, I couldn't tell up from down, but the pursuit ships were afraid to follow, afraid of a midair collision with me or each other. In clouds, they couldn't tell up from down either. Even if they tried, they couldn't find me. Hell, I couldn't find me till I broke out the other side or spun out the bottom. Many a time I would deliberately go into a spin hoping I came out the bottom with enough altitude to pull out. I stayed alive and got my observer and the information through all but once. I crash-landed just behind my own lines, but my observer was already dead, shot right through the heart. I finally got my wish, got assigned to a pursuit squadron. I thought that would be great after flying a slow observation craft, but hell, I had more close calls than before. It really wasn't much fun, John, the war I mean, but I miss the flying."

Robinson took the Great War flyer's knowledge and instruction in aerial combat seriously. He filled a journal with notes and sketches of maneuvers the slow-talking Carolinian patiently explained to him. John had taken instruction in basic aerobatics, loops, rolls, Cuban-eights and the like, but he had never thought of them in terms of evasive or aggressive tactics. He did now.

John enjoyed the man's company, the only company he had on the voyage. In turn, his new acquaintance from South Carolina seemed to enjoy the chance to talk about the flying he missed and take it upon himself to do all he could to improve Robinson's chances at survival in a conflict he believed, from what he had read in recent newspapers, was sure to come.

The two did not limit their conversations to serious matters. Both shared funny stories about their flying. The Carolinian told of landing an old Jenny one day with a whole line of women's laundry tangled in his undercarriage and streaming out behind—bloomers, nightgowns, and other unmentionables. He told John, "I had buzzed my girlfriend's place right between the back porch and the barn. I caught plenty of hell from my instructor, but not near as much as I caught from the mother of a girl who quickly became my ex-girlfriend."

The greatest laugh they had together was when John told of the Decatur Country Club and the destruction of Janet Bragg's OX-5 biplane. The Carolinian laughed until tears ran down his cheeks.

"It wasn't very funny at the time, I tell you." John laughed. "No, sir! It was not funny at all. It did no good for Coffey and I to try and blame each other. We thought that woman was going to kill us both. It took us a year and a half to pay for the plane. "

John knew he needed a little laughter. His pilot friend was the only fellow passenger who spoke more than a few words to him. Most ignored his presence. Some shunned him altogether.

I guess these white folks never saw a black man in first class, at least one who wasn't waitin' tables, making beds, or cleanin' up after 'em.

Late at night in the dark of his cabin, self-doubt crept in to taunt John. The faintly detectable rhythm of the ship's engines reminded him of the ever-increasing miles separating him from home. Once, when the liner was in the middle of the ocean, he followed the promenade deck all the way aft to stand at the stern and watch the ship's frothy wake stretch into the distance and fade away.

It was a grand ship, but for the most part, a lonely voyage for Robinson.

Chapter 12

Marseilles

THE SHIP APPROACHED THE STRAIT OF GIBRALTAR EARLY IN THE morning. The great promontories rising from Spain to the north and Morocco to the south guard the narrow, eight-mile-wide strait separating the Atlantic Ocean from the Mediterranean Sea and Europe from Africa. In antiquity, the highest pinnacles on each side were called the Pillars of Hercules. John joined a multitude of early risers crowding the ship's rails to view the narrow passage. From the port side of the ship, John could see Spain and the famous Rock of Gibraltar. He quickly crossed to the starboard side to get his first view of Africa: Morocco. His intermediate destination, Marseilles, France, was still some thirty-four hours away. The ship turned away from Morocco and Algeria to set a course along Spain's Mediterranean coast. In darkness it passed between the island of Majorca and the Spanish mainland. The historic cities of Valencia and Barcelona and the Pyrenees Mountains forming the border with France slipped past, unseen by the sleeping passengers. In the morning they docked at Marseilles. The ship and most of its first-class passengers would continue on the next day for a grand Mediterranean cruise, but not John Robinson.

At the base of the gangway, a well-dressed black man wearing western clothes held a sign with the name Mr. John Robinson on it. He was an Ethiopian envoy whose job was to meet John and escort him to his hotel overlooking the old harbor. He gave Robinson a ticket and travel papers for the ship *Lamoriciere,* which he said would leave Marseilles the day after tomorrow and take Robinson to the French Somaliland port of Djibouti.

"Mr. Robinson," the man said, without giving his name, "we think it would be better if you did not broadcast your destination here in this city. Marseilles has a long history as a center of smuggling and intrigue. Your purpose and destination are best left undeclared."

John had not thought of his mission in terms of international intrigue, but the envoy suggested, quite seriously, that there were some who might find it *convenient* if certain *experts* traveling to aid Ethiopia did not reach their destination. He did not mention Italian Fascists, but John understood he had just been given a warning. After asking if John needed anything further, the envoy excused himself and left John in his hotel room to ponder his new international status.

Robinson did not take the warning too seriously, but the next morning he decided to join an organized group to see the sights rather than wander about on his own. The hotel concierge arranged for him to join a small tour group. John laughed at himself. *Safety in numbers is what they say.* The hotel concierge nor anyone else made anything of the fact that he was black.

Marseilles was France's gateway to North Africa and the Orient beyond. As such it was a city where one could see a colorful mix of people: French, Spanish, English, German, Italian, Indians, Turks, Chinese, black Africans, and, most of all, Arabs. Marseilles was less French than it was an exotic montage of humanity. Though large, it was not a pretty city. Still, there were structures to impress a black child who had grown up in Mississippi; the Hotel de Ville and the old fortresses of Saint Jean and Saint Nicholas still guarded the original ancient harbor. Too small and shallow for modern ships, it was now used by fishing boats and yachts.

Robinson's group visited the Palais Longchamps with its dramatic fountains and colonnade, and high on a windy bluff overlooking the city and blue Mediterranean, the Basilique Notre Dame de La Garde. In the afternoon, John joined a half dozen tourists with a guide to explore the Quartier Panier, the old town that climbed the hills overlooking the old harbor. They were warned to be watchful of pickpockets as they entered the warren of narrow, dark, climbing, twisting streets, some so steep they were made of stone steps. Old houses and shops lined the streets, many with colorful awnings. John was glad to have a guide; one could easily get lost. If exploring alone, he would be an easy target if there really was anyone interested in doing him harm. (During World War II, the Germans raised most of the Panier to disable the confusing warren as a hiding place for the French Underground.)

Back at his hotel, John asked the concierge for recommendations for dinner. "Monsieur, Marseilles is famous for its bouillabaisse," he replied, as if everyone, even a black tourist, should know about Marseilles bouillabaisse.

John, not easily intimidated, asked what that was.

The concierge replied as if the whole of France had been slighted. "It is a marvelous seafood soup of course, Monsieur." He directed "Monsieur Robinson" to "the best restaurant in the city." And while John found the famous bouillabaisse tasty, it was expensive—and not as good as his mother's seafood gumbo.

After a day spent walking for miles, much of it uphill, while enduring warm breezes sweeping across the Mediterranean from the deserts of North Africa, Robinson was bone-tired. He turned in early. *Another ship tomorrow, Johnny boy. What have you gotten yourself into?* He was too fatigued to worry and dared not think of home. Sleep came heavy and dreamless.

The French ship *Lamoriciere* stood at the dock along the Quai de la Joliette at Marseilles's Port Moderne. Her hull was painted black while her superstructure was white. She had been built in 1920 specifically for the Marseilles–North African trade. A little worse for wear, she was much smaller than the luxurious transatlantic French liner John had travelled in from New York. Only three hundred and seventy feet long, she had a capacity for only four hundred passengers in three classes. John boarded her and was shown to his first-class cabin. It was small, rather plain, but comfortable. After checking his trunk to ensure it had not been tampered with, he walked on deck to join other passengers standing at the rail. They watched as the mooring lines were cast off and the ship eased from the dock. *Lamoriciere* maneuvered out of the Bassin de la Grande Joliette. With smoke pouring from her two stacks, she headed south into the blue Mediterranean.

Unlike the trip across the Atlantic, John was surrounded by passengers of all colors: black Africans, both light- and dark-complexioned Egyptians and Arabs, a few Indians, small groups of Chinese or Japanese, and the usual mix of European businessmen and world travelers. Nonetheless, John felt alone. He did not find another American on board. At his assigned first-class dining table sat an Indian, an Englishman, and an Egyptian who spoke English. He could not hide the fact that he was American, but he followed the advice he had been given in Marseilles to keep the nature of his mission to himself. It appeared to John that his fellow passengers did much the same. He got the impression that *the world is nervous.*

Lamoriciere sailed around the south end of Sardinia for the French colony of Tunis where it docked. The ship's purser recognized John standing near the gangway and asked if he cared to go ashore, see the sights. "The ship won't sail for six hours," he assured John.

"I can see 'bout all the people, goats, camels, and old buildings I care to right from the deck here," he answered.

Truth was, every new exotic port of call, filled with strange sights, sounds, odors, and people, reminded him of just how far from home the course he had chosen was taking him. Each morning brought another bright day, fresh wind across the deck, his pilot's eyes on the sky where he had always been most comfortable, his spirits most high, but each night in the cramped, hot cabin, he spent hours fighting in the darkness the mocking demons of self-doubt and loneliness.

From Tunis the ship sailed south of Sicily to the Italian-controlled port of Tripoli, Libya, and from there to the Anglo-Egyptian Port Said at the northern end of the Suez Canal. The ship rarely spent more than half a day at any port of call. John lost any desire to go ashore among the vendors and crowds congregating in the harbor areas. At each port a few tons of cargo was exchanged. At Port Said, John watched a Rolls Royce touring sedan carefully lifted from the forward hold, swung outboard, and land dockside.

I bet if they dropped that, some potentate would chop off a head or two. I wonder if they behead people in Ethiopia. I forgot to ask about that.

As *Lamoriciere* made its way down Suez, John was amazed at the French ditch cut through the desert sands.

At a distance from out on the desert, I bet a ship looks like it's plowing right through the sand.

The ship continued down Suez and into the Red Sea for more than a thousand miles, much of the time with Arabia off the port side and Sudan to starboard. At the southern end of the Red Sea, *Lamoriciere* passed through the straits of Bab al Mandab and barely kissed the Gulf of Aden before turning into the French Somaliland port of Djibouti.

The ship dropped anchor off shore. The harbor was too shallow for ocean-bound vessels. Small, ancient sailing craft loaded with trading goods crowded the old harbor where the tri-color flag of France flew over the customs building. Laborers carrying heavy sacks on their shoulders swarmed about like ants, loading or unloading lighters to transfer cargo, mostly coffee, to the few steamers waiting at anchor. Ship's tackle clanked and clanged as booms hoisted loads to or from the lighters.

John closed his steamer trunk and made sure his cabin attendant understood it was to be put ashore. He then went on deck. As soon as the accommodation ladder was lowered in place, John and other passengers disembarked onto a small, sea-worn vessel that served as a water taxi. The boat's wheezing gasoline engine labored to shore. From the dock, the Djibouti John saw consisted mostly of whitewashed buildings with roofs of straw or corrugated iron. The air was thick with humidity.

John had barely taken a step ashore when he heard his name.

"Mr. Robinson?"

The man who called Robinson's name was a slim bearded black man with high cheekbones and an aquiline nose. He was dressed in fine white cotton, jodhpur-like trousers with puttees, a white shirt, and a dark cape-like garment.

John nodded. "I'm Robinson."

"May I introduce myself? I am Ras Mebratu." He bowed slightly and offered his hand. John shook it. "I have been sent by the emperor himself, to whom I am a second cousin. He has honored me with the privilege of escorting you to Addis Ababa. All arrangements have been made. We will leave by train in the morning. I know you must be tired from your long journey. We will have ample time for a briefing and your questions during the train trip. For now, we have a room for you at the hotel. We will dine there this evening." The envoy spoke English with a distinct British accent.

"Thank you for meeting me. I have to admit this is all new to me, all unfamiliar—the travel, the lands I have seen, and," John swept his arm in a large arc, "so many different people, so many customs and languages. I reckon I got a whole lot to learn."

"It will not be so difficult. You will see. Good food and rest and you will be ready for the train tomorrow. Come. Your luggage will be brought to the hotel." They took an ancient Citroën taxi.

The hotel was small, old, but John found the food and service good. During dinner there was polite conversation but little serious talk. When John tried to turn the conversation to matters at hand, the envoy answered, "Mr. Robinson, you have come far and I know you must have many questions. Tonight let's just enjoy the food and good French wine. There will be plenty of time on the train to discuss serious matters. I assure you I will answer all your questions. Please have a good night's rest. Your journey is not quite finished."

John was not much of a drinker. To be polite he sipped at his wine a little during the meal. After dinner, he thanked his host, purchased a copy of the only English-language newspaper available, a two-week-old copy of the *Herald Tribune* published in Paris, and found his way to his quarters. There was a basket of fruit, a bottle of wine, and a bottle of mineral water on a small table beside a lamp. His steamer trunk was in a corner. Surrounded by sweltering heat, he turned on the ceiling fan, undressed, and flopped on the bed. The old fan made a rhythmic *wump-pa-wump* tattoo while drawing the exotic sounds and smells of Djibouti in through the open window. Still awake after an hour, John moved to the chair beside the table, turned on the lamp, opened the bottle of mineral water, and picked up the copy of the *Herald Tribune*.

Anything to get my mind off home and what the hell I'm doing here.

He skipped over an article concerning Italy's protest over the alleged sale of American arms to Ethiopia, but could not avoid a front page article stating, "Mussolini Doubling Troops Already in East Africa."

John, my man, you're in one hell of a spot and nobody to blame but you.

He turned to less troubling articles. There were several on aviation. Amelia Earhart had set another record, flying nonstop twenty-one hundred miles from Mexico City to Newark, New Jersey.

I wonder if a black woman had done it there'd be headlines like that. Janet Bragg or Willa Brown could have done it if they had the money and backing.

One article, headlined "Greatest Mass Ocean Flight Ever Attempted," stated that the US Navy had begun a flight of forty-six planes flying from Honolulu Pearl Harbor 1,323 miles to Midway Island. Another article that caught John's eye said that England's Royal Air Force was seeking recruits to keep pace with Germany's growing challenge.

Wonder if they'd take a black man from Mississippi?

The news stories did little to raise John's spirits. He turned to the entertainment section. American movies playing in Paris included *Devil Dogs of the Air* with James Cagney and Pat O'Brien and *Bride of Frankenstein* with Boris Karloff. The most popular film appeared to be *Mutiny on the Bounty* with Charles Laughton and Clark Gable. John had seen none of them. The only movies he saw growing up were from the colored balcony of a motion picture theater in Gulfport that had a separate box office window and stairs in the alley for black ticket-holders. He hadn't seen many movies as a child and they were all silent films back then. He saw his first talkies on the south side of Chicago in a theater with a mostly black audience. Howard Hughes's *Hell's Angels* was his favorite.

Just as the young pilot was getting sleepy, his eye caught a small article near the bottom of an inside page that set him wide awake. It read, "Captain Anthony Eden, Britain's traveling salesman of peace, returned from his Continental tour bearing a report of Benito Mussolini's avowed intention to wage war against Ethiopia." Sleep was a long time coming.

Chapter 13

Train From Djibouti

THE MORNING CAME TOO SOON. JOHN FELT HE HAD HARDLY GOTTEN to sleep before the bright sun of a new day awakened him. He took a sponge bath, since there was no shower in his room, put on fresh clothes, packed, and was waiting in the hotel lobby when the Ethiopian envoy arrived. His English-speaking host of the previous night was again dressed in white jodhpurs and puttees and wore a wide-brimmed felt hat. He greeted Robinson and, after arranging for John's baggage to be collected and delivered to the railroad station, suggested breakfast in the hotel dining room. Both ordered French pastry and coffee. After breakfast Ras Mebratu paid John's hotel bill and called for a taxi, this time a ten-year-old Renault a little worse for wear.

At the station, John was introduced to several other Ethiopian members of his escort party. Only one of the men besides Mebratu spoke English. The grime-streaked train consisted of a small wood-burning locomotive, a tender overflowing with firewood, two freight cars, and three white passenger cars The European-style passenger cars were divided into compartments boarded directly from the platform. John and the Ethiopians boarded their reserved compartment and settled in for the 488-mile trip to the Ethiopian capital of Addis Ababa aboard the French-built, narrow-gage rail line. Robinson's anxiety from the night before was displaced by anticipation of the exotic, primitive land that lay before him.

A few shouts up and down the platform followed by the shriek of conductor's whistles, and they were off. The morning temperature along the Red Sea coastal plain was nearly one hundred degrees Fahrenheit as the train began its slow, labored climb toward Addis Ababa, which was situated on the cool, fertile Ethiopian plateau at an elevation of nearly eight thousand feet.

John knew going in that he would not be flying over the friendliest geography a pilot could wish for. In preparation for the job before him, John had read all the resources he could find on Ethiopia—its history, people, geography, and climate. The highland plateau ranges in elevation from three thousand to ten thousand feet and is surrounded by mountains reaching up to and above fourteen thousand feet. Ethiopia, he learned, is the source of the Blue Nile and, because of the snow-capped mountains, is sometimes referred to as the Tibet of Africa. The high plateau is slashed by plunging valleys. In rugged parts of the highlands there are strange-shaped *ambas*, not unlike the buttes of the American West. The Great Rift Valley slices from Kenya through the plateau, opening into the lowland desert and ending at the Red Sea. To the southeast is the harsh desert bordering Somaliland. To the southwest lay humid tropical lowlands.

The dirt-streaked window of the compartment had been opened, the only relief from the smothering heat. John sat in silence. Looking out the open window, he was struck by the primitive beauty of the rugged terrain but shocked by the almost total lack of anything common with the modern Western world he had left behind. He saw people living in sunbaked mud huts and occasionally a camel caravan, scenes that appeared to have not changed for a thousand years.

Ras Mebratu must have sensed John's thoughts. He broke the silence and began to discuss the recent history of his country.

"You know, Mr. Robinson, Ethiopia is the only African nation that has been exclusively under black rule for at least three thousand years. It has been a Christian nation since 400 AD. Because of that, and the fact that we have been surrounded by natural boundaries of mountains, deserts, and swamps, and by countries of the Islamic faith since 700 AD, we have been mostly isolated from the modern world.

"Since Ras Tafari became Emperor in 1930 and took the name Haile Selassi he has worked even harder to awaken our land to the modern century. In 1931 he gave Ethiopia its first written constitution. But you have to understand that for Ethiopia, as for much of Africa, the bridge to the twentieth century spans a vast distance and must be crossed slowly if a culture is not to be ripped apart. Justice was traditionally in the hands of the chieftains of each district. They are still powerful and many look upon reform as a threat to their power as do many leaders of the Coptic Church."

John accepted a cup of tea and several plain cookies from a silver tray offered to him by a servant dressed in white. They passed the border of French Somaliland into low hill country. The train swayed and jerked on the narrow-gauge rails, slowing almost to a mule's pace as it struggled up the grade in its climb toward the highlands. On the rocky hillsides John could see an occasional round hut made of stones or mud and wattle, the walls often whitewashed, the structure covered with a conical straw roof.

"You will see many such structures," Ras Mebratu explained. "They are called *toucouls*, sometimes spelled tukuls in English." John nodded, still looking out the window at weird-looking cacti scattered across the surrounding semi-desert of which much was covered in black lava sands. Ras Mebratu took a sip of tea and continued.

"The emperor has outlined administrative reforms and has enlisted the aid of such experts as de Halpert of Britain, Auberson of Switzerland, General Virgin of Sweden, and Evertt Colson of your own country, but as I have said, changes must come slowly. The emperor cannot overwhelm his people and still retain their loyalty. I am afraid you may see slavery in practice while you are here. The Italians use that sad fact against us in their propaganda. His Majesty has worked many years to stamp out its existence. Nevertheless, a practice so long rooted in custom is not easy to abolish, as the history of your nation clearly illustrates. His Majesty has set up a bureau to administer the repression of slavery, but still the Italians use it against us before the League of Nations."

Mebratu paused, giving Robinson a chance to ask a question that was foremost on his mind. "What of your military situation? I have heard that some feel the emperor may have placed too much faith in the League of Nations."

His host was very quick to point out that it was not his place or desire to comment on the judgment of the emperor. He then smiled. "But it is my task to inform you of the situation here and I will be candid. We had hoped to receive some aid from England and France in the event the League of Nations cannot prevent war. Now we realize we will receive very little aid if any. What is worse, the League of Nations has declared an arms embargo against both Italy and Ethiopia. That must make Italy happy. They manufacture arms, tanks, and aircraft. We have only agricultural products and must import all manufactured goods including, of course, modern arms. We have an army of maybe three hundred thousand men. Only a quarter of them have had any form of modern military training. Some of our young officers have been trained in England, some in France, some trained here by a Belgian military advisory group led by Colonel Leopold Ruel. Most of our armies will be led by their chieftains, those loyal to the emperor. We have four hundred thousand rifles of various types, very few machine guns, about thirty light and heavy antiaircraft guns, Oberlikons, Schneiders, and Vickers. Most of our two hundred or so artillery pieces are antiquated. Ammunition and spare parts for such varied weapons is a problem. We have a small mixed batch of Ford and Fiat armored cars. The Imperial Guard is well trained and equipped, but it is not large and is used to protect the emperor."

John had known before he left home that the situation in Ethiopia would not be promising if war actually occurred, but he was stunned by the facts being given to him. "I just read that there are one hundred thousand well-armed Italian troops already on your border, with more on the way. The article said they are backed by two hundred trucks and tanks and two hundred aircraft. If war comes, what can you do to hold against such odds?"

"You are certainly straightforward with your questioning." Mebratu smiled. "But why not? You have come a long way to offer your help. But I must caution you. There will be journalists and others in Addis Ababa that will want to talk with you. Your question and my answer must remain between us."

Robinson nodded that he understood.

"The emperor has withdrawn his troops from the borders to avoid any further incidents that could be used by the Italians as an excuse to attack. If there is war, it will come from the Italians and the world will know it. If the Italians cross our border, we will withdraw still further to lengthen their supply lines. We have few roads. Their mules will be of more use than their trucks over much of our land. To use mechanized vehicles, they will have to construct roads and bridges in many places. Our advantage is in our rough terrain and our soldiers: We have not been beaten in two thousand years by any outsider. Our warriors need little. They are tough, and they are zealous in their honor. In battle you will find them desperately courageous. They are fanatical fighters. They will stand or die for their homeland."

Mebratu fell silent a moment. "But to win against modern tactics using mechanized infantry, planes, tanks, and artillery all coordinated together in the attack? Who has faced that? Could France or England or Poland win against such strength and tactics? Who knows?"

Mebratu paused again to gather his thoughts. "If war comes, the emperor will try to delay the enemy's advance and appeal to the leaders of the Western world to stop the fighting. If they will not or cannot, we will fight for our country as long as we can."

John sat stunned. For the first time the reality of the circumstances that he faced lay stark and naked before him. His ambition and enthusiasm to find an avenue by which he could prove beyond doubt that a black pilot could handle any challenge in the air had landed him in an ancient land facing war against terrible odds.

Well, Johnny boy, you got what you asked for. You gonna do the best you can. Nothin' else you can do now. Ain't gonna run. Just have to crawl over your fear. That's the first thing you got to do, and I reckon you got a mountain of it to crawl over.

John hoped the fear that had crept up his spine did not show in his face. He looked directly at his host. "I've come a long way. Can you tell me where I will be needed and what I will be asked to do?"

"Of course, Mr. Robinson. We have only a few radios, our telegraph service is poor, and we have few roads linking the outlying areas of our country due to lack of money and the very rugged nature of our land. We will have to use every means we have to establish and maintain communications with our armies, even the ancient methods of drums and runners. We have less than two-dozen aircraft, none of which are suited for combat. None is even armed. With the embargo we are not likely to obtain more. But the aircraft are vital for this reason. Even the few radios we have do not work well in the mountainous regions. An aircraft can cross in one or two hours rugged terrain that would take days or even weeks for messengers to cross. Aircraft will often be our only means of rapid communication and liaison between the front lines and the capital. They will be essential for message delivery, observation, and vital transport, besides any special assignment the emperor may request."

Ras Mebratu paused to give John a chance to respond. Robinson's mind was in a whirl. *Less than two-dozen unarmed planes against Mussolini's two hundred bombers and fighters. How the hell can we even begin to think about maintaining communications when the more pressing question is how can we hope to survive against such odds? I don't even know what kind of planes Ethiopia has. How will they maintain the ones that survive more than a flight or two? Where will they get parts? And, God help me, I'm going to fly them!* John tried to swallow but his mouth was too dry. He had no reply.

Mebratu continued. "His Majesty is anxious to meet you. You have come highly recommended. As you know, he was very disappointed in the flying ability of another black North American, Hubert Julian. Julian has returned to Addis Ababa."

John looked more than surprised. He looked startled. With a smile, Ras Mebratu waved his hand in a gesture of dismissal.

"Julian is assigned to the infantry and will not be allowed to fly. The emperor is not in a position to turn down volunteers, but he did firmly forbid Julian to fly. He should be no problem to you. The only value Julian has to Ethiopia is hopefully to enlist support and funds from America."

"Now, more to the point of your duty, Mr. Robinson. You will be offered the rank of captain to begin with, along with the authority you need to conduct air operations. We have, of course, some trained Ethiopi-an pilots now, and French aviators, but we expect the Frenchmen to leave if war is declared. It is the emperor's hope that he will be able to rely upon more than your flying ability. He was particularly interested in reports he received of your leadership experience. We know you helped organize a black owned and operated airfield, a pilot's organization, a mechanics school at Curtiss-Wright, and a flying school. It is the emperor's hope that your experience will be put to good use."

John remembered the words of the Carolina pilot from the Great War whom he had met aboard the ship crossing the Atlantic. The man had said that when he volunteered for air service duty in France, no one was able to talk him out of it. With a knot forming in the pit of his stomach, John now knew what the man had meant. Everyone John knew had begged him not to go. He now wished he had listened. Ethiopia's plight was far more serious than his worst fears. *I had the foolish idea that by coming on this "adventure" I could help open the field of aviation to blacks. If I'm killed it will do nothing of the kind.*

Well, you're here, Johnny. It's too late to look back and I'm not gonna run away. You've been afraid before, John boy, but you've never been a captain. The thought struck him as funny and he laughed out loud, startling the somber group around him.

At first the countryside that slid slowly past the window was drab and sparse with only an occasional round, thatched roofed house to be seen, but as the small engine pulled them ever higher, the vegetation became greener and there were more such farm houses. They passed the primitive villages of Aisha, Diredawa, Awash, and Hadama, all consisting of squat mud and wattle buildings, some whitewashed, most left natural. The train made frequent stops to take on firewood and water. John welcomed such breaks from the long hours of sitting in the rocking, soot-soiled coach. The stops gave him a chance to stretch his legs.

From time to time they would see a goat herder or a farmer tending his fields with primitive tools. Robinson saw a graceful impala, later a wart hog, and was startled to see zebra. Once, they passed a small band of warriors clothed in white shammas, waving rifles, spears, and swords at the train in salute. Some had shields made out of animal skin. *God almighty!* thought John. *The Arabian Nights in a contest against modern steel.*

He watched the sunset and thought of home as the train chugged into darkness, its hissing and puffing echoing off the hills and canyon walls.

Chapter 14

Addis Ababa, 1935

F ROM A DISTANCE, ADDIS ABABA STOOD IN THE DUSTY MORNING haze like an outcropping from the parched Abyssinian plain. The rainy season, which runs from June until September, had not yet given the city a cleansing bath or turned the high plain green. Unlike the circular farm homes with thatched, cone-shaped roofs that John had seen from the train, the structures on the outskirts of the city were mostly square huts of sunbaked brick or mud and wattle, some plastered, some whitewashed, most with corrugated iron roofs in various shades of rust. A few structures were two-story. Some had outside staircases leading up to rooftop galleries shaded by awnings. Nearer the center of the city there were Western-style houses, apartments, hotels, and shops. John was told that accommodations were waiting for him at the Hotel de France. One thing he noticed immediately was the mild temperature. The city might be near the equator, but it sat at an altitude of 7,600 feet. When he stepped off the train, the temperature was seventy degrees Fahrenheit and the air was pleasantly scented by the thousands of eucalyptus trees growing throughout the city.

Ras Mebratu ushered John into an ancient taxi for the ride to the hotel. Robinson felt he had passed through a time barrier into a strange world that reminded him of the Bible picture books he had seen in Sunday School as a child. Caravans of camels and donkeys carrying everything from spices and foods to carpets, tins of fuel, firewood, and sacks of charcoal moved through the stony dirt streets. The marketplace was filled with merchants under awnings and customers milling about, all wearing the contrasting costumes of different tribes and peoples. John's host pointed out Gallas and Danakils, Somalis, Tigres, Cottus, and the Hamites from north of Lake Tana, all identified by their clothing. The people spoke in multiple languages: Amharic, the official language of Ethiopia, Tigrinya, Gallinya, and ancient Ge'ez.

Women wore brilliantly colored garments. Some had veiled faces. Others had gems in their noses or wore amber necklaces or gold earrings. John noticed a slim woman who wore a flowing white shamma. She flashed a quick glance at him with beautiful almond eyes and disappeared on the far side of a black-robed man who rode slowly along on a donkey in the shade of a huge umbrella carried by a servant who trotted alongside. Always a lady's man, John would learn that many young women from the Amhara-Tigrean area of Ethiopia were slim, almond-eyed, and easily considered beautiful by Western standards. John recalled a term he had read about Ethiopia: *Here I am in the capital of what some in the West call the Hidden Empire.* It was all beyond his wildest imagination.

The Hotel de France was located in a district that more closely resembled the modern West. The streets were made of hand-placed rocks similar to cobblestones. They passed the Cinema Empire. John would learn that both it and Cinema Adowa were owned and run by Eda and George Nageliz. The presence of other foreigner *faranjis*, the Ethiopian term for foreigners, was evidenced by the flags of various countries flying over consulates scattered helter-skelter about the capital.

Upon his arrival at the hotel, Robinson was introduced to the owner, Monsieur Teras, and was shown to "one of our finest rooms." It was small but comfortable. What made it "one of our finest" was the fact that it had a private bath, most rare in Addis Ababa. Before leaving, Ras Mebratu told John that there would be a small dinner gathering that evening where he would meet some of the people with whom he would be working.

The first thing Robinson did was bathe the soot and dust of the train ride from his tired body. Afterward, he dressed in a clean shirt and trousers and ventured down to the hotel lobby with a bundle of dirty laundry. Using sign language, he got across to a hotel servant that he was behind in his laundry. The man bowed, took the bundle of clothes John handed him, and disappeared.

From there, Robinson walked into the hotel bar. It appeared that the entire press corps of Ethiopia was waiting for him. *So much for keeping things secret.*

Robinson was embarrassed to learn that he was already gaining a small amount of fame at home in the States in a way that was not necessarily to his liking. Some US news wag had dubbed him the Brown Condor of Ethiopia, and the sobriquet had caught on and would be used in future stories about him in newspapers and radio broadcasts.

"Who the hell started that? How'd something stupid like that get clear over here ahead of me?" he asked

"Shortwave radio travels a lot faster than ships," someone answered, which was met with laughter from the crowd.

That embarrassed John further. "Guess I asked a stupid question."

Every reporter who spoke English started shouting at John. He threw up his hands. "Gentlemen, I just arrived today. I don't have answers for you yet. Y'all give me a little time."

"Just one question then, Mr. Robinson," someone in the crowd said. "Did you have anything to do with the emperor's decision not to let Hubert Julian, the Black Eagle, fly?"

"Where'd you get that? I don't know Julian and I have not yet met the emperor."

One of the reporters held out his hand. "Mr. Robinson, I'm Jim Mills of the Associated Press."

"Thank goodness, an American," John replied, and he shook the man's hand.

Mills asked, "May I offer you a drink? "

"I'm not a drinkin' man, but if they have something with ice I'll take it," John answered. "What a relief to meet an American. You staying here?"

"I'm afraid us lowly reporters can't afford the tariff. Most of us were sent over here with little time to prepare when it looked like we might have a war to report. None of us knew what to expect. Some of us, including me, couldn't find Abyssinia on the map. You ought to see what some of the boys brought with them: jungle gear, including tents, suitcases full of medicine for exotic plagues, pistols and hunting rifles, mountain climbing gear, riding boots, and of course typewriters and cameras. One guy arrived with a string of six mules. Laurence Stallings of Fox Movietone News arrived with a red Indian motorcycle with sidecar. Wish I had done that. There's only one commercial wireless in the country. We have to wait in line to get out a story. All of us are staying at the Imperial Hotel. It's not so imperial . . . more like a long two-story barracks, one bath to the floor. It's owned by a Greek named Bollo Lakos. Now that's a name for you."

Still standing at the bar, John asked Mills, "Where'd they dig up that question about Julian? I've not met the emperor yet. I sure couldn't influence any decision about Julian or anything else." Robinson took a sip from a glass of mineral water. "I will admit after I was told he was over here, I was relieved to learn he won't be flying. He's done enough to damage Negro aviation back home."

"Well," replied Mills, "you have to admit it would make a good story: Two black pilots from America compete in the sky over Ethiopia."

"I don't think he's really American. I heard he comes from Trinidad, learned to fly in Canada. I'd thank y'all not to brew up trouble for me before I even get unpacked."

Jim Mills was about to protest innocence when in walked Hubert Fauntleroy Julian who had, as it turned out, just been asked the same question by a reporter on the front steps of the hotel. The reporter, eager for a story, told Julian that Negro papers in America were claiming that Robinson had been the one to convince the emperor that Julian should never again be allowed to fly for Ethiopia.

Julian, the Black Eagle, dressed in an infantry officer's uniform, appeared more than a little irate. When someone pointed out Robinson, he walked up to John and accused him of smearing his reputation and trying to steal his style.

Although John had a quiet and serious demeanor, there was beneath the surface a short fuse when it came to being pushed around. Before Mills could stand between the two, the Eagle pushed the Condor, and suddenly there was mayhem spilling out of the bar into the lobby. Some say Julian pulled a knife, though that was never proved. What did happen is that it took the entire press corps to separate the two. Julian was escorted out of the hotel and Robinson was convinced to retire to his room. That was barely accomplished before messengers dispatched from the Royal Palace delivered orders directly to Robinson, Julian, and the members of the press making it clear that there would be no more such displays and no report of the incident in any news stories—or heads would roll. The members of the press, doing what they could to straighten up the furniture in the bar and lobby, were not at all sure the warning about "heads rolling" shouldn't be taken literally.

What was made very clear to all involved was that with an Italian army on the border, the emperor wanted no personal feuds between the two American black pilots. Both could aid in recruiting volunteers, funds, and support from the United States and elsewhere. They were therefore too valuable to be allowed to create petty scandal. (According to Julian's biography, *The Black Eagle*, he was later expelled once again from Ethiopia under charges for taking money from and working for the Italians—an allegation never proven.)

After another bath and a change into freshly laundered clothes, the only evidence that Robinson had been in a fight was a bump on the side of his head where Julian had hit him with a broken chair leg.

Answering a knock at the door, John was greeted by the same man that had taken away his laundry. "Dinner" was the only word the man spoke that he could understand.

Robinson ventured once again to the downstairs lobby, where he was met by Ras Mebratu and two men he did not know, one black, one white. Mebratu greeted John. "May I introduce your companions for this evening: Monsieur Paul Corriger and Ato Mulu Asha, both pilots. You will be happy to know they speak English. Gentlemen, Mr. John Charles Robinson."

The men shook hands all around.

"Mr. Robinson, you will be free to rest and tour the city for a few days. As you can understand, the emperor is very busy these days. He will not send for you until next Friday at the earliest."

Mebratu then took his leave announcing, "Forgive me, but I cannot join you. I have a meeting at the palace."

A few moments later the hotel clerk informed the little group, "Gentlemen, your car is waiting."

The three pilots crowded into the back seat of a 1930 Citroen C-4 sedan. They drove across the capital leaving behind the only paved stretch of road in the country, a broad avenue called *Babur Mangued,* which roughly translates as Steam Train Avenue because at one end there stood the train station, a small version of the grand French design. The avenue had been paved in preparation of the negus's 1930 coronation to allow foreign dignitaries and other guests arriving by train a smooth ride to the palace, and to provide a parade route for the celebration in which the newly crowned emperor rode in the open back seat of his maroon Rolls-Royce.

After passing out of the city, the driver settled down to a speed of twenty-five miles an hour, the most the rough country road would allow without shaking the car to pieces. The night was chilly and the cool air flowing through the open windows afforded the only comfort the three passengers had as they were jostled shoulder to elbow in the hot backseat of the road-worn Citroen.

John asked, "Do I call you Ato or Mulu?"

Mulu Asha laughed. "Mulu please. *Ato* is Ethiopian for mister or, in Paul's language, Monsieur."

Paul Corriger added, "While we are at it, *ras* as in your host's name, Ras Mebratu, means chieftain or prince."

"I sure didn't know that. I have a lot to learn. I hope you two will keep me out of trouble."

As the car bumped and jostled them, the men talked a little about flying. Corriger was one of several French pilots and mechanics brought in several years before to do the flying and aircraft maintenance for Ethiopia. Mulu Asha was one of a rare handful of Ethiopians who had recently returned from England where they had gone to school and then received pilot training from the Royal Air Force.

After a while the trio settled into silence as they rode into the night. Left to his own thoughts, John worried about the scuffle with Julian earlier in the evening. Would it find its way into the papers at home? He had come halfway around the world, volunteered to risk his life to promote black aviation, only to begin by displeasing the emperor and giving the press exactly the wrong kind of publicity. He cursed himself for allowing the stupid incident to happen.

The driver turned off the main road onto a narrow unimproved lane. John had been told that tonight's dinner would be a small informal affair at the home of Ras Tamru, a wealthy chieftain, friend and supporter of the palace. When they reached the home, John was surprised to see that it was architecturally like the *toucouls* he had seen from the train, a traditional round mud and wattle structure with a conical thatched roof. The difference in this one was its size. It was much larger than any he had seen and its walls were covered in whitewashed stucco. John soon discovered that any resemblance of Ras Tamru's home to the *toucouls* of the poor ended with the outward appearance. The thick wooden front door opened to reveal an interior of huge proportions. A stone and copper fireplace dominated a large center area. Thick draperies formed small partitioned areas within the round structure. The floor was covered with beautiful, thickly woven carpets. Two lion skins were spread near the fireplace which served as the center of activity and was used both for heating and cooking. Around the fireplace were Western-style furnishings. To one side, a group of chairs were arranged around a table. Other than the fire the only additional illumination was provided by oil lamps. At the top of the cone-shaped roof was a round opening to the sky, which served as a natural chimney above the fireplace.

John was introduced to his host, Ras Tamru, though not to the interpreter who remained in the shadow of the chieftain. The man would step forward whenever his services were needed only to retreat into the shadows. After everyone was comfortably seated, two women who had been busy preparing food brought cups filled with *talla*, a native beer brewed from barley. The host wanted to hear about John's trip and whether he found his accommodations satisfactory. Following more polite talk, the host motioned the group to the table. When all were settled their cups were refilled with talla.

Ras Tamru, through his interpreter, asked Robinson, "What is the mood in America concerning the Italian threat of war with Ethiopia?"

"To be truthful," John replied, "from what I read in the newspapers before leaving home, many Americans have become what they call isolationist. They do not favor getting into any more foreign wars following America's involvement in the Great War."

Ras Tamru replied, "Our emperor, through his appeal to the League of Nations, has tried to convince the Western world that Mussolini's appetite might include more than our small African nation. A hungry lion does not take just one taste from a farmer's goat. He finishes one goat and takes another and another and sometimes the farmer himself."

There was a momentary sense of uneasiness at the table. Ras Tamru sensed it and changed the subject. "But, it is time for you pilots to talk of flying."

Corriger and Mulu told a few light stories about their own flying experiences, then began a serious discussion about the kind of terrain and weather John would encounter. They expressed their confidence in

Robinson based upon his flying reputation, and they recited to their host facts they knew about him.

One thing was clear to John. *These people know a great deal about my qualifications and flying experience and a lot more about my country than I know about theirs.*

Food arrived at the table. A huge, thin, pancake-shaped bread was placed in the middle of the table. Mulu Asha explained that it was *injera*, the staple bread of Ethiopia made from a native grain called *teff*. He said he hoped John would like it because he would be eating a great deal of it if war came and he found himself away from the capital and its few Western restaurants. The injera almost covered the small table.

From a pot, a thick, spicy sauce with small chunks of meat was ladled right onto the injera. Mulu told him the meaty sauce was called *wat*. From other pots, a variety of vegetables were spooned onto the bread in separate piles. The diners' cups were refilled.

John had not been given a plate or fork. He turned to Corriger and asked how they were to eat. Corriger shrugged with a smile. Mulu said something in Amharic to the host who laughed. Ras Tamru turned to John and motioned for him to watch. With his fingers he tore off a wedge of the injera, folded it slightly, scooped up some of the wat and put it in his mouth followed by a sip of talla. John nodded, tore off a small piece of the bread, scooped up some wat and managed to get most of it in his mouth, spilling only a little down the front of his suit.

As the meal continued, he was surprised to find that not only did he have to eat with his own fingers, but from the fingers of others. It seemed to be a part of Ethiopian hospitality. Everyone fed everyone else. There was more than one course. Different foods were added here and there to the shrinking bread pancake. When John got up enough courage to ask what might be in the fiery morsels that seemed to be flying into his mouth from all directions, Mulu and Corriger took turns checking off the list: lamb, goat, beef, chicken, eggs, ox tongue, cheese, peppers, spices, and anything else that might be handy. To his surprise, John found it all tasted pretty good, but he wondered whether the concoction would blow his insides apart. When he mentioned this to his companions, Mulu interpreted John's comment to their host. Ras Tamru laughed and called to a servant to bring fresh cups. They arrived filled with a golden orange liquid. Mulu explained that it was called *tej,* made from fermented mead and honey, and that if a cup or two failed to quench the fire of the belly, several cups would certainly take one's mind off the problem. After a few sips, John wasn't sure it wouldn't just take one's mind, period.

The ability to understand one another's language appeared to grow in direct proportion to the flow of the native amber wine. Amharic, English, and French were all exchanged as if everyone understood perfectly what each person was saying, the tej not only making everyone at the table multilingual, but also placing the entire group in agreement with whatever was being said at any given moment.

When it was suggested that the group venture back to town to further acquaint their new American friend with the cultural aspects of Ethiopia, all present voted in favor. The host and his three guests loaded into the Citroen sedan. The driver, who may have had a little talla himself while waiting, charged forth.

Once again the cool air blowing in the windows helped make the crowded sedan a little more comfortable. It also helped to steady John's stomach, which he was sure had been on fire shortly after the meal ended. Wherever they were going, John was determined to conduct himself in a manner befitting what he had been assured was his new rank, that of captain.

That is, if I still have a chance of any rank at all after the run-in with Julian.

When they re-entered the city, John was reminded of just how great a task Haile Selassie had in trying to modernize his nation. The sanitary problems alone were enough to stagger any civil engineer. In the suburbs of mud brick structures surrounding the city center, there was no sewerage or waste disposal system. Outdoor privies were the best solution they had for sewerage. Garbage and trash were simply tossed into the streets to be rummaged through by the poor and occasionally picked up by trash wagons.

That night John witnessed a waste disposal system provided by nature. As the sedan rounded a corner, its lights illuminated the surprised faces of a pack of spotted hyenas feeding on the evening's garbage. Before he could speak, the beasts were lost in the darkness behind them. Since none of his companions paid the least attention, John wondered if he hadn't had a little too much tej.

The Citroen pulled up in front of a fairly modern structure with a large archway spanning two heavy doors, one of which was open. The four men got out and walked inside. The place was crowded. It took a moment for their eyes to adjust to the soft light provided by a few electric fixtures and oil lamps. Around small tables, groups of Ethiopian men were eating, smoking, drinking, and talking jovially. There were a few Ethiopian women scattered among the patrons.

John noticed several white faces in the room, ferenjis, members of the Western press, diplomatic staffers, and perhaps a few military advisors and medical team volunteers he had heard about. He and his new friends seated themselves on cushions around a small low table. Cups of wine soon arrived. John was determined to sip very slowly and only a little.

A group of musicians struck up a wild rhythmic tune just as a voice from behind him called his name. Surprised, John turned to see Jim Mills, the Associated Press correspondent whom he had met at the hotel bar, sitting at the next table.

"You're not doing badly for a new boy on the block."

Before John could reply, a burst of applause arose from the crowd. To the delight of the customers, several dark-skinned girls entered the cleared area in the center of the club and began to dance to the exotic music.

John, glad for the company of a fellow American, turned to Mills, "This beats hyenas for entertainment."

Mills laughed. "Speaking of entertainment, would you like a little company now and then during your stay?" Before John could answer, Mills added, "Of course, you might have to marry one."

"In that case, no thank you."

"Oh, it's not all bad. Which type of marriage do you want?"

"Which type? Just how many kinds of marriage they got here?"

Mills explained, "Under Ethiopian custom there are three."

"Three?"

"Just listen and learn, my friend. The first, foremost, and least common is the church marriage or *Qurban*. Now that one you have to be careful of. It is considered sacred and indissoluble. Young people are considered too unstable for this type of marriage. The second type called *semanya* is more common. It is a civil contract marriage blessed by a priest. It can be dissolved by mutual consent or court decision."

"And the third type?" questioned John with a little more interest.

"The third type," replied Mills, "is called *damoz* or wage marriage. Traditionally, this kind of marriage is provided to a man traveling far from home. You certainly qualify there. Its purpose is to provide such a man with a temporary wife for which he pays a fee. At the end of the marriage, no further obligations are owed unless a child has been born."

"That's the smartest approach to marriage I've ever heard. Mussolini says he is coming here to civilize the savages of Abyssinia. He might do better to send the Pope over here to study civilized marriage. You ought to put that in your paper."

Mills replied, "Oh, but that won't sell as many newspapers as the idea of the seat of the Christian world making war on the oldest Christian nation in Africa. Hell, Italy declared a Fascist Sunday to convince all those young conscripted Italian soldiers and their families that God is on Mussolini's side. That bastard Mussolini means to have a war with these Ethiopians." Jim Mills looked around the room. "These bright, funny, proud, and hospitable friends of mine just can't move this ancient nation into the twentieth century in time to meet the threat of modern warfare. Anyway," Jim raised his cup, "here's a toast to you, my Brown Condor, and to me and all the other poor bastards who trade home for the wild winds of fortune."

Jim smiled and added, "Happy flying."

Chapter 15

Rocks in the Clouds

THE THREE WRIGHT WHIRLWIND J-5 ENGINES OF THE 1930 FOKKER F-VII b/3 tri-motor droned steadily. In spite of experienced hands adjusting the throttles, the trio of propellers moved slightly in and out of synchronization, playing their own harmonic tune. John was flying left seat with Paul Corriger in the right seat acting as check-pilot. The high-wing tri-motor was the largest aircraft in Ethiopia's stable. All seats in the cabin area behind the cockpit had been removed to make room for a cargo of six hundred gallons of aviation fuel carried in one hundred and twenty five-gallon tins stacked on pallets carefully secured with cargo nets and straps. The total weight of the fuel, tins, and pallets was barely within the maximum allowable cargo limit. Both Corriger and Robinson were aware of the dangerous cargo. They took turns at frequent intervals going back to check for leaks and to make sure the tins were all secured.

With the fuel in the wing tanks and six hundred gallons in the cargo bay, John had made the most careful takeoff of his flying career. At sea level and gross weight, the Junker would climb at a little over six hundred and fifty feet per minute. Taking off from the nearly eight-thousand- foot elevation of Addis Ababa, it was a struggle to reach two hundred feet per minute climb. He cringed at every bump and thump the landing gear took on the long takeoff run, praying the loose rocks wouldn't blow a tire. It took nearly thirty minutes of circling to climb forty-three hundred feet above Addis Ababa to reach their cruising altitude of twelve thousand feet. The Fokker FVII b/3 had a service ceiling of only fourteen thousand feet at gross weight, but with no oxygen for the pilots, twelve thousand was as high as they cared to fly. That would get them through the mountain passes.

The cargo of fuel would be off-loaded and stored at the ancient city of Adowa located some four hundred and fifty miles north of Addis Ababa near the Italian Eritrea border. It was at Adowa thirty-nine years before that the Ethiopians had soundly defeated an invading Italian army. News accounts of the day accused the Ethiopians of commit-ting barbarous atrocities and told of the death of ten thousand Italian soldiers and the loss of seventy-two cannon. Il Duce had been thirteen when that disastrous event had occurred. Now, as his Italian army was massing on the Italian Eritrean border in preparation for a new invasion, Mussolini promised the Italian people he would avenge that defeat.

The figures concerning the cannon had stuck in John's mind. Shortly after hearing the story of the Italian defeat, he learned that almost half of the present artillery strength of Ethiopia was comprised of those same antiquated seventy-two cannon captured in 1896. After looking over the Ethiopian inventory of aircraft, he was convinced they captured half their aircraft in the same battle. He had seen the list of aircraft presently on fly-ing status. Listed were eight French Potez 25s powered by 450-horsepow-er, Lorraine-Dietrich engines—planes that were only slightly improved over the aircraft of the Great War. There was one tri-motor Fokker FVII b/3 (the one they were now flying), one old Farman F-192 single-engine transport, and two large Junkers W 33c single-engine transports. Not one of them was armed. About eight other planes were listed as "currently unserviceable."

The flight Robinson and Corriger were making would serve three purposes: transporting a stockpile of fuel to Adowa, giving Robinson a checkout in the Fokker FVII b/3, and also familiarizing Robinson with some of the country over which he would be flying.

John looked down at the jagged terrain below. Their route of flight followed a road leading from Addis Ababa past Dessie, then a turn slightly to the left to cross the beginning trickle of the Takkase River and on toward the village of Skota. From there they picked up another trail that would lead them to the town of Adowa situated on the cusp of the rugged, hot, desert lowlands fifty miles from the Italian Eritrea border.

There were few maps of Ethiopia, none accurate enough for precise navigation, and no radio beacons or modern air navigational aids. A compass, a watch, a good memory for landmarks and terrain features, and a pilot's own notes were the most dependable means of navigation available to a pilot in Ethiopia in 1935.

During John's orientation, Corriger pointed out that it was extremely important to learn every valley, canyon, riff, riverbed, road, village, and other distinguishable terrain features. He reminded Robinson that unless he did, he could easily become lost. "Without such knowledge," he said, "a pilot might fly up an unfamiliar canyon only to find that it narrowed too much to allow a turnaround and that the canyon walls rose faster than the plane could climb. If such a canyon terminates in a dead end, so will the plane and pilot. If you go down in the wilds of this country, even if you survive, it's likely you won't be found, at least before you die of thirst."

Corriger had John's attention. He recalled what he had read about the early mail pilots in the States. They drew their own maps, sketching important features along their route. Some of the notes might read, "Large barn with twin oaks at south end and windmill at east side by pond," or "river fork with two sets of rapids points north. Course 320 degrees from fork." If a pilot was flying above broken cloud or fog, his life might depend on his ability to recognize in one brief glance some feature on the ground that would tell him his present position.

As important recognizable features appeared below, Corriger shouted over the engine noise to point them out. John jotted down the information in his notebook along with compass courses and altitude, often adding crude drawings.

The central plains were at elevations between four thousand and ten thousand feet. The highlands had mountain peaks that towered above fourteen thousand feet. On this day, with the monsoon blowing moist air up from the sea, clouds and rain had kept them company. Flying at twelve thousand feet, sometimes above cloud cover, John could see mountaintops projecting out of the white fluff. He realized that the clouds of Ethiopia could have rocks in them.

Robinson appreciated the fact that had Paul Corriger not known every trail, ridge, stream, and rock outcropping along the way and not carried a notebook listing the compass course from one prominent terrain feature to the next, they could have easily made their mark in life at about the twelve-thousand-foot level on the side of some ridge, canyon wall, or mountainside. John entered every feature Paul pointed out to him in his own notebook. Ethiopia is about the size of Texas and Oklahoma combined. He had a great deal to learn.

John noticed the terrain had begun to drop toward the lowland desert. The rain and clouds faded behind them. Their destination was not far ahead.

Adowa, like most of Ethiopia's towns and villages, had no airport. Corriger told him that a flat stretch of ground near a village would have to do for an airfield. John knew that the high-wing Fokker FVII b/3 tri-motor had a stout, fabric-covered steel tubing fuselage and plywood-skinned wooden wing. It was as strong as a bridge. Its thick-chord wing was capable of lifting almost any load that could be put in the plane. It incorporated a tough landing gear with large wheels and tires, which, by design, allowed the plane to operate from rough, unimproved fields.)

As instructed, John made a low pass over the village to alert the work detail of their arrival. Then he circled a landing area that had been cleared by the villagers and made a low pass for a close look at the landing zone. It was a flat, rocky stretch of ground.

"That's it? Looks rough to me."

Corriger answered, "Yes and yes."

Circling once more, John lined up for the final approach to landing. He was sweating and not just from the heat. This was a test and he knew it. John spread his right hand over the three throttles on the center console. He eased them back a little and re-trimmed the aircraft. A few feet off the ground, John eased the three throttles back further, keeping a little power on to gentle the heavily loaded plane onto the ground.

The clattering sides of the Fokker FVII b/3 and the banging struts of the landing gear announced contact with Mother Earth. John pulled the throttles to idle. With use of the rudder and judicious application of brakes, he held a straight path. The plane waddled over the rough field, raising a cloud of dust before coming to a stop. After shutting down all three engines, the only thing Robinson could hear was a ringing in his ears. It was (and is) a common ailment of pilots who fly piston engine aircraft.

John sat slumped in his seat for a moment. The fatigue of the flight was settling on him. It always takes a little while for a pilot to transition from sky to ground. John reached down to unfasten his seat belt and noticed that the Frenchman was already out of his seat.

"Not bad," Corriger said. "Not as good as *Corriger*, of course, but not bad. Now," he continued, "we'll be here for the night. By the time the work crew gets out here, unloads the plane, and refuels it, there won't be enough daylight left to make the return flight to Addis Ababa. Clouds, rain, and the mountains are a challenge to any flight, but even for Corriger, night flying over this terrain is suicidal. There are few lights visible below and no way to recognize landmarks."

Squeezing past the pallets of fuel tins to the rear door, Corriger took a large funnel from its storage place behind the rear cabin bulkhead. He and John stepped out into the heat of Adowa. It was a shock after the cold air that had filled the drafty cockpit at twelve thousand feet. Both men were quick to pull off their leather jackets and seek shade under the wing while they waited for the workers to arrive.

"Time for another lesson," Corriger said. "We'll oversee the refueling. Never trust anyone to fuel your plane unsupervised. Check the fuel from every tin and filter every drop that goes into your tanks. I discovered a tin from which someone had stolen half the petrol and replaced it with water, or maybe camel piss, both are about the same color around here. On another occasion, an opened tin had been tipped over and some of the fuel spilled. The poor devil who spilled it was so afraid he would be in trouble that he scooped up the puddled fuel with a pan and put what he could save back in the tin. Petrol is precious as gold here, but not when it's full of sand or water. I think you see my point."

John shook his head. "This is getting to be more fun all the time. How long have you managed to stay alive at this game?"

"Four and a half years, but if war comes, it will be all your game. My government will frown on a Frenchman fighting their neighbors the Italians."

"Oh! That's just great."

"Don't blame me. After all, war, if it comes, will be between you Ethiopians and Il Duce."

"What you mean 'you Ethiopians'? You know I'm not Ethiopian. My country don't want this boy fighting Italians, either. Remember, I'm supposed to be over here selling airplanes that the League of Nations won't let me import."

"You will be." Corriger looked at John with a peculiar smile.

"Will be what?"

"Will be an Ethiopian, *mon ami*."

"Now tell me just how you figure that."

"It's simple. When the emperor receives you, he will already have my report on your excellent ability and qualifications. He will honor you by bestowing upon you rank, salary, and Ethiopian citizenship. Surely you will not refuse such an honor from the emperor himself."

"Did he offer you citizenship?"

"I am afraid the color of my skin prevented him from making such an offer, but he has been most generous in the area of pay. It would be ungrateful of me to complain. *C'est la guerre.*"

A dozen Ethiopians arrived to unload and fuel the plane. John climbed up on the wing and took the funnel from Corriger. It had a chamois skin filter. After chamois leather has first been soaked in fuel, water will not pass through it. The work crew formed a line to pass the tins of fuel down from the plane and carry them to a storage area nearby where they would be hidden under desert-colored canvas and scrub brush. The Fokker FVII b/3 had a range of seven hundred miles. The round trip would be close to nine hundred miles. The last forty tins were passed up to the wing, opened, and their contents emptied into the Fokker FVII b/3 fuel tanks using the chamois filter.

John looked down at Corriger. "You crazy bastard, you won't leave if the Italians start a war."

"Of course not. But we won't tell France that I am here fighting the Italians and we won't tell America that you are an Ethiopian. We crazy bastards must stick together, no? Now pay attention to the fueling. The precious two hundred gallons they are filtering into our tanks added to the remains of our fuel from the trip out here ought to get us back to Addis Ababa tomorrow . . . if you don't get us lost."

House at 1905 31st Ave. Gulfport, Mississippi, in which John C. Robinson grew up.

John C. Robinson (far left) with teenage friends. The boys had just swam across the harbor to impress the girls.

Janet Waterford-Bragg (right, in flying clothes) who lent Robinson her plane to fly to Tuskegee Institute.

Robinson is welcomed by President Moton and Dr. Patterson of Tuskegee after landing on the campus in 1933 to promote the idea of a Tuskegee school of aviation.

Airport at Robbins, Illinois, that Robinson helped found. Robinson is at far right.

Curtis Wright Aviation School. Robinson became an instructor there after graduating from their flying school.

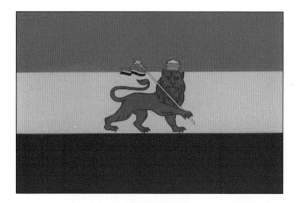

Imperial flag of Ethiopia, 1935

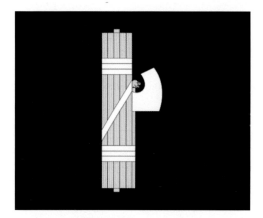

Fascist flag of Italy, 1935

Ethiopian Imperial Air Force aircraft roundel insignia

John C. Robinson, as a Captain in the Imperial Ethiopian Air Force (second from left), with French pilots hired by Emperor Haile Selassie.

Robinson (left) with French pilots hired by Emperor Haile Selassie. Note the Potez 25 biplane in background.

Photo Credit: John Stoke

Col. John C. Robinson
Ethiopian Air Commander c.1935
Photo donated by his cousin
Gwendolyn Woods

Photo Credit: Gwendolyn Woods

Col. Robinson standing beside Junkers W33c transport. Note the Imperial Lion of Judah insignia on side of the aircraft.

Col. Robinson prior to takeoff in Junkers W33c transport.

Potez 25 aircraft like the one Col. Robinson flew on patrol

Italian IMAN RO 37 Used by Regia Aeronautica Italiana (Italian Air Force) in Ethiopia.

Sovoia-Marchetti SM 81 bomber.

IMAN RO 37 hunting targets of opportunity over Ethiopia.

Photo credit: T. Simmons Collection

Col. Robinson giving flight orders to Ethiopian pilots.

ETHIOPIA'S FLYING ACE

(A. P. Wirephoto)
First photo from Ethiopia of John C. Robinson, Chicago Negro, known as the "Brown Condor," who was appointed chief of air force in Ethiopia by Emperor Haile Selassie.

Italian Army CV 33 Tanketts used in Ethiopia.

Col. Robinson with Beechcraft model B17R Stagerwing in which he flew Emperor Haile Selassie between Addis Ababa and his front lines.

Col. Robinson returning to the U.S. aboard the North German Lloyd Lines ship, *Europa*.

Col. Robinson aboard the North German Lloyd Lines ship, *Europa*.

Col. Robinson stepping from Transcontinental and Western Air (TWA) DC 3 at Chicago to a welcome by members of the Challenger Air Pilots Association which he helped organize. His friend Cornelius Coffey is at lower left.

Photo taken from the balcony of the Grand Hotel at the intersection of 15th and South Park Avenue. An estimated 20,000 people turned out to hail their hero, Col. Robinson, who was standing on the balcony.

Col. Robinson's new Stinson SR Reliant. Mrs. Malone, founder of Poro College, stands beside the plane waiting to begin a tour of several cities to promote her cosmetic products.

Photo credit: Jim Cheeks

Col. Robinson in Gulfport with his Cadillac convertible.

Photo credit: John Stokes

Col. Robinson in his commercial pilot uniform at an Army Headquarters flight line shack.

Col. Robinson with his chosen American cadre of pilots to begin training a new Ethiopian Air Force. The group at their villa in Addis Ababa.
Standing L to R: Jim Cheeks, Ed Jones, Haile Hill and Joe Muldrow.
Front: L to R: Andy Hester, Col. Robinson.

Starting engines after complete overhaul on a U. S. surplus Cessna UC 78.

Col. Robinson with an English Army sergeant at the airport in Addis Ababa, Ethiopia, 1944.

Jim Cheeks standing by the tail of the Cessna UC 78. Note the Ethiopian roundel on the fuselage.

The first class of flight cadets trained in the UC 78, the only plane available at the time.

Colonel John C. Robinson beside the first Ethiopian Air Line DC-3.

Chapter 16

Audience with the Emperor

THE SUN BROKE THROUGH THE THINNING CLOUDS TO CHEERFULLY brighten the morning. John took it as a good omen on the day he was to meet Haile Selassie. The rain had turned the streets to mud but nobody seemed to notice. Robinson picked his way carefully trying to keep his shoes and pants clean until he reached the paved street that ran past the Arat Kilo Ghibi Palace, built by King Menelik in the late nineteenth century. The emperor lived in the Guenete Leul Palace but worked in the Imperial Ghibi Palace. The gate leading onto the palace grounds was guarded by two armed soldiers wearing greenish-khaki uniforms like those of the Belgian army. The smartly uniformed palace guards were special members of the seven thousand strong Imperial Body Guard, the most well equipped military unit in Ethiopia. The members of the palace guard itself were handpicked from a northern tribe noted for their height. Most of them were nearly seven feet tall. John presented the formal invitation he had received the day before. Written in Amharic characters and English beneath the royal seal, it requested his presence at the palace. The ranking guard examined the card, looked Robinson over carefully, motioned for him to wait just inside the gate on the palace grounds, and proceeded to the palace.

Moments later the guard returned with an equally tall man carrying a sword and dressed in white jodhpurs and puttees but no shoes. He motioned Robinson to follow him past two lions chained beside the walk leading up to the palace steps. One lion was asleep. The other watched with deep staring eyes as they passed.

At the top of the steps, John was turned over to the emperor's chamberlain who led him into the palace and down a hall to a pair of massive, beautifully carved doors. With no apparent order given, the doors were swung open by two uniformed guards. Robinson hoped the excitement he felt would not show.

The doorway opened into a large, high-ceilinged room. To the left side was a magnificent carved desk, to the right side stood a cavernous marble fireplace. The focal point sitting on a plush Oriental carpet was a gilt chair upholstered in red brocade and bearing in gold thread a likeness of the imperial crown. The chair, quite large and sitting on a raised platform, was occupied by small man, bearded and dark complexioned with an aquiline nose and the most penetrating black eyes John had ever seen. John bowed slightly before the emperor as he had been instructed by the chamberlain.

The man before him, dressed in an immaculate military uniform, appeared weary, but his eyes reflected both energy and warmth. Robinson was not the first to sense a calm dignity, almost an aura of regal bearing, when in the presence of His Imperial Majesty, Haile Selassie I, Emperor of Ethiopia, King of Kings, Elect of God, and Conquering Lion of Judah.

The emperor smiled. With a motion of his hand, he summoned the royal interpreter.

"Mr. Robinson, do you by chance speak French?"

"Just Southern English I'm afraid."

"I asked because His Majesty speaks French fairly well but English only haltingly." The interpreter turned to the emperor and bowed, indicating the audience could begin.

The emperor spoke in Ethiopia's national language, Amharic, and the interpreter translated. "His Majesty says we welcome you, John Robinson. We are honored and deeply grateful that you have traveled so far to offer your services to Ethiopia."

John replied that it was he who was honored to serve His Majesty, a man he had long admired. "I hope my ability as a pilot will be of some value to you and your country."

The emperor paused often for the interpreter to speak. "His Majesty has studied your qualifications and the reports of your performance by our own air group since your arrival. They are excellent reports. As you must know, we are in the process of training Ethiopian pilots, but none have yet attained the level of your skill and especially your experience. We have therefore continued to rely on our French airmen to lead our air service. If war cannot be avoided—and we pray it will be—but if it cannot, the French staff will be placed in an awkward position. France insists that these men cannot fight against her neighbor, Italy. Belgium, likewise, is anxious to avoid giving offense to Italy. The official Belgian military mission here will be withdrawn in the event of war. We have arranged for certain Belgian volunteers, some from the Congo, to discreetly return as advisors. However, they will not be allowed to enter actual combat and risk embarrassment to their native Belgium. If their nationals were captured, neither France nor Belgian would appreciate being caught in such an international incident. Because of the color of their skin, they certainly could not pass for Ethiopians. Also, in the case of the French pilots, we are afraid our people, under the stress of war, would have natural suspicions of any white ferenjis that might fall from the sky and be captured. We could not guarantee their safety."

The interpreter continued, "That being said, His Majesty would like for you, John Robinson, to consider the following offer: the rank of colonel and command of the Imperial Ethiopian Air Corps and, of course, Ethiopian citizenship which would protect your country from any similar embarrassment."

The emperor continued through his interpreter, "We understand your concern. We do not want to endanger your American citizenship. We have discussed this with the honorable Cornelius Van Enger, your country's chargè affaires here in Addis Ababa, and he feels this can be looked upon as dual citizenship. We will refer officially to your service as advisory.

"I admit that our selfish interest will be served by the publicity your activities will generate in the American press, but I ask if this is not one of the reasons you are here?"

John had to agree. "That's true, but not for me personally so much as to help open aviation to blacks in my country. If a black man can prove his flying ability here, a black man should be allowed to do the same in America."

The emperor nodded.

His interpreter continued, "His Majesty says you will, of course, be properly rewarded for your services. We realize that our offer presents you with a most serious decision. We respect your need for careful consideration. We will, should you refuse the offer, bare the expense of your return to America."

The meeting was over.

Back at his hotel, John sat in his room for a long while thinking about the offer and what he had seen and learned over the past few weeks. He thought of home and the security of the flying school he had established, which his friend and partner Cornelius Coffey was now running. He had been promised an appointment to head up a school of aviation at Tuskegee when and if necessary funds could be found to establish it. He also knew from what he had seen and learned that should war with Italy come, Ethiopia could not win without help. John was homesick and afraid, but he was no coward.

An aviator who had grown up in Mississippi was now a colonel in the Imperial Ethiopian Air Corps. Walking down a muddy street to his hotel, wearing a smart uniform cut in the style of Britain's RAF, he won admiring glances from young women in the marketplace.

Colonel Robinson hardly noticed. His mind was on more serious thoughts. In the breast pocket of his uniform he carried two passports, one American, one Ethiopian. He wondered if he would ever be allowed to use the former again. An 1818 US law forbade American citizens to accept commissions in a foreign army at war against a nation in peace with the United States.

In a letter to his mother, he tried to explain his situation. "I'm now a colonel, Momma. I'm sometimes in the company of an emperor who appeals for peace before the League of Nations. Why don't they do something to stop this Mussolini fellow? Do you read much about it the paper at home? I'm making more money than I ever have. I will send most of it home to you. The air corps here is small, but I have been given its command. I wonder if anyone at home knows all this or even cares. I love you, Momma. Tell Daddy I love him too. Don't worry about me. I'll be alright." He signed it "Johnny."

What he did not tell his mother, but knew full well, was that Ethiopia was in harm's way. He didn't have to tell his mother that. Haile Selassie would give her proof enough.

On any given Sunday, the emperor attended church services carrying a rifle to dramatize the fact that although Ethiopia was praying for peace, she was preparing to fight if necessary. Nearly ten thousand miles away, a picture of the emperor at church with a rifle was carefully cut out of the *Daily Herald* newspaper and placed with John's letter in the small drawer of a bedside table. Celeste Cobb sat on the edge of her bed and closed the drawer. "Lord," she prayed, "please look after my boy, Johnny."

John bought the latest English language newspaper available. It was dated July 1935 and carried little news from the United States. It did say that one senator, a Democrat from Missouri named Clark, was calling for a full investigation of all lobbying on Capitol Hill. John wasn't sure what lobbying was, but it sounded like the senator thought it was a little crooked. A front-page headline blared, "Japan at war with China."

The League of Nations is supposed to take care of things like that. Sounds like that War to End all Wars didn't do the job. War seems to be breaking out like chicken pox.

Two short articles on flying drew John's attention. The first stated that Wiley Post, a noted American aviator, was making final test flights for a new floatplane he and his friend Will Rogers planned to fly from Los Angeles to Moscow via Alaska. Another article was closer to home. A new aviation record had been set by two brothers over Meridian Mississippi. Al and Fred Key had set a world endurance flight in a modified Curtiss Robin monoplane using their own method of in-flight fueling. Their flight had lasted an incredible twenty-seven days, five hours, and twenty-four minutes.

That ain't bad for a couple of boys from Mississippi. Damn! If that in-flight fueling could be set up right, they could fly around the world without landing. Somebody's gonna do that one day.

Two political cartoons appeared on the opinion page. One showed Mussolini juggling arms and treaties while a bystander told Hitler and Stalin, "It might pay for you boys to watch this guy a little longer." The second cartoon depicted Hitler giving Mussolini a medal for breaking up world peace machinery and the ring of nations surrounding Germany.

Making one last appeal, Haile Selassie, with tears in his eyes, rose to plead for peace and protection for his country before the body of the League of Nations in Geneva, Switzerland. As he began to speak, Baron Aloisi of Italy walked out. Shortly after, the Italian consul in Addis Ababa received orders to withdraw from Ethiopia. To appease Italy, France and England had secretly agreed to keep out of "the Abyssinian thing." Both countries wanted to keep Italy on their side should Hitler start a war in Europe. Without France and England, the League of Nations could argue but not act to keep the peace. Dejected, disillusioned, Haile Selassie returned home to prepare to defend his people as best he could. Ethiopia would have to stand alone.

The rainy season ended. With Italian troops massed on the Ethiopi-an borders, there was little doubt what the dry season would bring. On September 28, 1935, Cornelius Van Enger, US chargè affaires in Addis Ababa, advised all US citizens to leave Ethiopia. He, his wife, and his staff would bravely stay.

Chapter 17

Gathered at the River, 1935

Ethiopia had chosen to join the League of Nations in 1923. Haile Selassie, agreeing with the stated principles of the League, believed his country safer by virtue of the protection that the self-esteemed body promised member states under its Articles of Collective Security. Just the year before, 1922, Mussolini had bullied his Fascist party to power in Italy. Selassie was not blind to the potential threat that posed to his country. Italian colonies bordered Ethiopia on two sides. Now, eleven years later, that threat had grown to a clear and present danger.

To the north of Ethiopia was the Italian colony of Eritrea. To the south lay Italian Somaliland. Italian troops were massing on both borders. It was clear, not just to Ethiopia but to the world at large, that Mussolini was preparing to attack the proud, independent Christian nation once called Abyssinia. Emperor Selassie formally appealed to the fifty-two member League to act on its covenant to provide collective security to prevent or stop any aggression perpetrated by one member state against another.

While Selassie appealed to the League to honor its covenant, he ordered his troops to pull back thirty kilometers from Ethiopia's northern and southern borders to preclude any incident that might be used by Italy as an excuse for war. It was a futile gesture. The League went through the motions of addressing Selassie's appeal fully aware that its bureaucratic procedures and formal deliberations could drag on for months even without internal interference. In the matter of Ethiopia, Italy provided internal interference at every turn, often aided by France.

French Premier Pierre Laval was concerned about its Fascist neighbor, Italy, as well Germany's new government formed by the National Socialist German Workers' Party under Adolf Hitler. In January 1935, as an act of appeasement, Laval secretly concluded an agreement with Mussolini that conceded France's disinterest in Ethiopia in return for Italian concessions in favor of French citizens living in Tunisia. The attitude of the British government's foreign office was no better. The British foreign minister, Sir Samuel Hoare, privately assured Italy that the British Empire had no interest in Ethiopia whatsoever. He was concerned about any threat Fascist Italy's West African colonies might pose to Anglo-Egyptian Sudan. England and France thought it better for Mussolini's attention to be directed toward conquering and colonizing a backward African country rather than stirring up trouble in Europe. What both France and Britain failed to take into account was that by accommodating Mussolini in his egregious grab for Ethiopia, the act would destroy the credibility of the League of Nations, its post Great War ideal of collective security, and, most damaging of all, the perceived balance of power in Europe. (One nation that did not fail to notice the weakness displayed by the League in regard to Fascist Italy was Hitler's Germany. His National Socialist German Workers' Party had adopted Mussolini's Fascist rationale by 1933.)

Emperor Selassie realized too late that the faith he had placed in the League of Nations had been a mistake. It became sadly obvious to him that neither the League as a body nor a single member nation would step forward to try and prevent Fascist Italy from violating Ethiopia's borders. Even worse, none offered Ethiopia any support or material aid. Italy, an industrialized European nation, home of the Vatican, seat of the Christian world, was poised to invade an ancient, agrarian African nation of twelve million people, a Christian nation since Biblical times, the only African country that had successfully resisted colonization by both the Islamic Ottoman Empire from the East and Christian Europe from the West.

Selassie knew the coming war would be one his people could not win, but they would fight rather than capitulate. His hope was that by fighting he could buy time, time to gain the attention of the world, time for the League of Nations to at least prevent Ethiopia from becoming a Fascist colony. The clock was ticking.

On September 27, 1935 in Asmara, capital city of Italian Eritrea, a telegram from Mussolini was delivered to the Italian field commander General Emilio de Bono. It read, in part, "You will attack at dawn on the third, repeat, third of October."

As fate would have it, the next day, September 28, the following order was issued throughout Ethiopia by means of handbills and telegraphs, transported by donkey, runner, drums, and a handful of liaison aircraft:

All men and boys old enough to carry a spear will be mobilized and sent to Addis Ababa. Married men will take their wives to carry food and to cook. Men without wives will take any woman without a husband. Women with small children need not go. Those who are blind, cannot walk, or for any reason cannot carry a spear are exempted. Any able man who is found at home after receipt of this order will be hanged.

Signed: H.I.M. Haile Selassie I.

In the early morning darkness before dawn on October 3, young Italian troops moved sleepily to their assembly points on the north bank of the shallow Mareb River. Each man was issued four days ration, a half-gallon of water, and 110 rounds of ammunition. Some sat on the ground finishing breakfast. Some nervously checked and rechecked their equipment. Others gathered in small groups. There were the usual attempts by the young and inexperienced to smother pre-battle fear with jokes and bravado. Most left unsaid any reference to the battle Italy had fought and lost to the Ethiopians thirty-nine years before at Adowa in 1896. More than ten thousand of

Italy's finest troops had been killed in the humiliating defeat made more so by the fact that, for the first time, a modern European colonial power had been driven out of a black African nation.

The soldiers gathered at the river knew that a long, hard, uphill trek lay before them. There were few trails capable of use by motorized vehicles. Mules, not trucks, would have to serve as primary supply transport until passable vehicle routes could be built. Their initial goal, the town of Adowa, was situated at an elevation three thousand feet higher than their starting point. The Italian columns would have to climb rising desert terrain sparsely covered with thorn bush and laced with deep canyons and lava-strewn ravines. If existing routes could not be found, trails leading up steep escarpments would have to be cut. The troops were worried about being ambushed in such terrain. What made them even more nervous were rumors that in the war of '96, the Ethiopians castrated Italian prisoners. It gave the young soldiers pause to consider the part they were being ordered to play in building Mussolini's New Roman Empire. As time grew short, their mouths became dry and talk died away. In the uncomfortable silence, each man was left to his own thoughts.

The order to advance came at the first light of dawn. Flag bearers unfurled their banners and trumpets blared in a triumphal procession befitting the new conquerors from Rome. The rising sun illuminated a hundred thousand soldiers wading across the shallow Mareb River in three large columns spread along a forty-mile front. In addition to modern rifles, de Bono's army carried 6,000 machine guns and had at its disposal 700 pieces of artillery, 150 tracked CV 3/35 tanketts (small, two-man tanks carrying twin 8mm machine guns), 140 aircraft, several thousand motorized vehicles, and 6,000 mules. Held in reserve were 100,000 additional soldiers. At the same time there was a lesser, but formidable number of troops massing on Ethiopia's southern border with Italian Somaliland. The crossing of the Mareb River on that morning, October 3, 1935, was the first step of a Fascist march that in four short years would engulf the world in war.

High above and slightly to the south of the Mareb, a tiny speck in the sky went unnoticed by the columns marching below. It was an obsolete French Potez 25a2 biplane, its single 450-horsepower engine throttled back to reduce noise. From five thousand feet above the river (eight thousand feet above sea level), a young black pilot from Gulfport, Mississippi looked down on the invading army below. Just seventeen years after the end of the Great War, Colonel John Charles Robinson unwittingly became the first American to witness the first Fascist step in the march toward World War II. (The Great War was not referred to as World War I until World War II broke across the globe.)

John had taken off from Adowa in the dim glow of false dawn to begin another routine patrol of the section of the northern Ethiopian border along which the Italians were encamped. As the African sunrise made a golden ribbon of the shallow Mareb River, the lone pilot knew this day was different. Clouds of dust streaming in the shallow light of a new day left no doubt that the Italian army was on the move. He was stunned by the panorama of troops and equipment advancing into Ethiopia. Robinson knew his job now was to gather as much information on the ongoing invasion as time allowed, and he knew time was short. Italian aircraft would be lifting off from the airfield at Asmara, Italian Eritrea, just 140 miles away; they would have armed aircraft—single-engine Imams or tri-engine Marchettis or Caproni 133s, any of which could outrun his obsolete, Lorraine-Dietrich powered Potez biplane.

John cursed himself for leaving his silk scarf in his room. Constantly turning his head to search the sky for enemy planes, he was rubbing his neck raw on his stiff uniform collar. He flew westward parallel to the Mareb River for a distance he estimated to be fifty miles before he arrived at the western flank of the invading army. Across that distance he had observed three massive columns sloshing across the Mareb into Ethiopia. There seemed to be no end to them. As he wheeled back to an eastward heading, his sharp eyes spotted six tiny dots in the sky to the northeast. It was time to run. John turned southward pointing the nose slightly down to gain speed toward Adowa where he would have to refuel before flying on to Addis Ababa with the terrible news. He found himself shivering and wondered if it was from the altitude chill of the open cockpit or cold fear.

Constantly checking the sky behind him, he began to relax when he found no following aircraft. His thoughts turned to the weeks that had so quickly passed since his arrival. He had to admit that up to now his time in Ethiopia had been fun—challenging and hard work, but fun. He enjoyed the training flights over the rugged, beautiful country. There were inhospitable stretches of mountainous desert that reminded him of pictures he had seen of the western badlands of North America, high fertile plateaus of grain and coffee farms, grasslands, rugged desert lowlands, beautiful lakes and rivers, jungle wilds, snowcapped mountain ranges, and the great Rift Valley. He had been surprised to find such friendly people in this exotic land. John smiled, remembering the military parade staged in the capital city. Belu Abaka, the nearly seven-foot-tall drum major of the Imperial Army Band, had led the procession past the emperor's magnificent pavilion especially erected for the occasion in Cathedral Square. Invited to stand with the royal entourage, John had to bite his tongue to keep from laughing when the emperor's royal lions that had escaped from their cages suddenly made an appearance. The crowds of spectators lining the parade route scattered in all directions. The emperor was not amused.

John was still smiling when Adowa appeared out of the haze a few miles ahead. Robinson thoughts quickly returned to the present. *My God! How long have I been flying straight and level?* He quickly whipped the Potez into a hard bank to the right and then to the left to check the sky behind. *What the hell am I doing letting my mind wander?* Turning his head as far to the left and right as his safety harness would allow, he made one more "S" turn to survey the sky for enemy planes before easing off the throttle and descending toward the rocky plateau ahead.

There was no airfield at Adowa, just a stretch of flat rocky ground at an elevation of six thousand feet on the edge of town. It would serve well enough. The townspeople had cleared the area of brick-size and larger stones. Weeks before, John had landed a Fokker tri-motor transport on the same stretch of ground.

Before landing, he flew low over the town to alert the ground crew that he was coming in for fuel from the supply he had delivered in the tri-motor transport. It would have to be a quick turnaround. Enemy planes launched from Asmara Eritrea could appear at any time. Robinson wasted no time getting back into the air.

On the ground in Addis Ababa in just under four hours, he ordered his plane to be refueled before getting into a waiting car to be driven to the palace.

Once past the guards, he was greeted at the main entrance by the chamberlain and ushered through the palace halls directly to His Imperial Majesty, Haile Selassie, working in his study with two scribes. An interpreter was quickly summoned.

"Please be seated," Selassie, speaking Amharic, communicated through his interpreter. "Tell me what you have seen, Colonel Robinson."

John related all he had observed from the air, careful to speak slowly and pause often for the benefit of the interpreter. While the emperor listened to every detail with solemn attention, his scribes recorded the interpreter's translation of John's report and his answers to the emperor's questions.

"The same may be taking place on our southern border with Italian Somaliland," the emperor said.

John injected, "I expect Lt. Mulu Asha within two hours. He had the morning patrol over the southern border out of Kallafo on the Shibeli River."

The emperor hesitated a moment, picking his words carefully. "I know what you must be thinking. We do not have enough machine guns, artillery, aircraft. We have not had time to train enough soldiers in modern warfare and we have too few radios. I naively thought joining the League of Nations in 1923 and the 1928 Treaty of Friendship with Italy would protect us. I was terribly wrong. We cannot win if we do not get help. Nonetheless, we will fight them, we will try to hurt them, slow them down at every mountain pass, river and ravine, hit them and run, bite their flanks, ambush them wherever we can. Our only hope is to buy time to gain the world's attention. Surely someone will aid us in our struggle." The emperor paused. "You are an American, and you have left your home far away. I realize this is not your war. If you want to leave, I will understand. But know this, you must make the decision now. My people and I need you, John Robinson, in more ways than you know, but the choice to go or stay must be yours."

Robinson was silent for a long moment. He appreciated the frankness of the emperor's words, knew he spoke the truth, could not shake thoughts of the dire risks of staying, had considered leaving. He thought of home, of his parents he had seen so seldom since leaving college, thought of the flying school in Chicago that he had left behind, and the good times, the parties, the women, all the things he had taken for granted that had made his life pleasant, even fun.

Does anyone back home really need me in the way these people need me? Here I command an air corps, a small one that probably can't last long, but for now it's mine. Hell, some white folks at airfields back home won't even sell me gasoline. It's for damn sure they won't make me a colonel.

"Your majesty," John finally spoke, "I will stand by the offer I accepted. I don't know how long I can keep the Imperial Air Corps in the air, but I will do my best."

Haile Selassie nodded his head. John bowed and walked toward the door.

"Colonel Robinson?" the emperor asked.

John turned. "Yes, your majesty?"

"If you stay, you will be entrusted with great responsibility."

John answered, "I am staying, Your Majesty."

The emperor replied, "One last thing before you return to your duties. I know you have asked for faster planes. I have been informed that in the event of war, the League of Nations intends to declare an embargo of war material against our nation and Italy. It will hardly make a difference to Italy, but we will greatly suffer from such an embargo. We ordered new fighter planes, but I have been informed England and France canceled the orders. If I can't obtain military aircraft, perhaps you know of a civilian plane that might suit our purpose. It may just be possible for us to get such a machine."

John thought a minute. "Your Majesty, there is a small American firm, Beechcraft, that has just introduced a new, fast, cabin-model. They call it a Stagger Wing. I believe if we can get one or two with the largest engine option, it would make a good courier plane, better and faster than anything we have now."

The emperor nodded and Robinson took his leave.

When John returned to Akaki Airfield just southwest of the capital, he didn't have to call together his pilots and ground crew. They were waiting for him, waiting for the news he carried. He stood silent a moment looking at the faces gathered around him: French pilots Andre Maillet, Paul Corriger, Gaston Vedel, and Comte Schatzberg; French mechanic Demeaux; Ethiopian pilots Mishka Babitcheff (whose father was Russian), Bahru Kaba, Asfaw Ali, and Tesfaye; and German pilot Baron H. H. von Engel. Language was just one more problem John had to face. He had learned a little French and less Amharic, but only a few phrases in each. He had arranged for an interpreter to be at the airfield at all times to man the telephone and the one radio they had—the one on duty to translate his words into Amharic for those who did not understand English. Paul Corriger did the same for Maillet and Demeaux who were not proficient in English.

John didn't waste words. "We're at war," he told them. "The Italians are attacking from Eritrea. They may be attacking from Italian Somaliland to the south as well. When Mulu Asha returns, we will know what's happening there.

"Now y'all listen good. I've done no fighting in the sky, but what I am telling you is what I have been taught by someone who has. He said the plane you don't see is the one gonna kill you. We got no guns. They do. Our planes are slower than theirs. You see a dot in the sky or even think you do, run. It'll be an enemy plane. Any of 'em can kill you.

"From this minute on, all aircraft will be fueled upon landing, parked away from others, and covered under brush or whatever can be found to hide 'em. That goes for wherever you land. The big planes are going to be hard to hide. If you can't cover them completely, use anything you can find to break up their shape. The only time I want to see a plane in that hangar over there is when it needs work. The Italians gonna bomb every hangar they find.

"You pilots avoid contact with Italian aircraft any way you can. The emperor doesn't need you bravely dying for Ethiopia. What he needs is aircraft and pilots. Do everything you can to preserve them. To keep from being seen, fly very low following the contours of the terrain or fly very high. If an Italian pilot sees you, you can bet he will come after you. They will think it great sport to shoot us down. We are so few that Italian hotshots will run all over one another trying to get credit for knocking one of us down. If they see a plane on the ground they will destroy it. We are all probably worth a medal to them. If that scares you, good. It scares me. It ought to make you more careful. You're gonna have to use every trick you got. You know the country, the terrain, they don't. Fly down into canyons, hide behind hills and mountains, and duck into clouds. If they shoot at you, zigzag, slide, slip, do anything to throw their aim off. You gotta constantly look for the enemy. Keep your head turning all the time. Never, never fly straight and level for more than a few seconds.

"Our job is to maintain communication between commanders in the field and headquarters here in the capital. We will deliver ammunition and medical supplies in the transports when we can. We have a hodge-podge of flyable aircraft, not enough pilots, and little to no chance for parts or replacements. Every plane is important. Most of us gonna wind up flying all day, every day. Do all you can to protect both your aircraft and your hide. The Italians can outrun everything we have. We are couriers, not warriors. I don't want any heroes. The only advantage we have is knowing the terrain, knowing where to hide. Remember that and stay alive. Any questions?"

There was shocked silence. John dismissed everyone except his second-in-command, Corriger, who had been in charge of flying until John's appointment.

"I hope you aren't angry 'cause the emperor appointed me in command."

"Mon ami, I am the one who told you that would happen, remember? My pay is the same. I am glad not to be responsible. With this war, you have an impossible job. Besides, all Frenchmen will be ordered back to France. I've told you France doesn't want Frenchmen fighting Italians. Neither does Germany. Gaston Vedel, Comte Scharzberg, and Baron von Engel are leaving."[2]

"But you won't go?"

"I will stay as long as I can. So will Demeaux. Don't ask me why. I really have no answer."

John looked at his French friend. "I do. You are one crazy Frenchman."

Corriger shrugged his shoulders and held up both hands.

John smiled. "Okay. Can you write down everything I just told the group in English, French, and Amharic? Get copies to everyone, especially ground crews and pilots who weren't here?"

"Certainly."

"When Lieutenant Mulu gets back, tell him he is now a captain and in command of the southern front. Tell him to pick three pilots to work with him. I will take the northern front. Paul, anytime I'm gone, you're in charge here. Dispatch pilots and planes as ordered by headquarters. Always have at least two planes and crews warmed up and standing by from sunup to dusk. Demeaux's in charge of maintenance and fuel. And Paul, you are not to fly unless it's an emergency. Don't look at me like that. Those are the emperor's orders, not mine. Even in an emergency, he

---

2 It should be noted that although he left Ethiopia, Gaston Vedel and his wife fought bravely in the French underground during WW II. Both were captured by the Gestapo and sent to concentration camps. Somehow they both survived. It is not known at this printing what happened to Comte Schatzberg or Baron H. H. von Engel.

said you're not to fly over enemy-held territory. Hell, if you go down over friendly territory he's worried that his warriors will take you for an Italian and kill you. Any questions?"

Corriger shook his head.

Robinson nodded, walked out to the Potez, climbed in, and took off once again for Adowa.

Exhausted at the end of the first day's march, the Italians had advanced little more than five miles after crossing the Mareb River. The terrain made for slow going. Although by sundown no shots had been fired, the young Italians were wary. There was an old African saying: "The darker the night, the bolder the lion." The night could enfold black warriors in its darkness, warriors known to be silent and deadly with cold steel. Pickets were put out and camp guards doubled. The next morning several platoons awoke to find a single comrade among them with a slit throat. The news traveled fast. Few Italian soldiers slept much after that.

Because the Ethiopian army was not equal to the task of meeting the Italian invasion head-on, Haile Selassie's plan was to allow the Italians to advance well inside Ethiopia before engaging them, where they would be dependent on long supply lines. He established his initial battle lines fifty miles from the frontier. This meant the abandonment of Adowa and Aksum. The emperor believed that by doing so the civilians of the towns would be spared. John's orders were to standby in Adowa as long as possible in order to collect as much information about the Italian advance as could be gathered by Ethiopian scouts. Robinson was then to fly the information to headquarters in Addis Ababa.

In Adowa, Robinson reasoned that the rugged terrain coupled with hit-and-run raids by small Ethiopian bands would delay the enemy's advanced units from reaching the town at least three or four full days. John knew the Italians had been informed that Adowa was an undefended, open city. He expected the enemy to march in to occupy the town without shelling it, but in anticipation of the Italians scouting Adowa from the air, he hid his plane under brush a safe distance from the edge of town. That aircraft was the only available means of rapidly transmitting vital information to the capital. Robinson planned to stay in town on the fourth of October and fly out at dawn on the fifth. He figured that would give enough time for runners to bring in initial information on the Italian advance—what units were engaged, their order of march, weapons and equipment, rate of advance, and other intelligence that would help Selassie, his war cabinet, and chieftains plan tactical strategy.

On October 4, Ras Seyoum Mangasha withdrew his small raiding force after making a lightning hit-and-run attack on an Italian scouting force. He and his men took shelter in a cave on a mountainside near Maryam Shoaitu. While having breakfast at first light on the morning of the fifth, Ras Mangasha heard a sound he had never heard before. He ran to the mouth of his hideout. The strange noise was the drone of fifty-four aircraft engines reverberating across the valley and off the cave walls. What he saw was eighteen tri-motor aircraft heading for Adowa from Eritrea. Having rarely seen an airplane in the Ethiopian sky, he was awed by the sight.

John had enlisted the aid of three scribes and established a message center in a building in Adowa used as a court of law. All night, runners had streamed in with reports from various scouting parties shadowing the Italian advance. The scribes recorded on paper every runner's verbal report. Most able-bodied men had left Adowa when they received the emperor's call to arms. Except for John, the scribes, and a few men guarding the Potez and cache of gasoline, all that remained in the town were women, children, and old men.

At the first dim light of dawn, Robinson was stuffing the reports into a leather courier pouch in preparation to fly them to Addis Ababa when he heard the sound of approaching aircraft. The first bomb explosion startled him, the second blew down the door to the street and knocked him off his feet. At first stunned, he recovered enough to realize what was happening. He grabbed the leather message pouch and ran into the street just as a Caproni tri-motor flew overhead. Each of the three six-plane squadrons came in succession to drop their bombs on a helpless town of little or no military value.

The civilians had never witnessed squadrons of multi-engine aircraft roaring above their heads. They were terrified by the deafening staccato of exploding bombs.

Roofs collapsed. Walls tumbled into streets as the bombs were unleashed across the town. Lethal shrapnel, debris, and shards of glass mutilated bodies. The screams from the wounded and dying were more unbearable to John than the deafening explosions as he stood in the shattered doorway of the message center clutching the leather pouch with both hands. Blood streamed unnoticed from a cut on his cheek. His mind refused to work.

What seemed minutes to John was in reality a matter of seconds before rational thought returned in the midst of chaos. His job was to get the reports he had collected to Addis Ababa. As the noise of the Italian planes faded, Robinson began to make his way through wreckage-strewn streets toward the field at the edge of town where he hoped he would find the Potez in one piece.

The streets were filled with confused and frightened old men, screaming women, and terrified children, some walking, some standing dazed, many staggering in all directions through clouds of smoke and dust. The wounded, the dying, and the dead were everywhere. John stumbled and fell upon what he discovered to his horror was only half of what had been a human being. Getting to his feet, he saw a crying, blood-splattered baby lying beside a mutilated body. He lifted the child and passed it to a dazed woman sitting in a nearby doorway. Without looking at John or the child, she clutched the baby to her and began moaning and rocking back and forth. He continued toward his plane as the last of the Italian bombers disappeared northward toward Eritrea.

The Potez sat covered with brush as he had left it. Several white-clad, elderly warriors ran from hiding to help John clear the brush away from the plane. They had been guarding the cache of gasoline.

"Thank you" was one of the few phrases of Amharic that Robinson had learned. The men nodded, stepped away, picked up their spears, and walked solemnly toward the smoldering town.

God help them! These people are going to pit spears, swords, flesh, and courage—all they have—against machine guns, planes, tanks, and artillery.

John started the Potez's engine, checked the gauges, swung the plane around checking the sky for enemies, turned into the wind, and pushed the throttle forward to the stop. The Potez withstood the bone-shaking abuse of the stone-rough field as it struggled to reach flying speed before lifting at last into smooth air lightly smeared with wisps of drifting smoke from the destroyed town.

Upon landing at the capital, Robinson spoke to no one except the driver of the waiting car. "The palace, fast!"

Driven directly to the palace, he was immediately ushered into the War Room. Emperor Selassie and his war cabinet stood around a huge table covered with maps. John stood awkwardly by the door a moment, the leather pouch full of reports held close to his chest with both hands. Everyone in the room turned to stare at him in silence. He diverted his eyes down for a moment, and for the first time he was aware of his appearance. He was covered in dust and dirt, his uniform and hands stained with blood, that of the dismembered torso he had fallen over and his own blood from the cut across his cheek. The wound had bled a line down the side of his face and throat, spilled over his shirt collar, and disappeared into his jacket. What those in the room saw was a mass of clotted blood and dirt stuck to the lower right quarter of his face. Fortunately, the wound looked worse than it would turn out to be.

After a moment, the royal interpreter spoke. "His Majesty will hear your report, Colonel Robinson."

John handed over his courier pouch before describing in detail the aerial attack he had witnessed. He left out nothing: the description of the bombers, the terrified civilians, the destruction and death, everything he could remember. When he finished, there was dead silence in the room.

For a moment Selassie looked at John with deep sadness in his eyes. Seconds later, in fiery rage, the emperor slammed his fist on the table.

"In good faith we made treaties and agreements with Italy according to international protocol. They have not only violated every agreement they made with us, but the very precepts upon which the League of Nations was founded. Mussolini hasn't even bothered declaring war on us. He has slaughtered our people in Adowa when I deliberately declared it an undefended open city. The Italians could have marched in without firing a shot or dropping a single bomb. By their cowardly attack on women and children they have revealed their hand. In this undeclared and unjustified war, they aim to kill our people whether we fight or not. They are the barbarians! We will declare war! We will fight them until we can fight no longer."

The telephone rang. An aid picked up, listened for a moment, then hung up.

"Your Majesty, Captain Mulu Asha has just landed. The Italians have not moved from their line on our southern border with Italian Somaliland. The captain is on his way here to give a full report."

The emperor thanked John and told him to get some rest, that he would receive new orders soon.

By the time Robinson reached his hotel, he hardly had enough strength left to walk down the hall to his room. He was tired, lonely, and frightened. Safe for the moment, he could not clear his mind of the horrific images he had seen. Starkly aware that war had only just begun, John knew he had been lucky to find his aircraft unscathed and escaped. He wondered if he would be so lucky the next time. He was shaking, perhaps from lack of sleep and fatigue, perhaps from shock.

When he opened the door he was surprised to find his room spotlessly clean. There was a bowl of fresh fruit on the table by the couch. He was even more surprised when the door to his bath opened and he found himself staring at an equally surprised, slim, young woman with beautiful almond eyes. She wore a traditional white *kamis*, a long loose dress. It had a gold chain around the waist. She returned his gaze with equal questioning. She looked toward the door, then back at John. Her perplexed expression slowly turned to a shy smile.

"Please," she said and held out her hand.

"Who are you?" John managed to ask.

"Please," she repeated, as she was often to do. It was the only word of English she knew. She stepped forward, took John's hand, and led him to the bath, which was filled with hot, steaming water. John stood mute, wondering if the girl could feel him shaking inside. Before he could decide what he should do, he found himself naked, sitting in a tub of hot water with the girl kneeling beside the tub, bathing his filthy, aching body. He was too tired to be embarrassed and too in need of company to ask questions. The girl carefully cleaned his face and frowned at the cut across his cheek. The bleeding had stopped.

Whenever the lovely young lady said "please," he simply did as she motioned for him to do. When she finished drying him, she led him to the bed. There she smiled and gently kissed the cut on his cheek. John wanted to cry, laugh, hold her desperately close, but most of all he wanted not to be alone with the fresh images of war dancing across his mind. She moved softly next to him and he held on to her tightly. They did not speak. They did not kiss. John simply laid his head upon her breast and clung to her as a child might cling to his mother. He knew his worst fear was of fear itself, the kind that can turn a man into a coward.

She held him until he fell asleep, and then she quietly gathered his soiled uniform, laid out a fresh one on the chair next to his bed, and let herself out of the apartment.

The next day, October 6, the Italians marched into what was left of the town of Adowa. As Emperor Selassie had ordered, not a shot had been fired in defense of the town. Some of the Italian troops, looking at the bombed ruins and pitiful people, began to wonder if Ethiopia could possibly be worth a war, much less the risk of their own lives.

In Rome there was joyous celebration upon receiving the news that at last Italy had avenged its shameful defeat at the hands of Ethiopia in 1896. Church bells rang and people turned out in the streets for a victory festival. Mussolini bathed in the adoration.

At Adowa, General De Bono ordered several battalions turned out for review in formal celebration of his great military victory. The ceremony was complete with banners, bugle fanfares, drums, and motion picture crews. It was meant as a grand gesture to boost the morale of the soldiers and, of course, make General De Bono the star of Italian motion picture news. The average soldier, standing in formation after hard days of marching uphill, would just as soon have skipped all ceremony in favor of a hot meal, a cigarette, and rest.

Mindful of the hundreds of thousands of warriors that could be waiting ahead, De Bono halted the most powerful war machine Africa had ever seen in order to consolidate his forces and bring up his artillery, tanks, and supplies before preceding deeper into Ethiopia. De Bono was a cautious man.

Chapter 18

Dogs and Rabbits

On the same morning, October 6, that General de Bono was celebrating his victory at Adowa, John was having breakfast with Mulu Asha.

"When I got to my room yesterday, there was a girl there."

"I'm glad you brought that up. I did not know quite how to approach the subject. What happened was not planned," Mulu replied.

"You know?"

"Yes. She came to my family's house last night and told us. She is my sister's best friend. You must understand. She did not intend for you to find her there. She is no servant, my friend. She is the daughter of a chieftain, a Ras, and the former wife of a friend of mine, a student pilot. He was killed in a training accident more than a year ago.

"Word travels fast in Addis Ababa. You are better known to our people than you realize. When word came that you were back from Adowa and had gone to the palace, she and my sister took fruit and flowers and supervised two hotel servants to clean your rooms so everything would be fresh and clean. You have come a long way to help us. It was a small thing, but still something they could do to show our people's appreciation. My sister and the servants had just departed when you arrived and surprised the lady as she was leaving. When she saw you, I think she lost her head for a moment. Great God, man! You don't know how shocking you looked. She said you were covered with caked blood and dirt, there was oil and blood on your face, your uniform was torn, and you looked dreadfully shaken. She could not simply run past you out the door and leave you like that."

"Please, what is her name? I want to see her again . . . at least to thank her."

"My friend, it is best that you not know who she is for now. She is a little afraid to see you. And there is her family to consider. Her father is . . . well, a high ranking official. This is no ordinary lady. You will have to wait and see. Besides, my commander, it appears that you and I are going to be very busy flying from here on out."

"Well, damnit! I must have some sort of name for her . . . what is the Ethiopian word for 'lady'?"

"If she was single it would be *weiserit* for miss, but since she is a widow you would address her as madame. The word is *weisero*."

"All right. Tell her I don't have to know who she is, but I desperately want to see her, to be with her when there is time. We don't have to be seen by anybody. I won't embarrass her. Will you tell her that for me? Maybe the three of us could meet together, we could always have a chaperone. Do you understand the word chaperone?"

And so they did when there was time. The three met to dine or picnic, sometimes at the farm of their friend Ras Tamru. John learned some words of Amharic and his *weisero* learned a little English, but she did not reveal her true identity and John never asked. He just knew he needed her. In the months that followed, she provided him with beauty and peace when his world was filled with the ugliness, frustration, and horror of war.

The following morning, Paul Corriger joined John and Mulu at the Akaki airfield, which was commonly referred to as simply the new airfield. The first few years of flying activity in Addis Ababa had taken place on the racetrack and polo grounds. However, the foreign diplomatic set had been so irate at this interference with their Sunday sport that the emperor finally gave in to their complaints and ordered a landing field constructed on the outskirts of the capital.

"Paul," John asked, "how many aircraft are flyable?"

"Demeaux says it's a good day. We have ten that might get off the ground—two Fokker F-Vllb/3m, the Farman F-92, five Potez 25s, the Breda Ba15, and one Junkers W33c. Demeaux is doing the best he can. Parts are scarce. We have trouble getting them past the French customs at Djibouti. I'm surprised they let shipments of fuel through."

"Ten flyable planes and eighteen pilots, the new ones with less than a hundred and fifty hours total time. The Italians have two hundred modern planes and well-trained pilots. Not very good odds. When our planes are gone, daily contact with the front will be gone."

"Why worry?" Mulu said. "When the planes are gone, most of us will be gone."

"That's a happy thought."

"I'm just trying to be logical."

"The army still has a few field radios," Paul suggested, trying to change the subject.

"I've seen 'em," Robinson answered. "One man cranks a generator by hand while another works a telegraph key. In the mountains they often have trouble reaching the next relay station and those have trouble contacting the radio at the palace. As far as international traffic goes, there is one commercial station downtown. It's always busy with government traffic and three dozen news reporters fighting to get their stories out. I've been told the American consulate has just received a transmitter. Cornelius Van Engert begged Washington for one because he was frustrated trying to get his official traffic out through the commercial one in town. What they sent was an old transmitter and generator that came from an obsolete submarine from the Great War. Four American sailors came with it to keep the thing working."

Mulu brought up a subject he had tried before. "The Potez 25s came with machine guns but the army took them."

John sat down at his desk. "I know there's been talk of arming our planes, but adding guns would be like puting spiked collars on rabbits to fend off dogs. If they catch us rabbits, they'll shoot us out of the air, guns or no guns. Their IMAM RO 37 is at least thirty miles an hour faster than a Potez 25. If we put a gun, ammunition, and gunner in the back cockpit, the extra weight will slow us down even more. The Italians know we don't have a real fighter. We're messengers. That's our job. We can carry a message from the front in hours that would take runners days to deliver. Every month, every week, every day we have even a single plane left is important. We have to convince every pilot we have how important he is and that his only chance is to run if he sees a speck in the sky."

"We have told them," Paul answered.

"Well tell 'em again, dammit! Who went out this morning?"

"Bahru Kaba to the south, Asfaw Ali north. Tesfaye is transporting fuel to the southern front at Neghelle, and Mishka Babitcheff is here on standby," Corriger replied.

John nodded in approval. "Is the phone line to the palace working?"

"Yes," answered Mulu. "I checked it myself."

"See that it's checked every morning." John stood up. "Okay. I've got a meeting with the emperor. Probably to get more good news. Why don't y'all ride into town with me? I'll buy lunch."

Corriger smiled. "How could we refuse?"

The three, dressed alike in flight coveralls and leather jackets, climbed into the staff car, a dusty, dented 1929 Peugeot painted a dull green the same shade as their aircraft, and like the aircraft it had a roundel painted on the rear door of each side. The Ethiopian roundel consisted of a six-pointed yellow star with alternating long and short points in the center, a red circle surrounded by a yellow middle ring, and a bright green outer ring.

On the drive into town, the three sat in moody silence until Corriger started singing a bawdy French song popular among pilots during the Great War. He changed the words to inflict funny insults on the Italians.

He sang it in English for the benefit of his American friend. John and Mulu picked up on the chorus.

After the singing and laughter, the three lapsed into silence once more until Mulu said, "I'm the only sane one among us. I have to be here. It's my country. You both volunteered, you could leave this madness but you don't. You both must be crazy. You know none of us can last long in the air."

"You have that wrong, my friend," Corriger said. "We are all sane. It is the world that has gone mad. It is the same for us as it is for you. It is honor that won't allow us to run away. We sing and laugh, yes, because we are afraid to cry."

John returned to the hotel dining room after his meeting at the palace, sat down at the table, and did not speak so much as a word of greeting.

"I know what the emperor wanted," Paul said. "You are to be his personal pilot."

John turned to stare at him. "How the hell did you know that?"

"Ah, mon ami, the answer is simple," replied Corriger. "The emperor has already flown a few times to show his people he is not afraid. I know because I have been his pilot on such occasions as had Andre Maillet. He has also flown with the Junkers representative, Herr Ludwig Weber, but he is leaving for Germany. So you see, the poor emperor has no choice. His fantastic white French pilot," Corriger pointed to himself, "has been forbidden to fly to the front. If the famous Corriger was captured by the Italians, it would cause embarrassment to France, an international incident Ethiopia cannot afford. If Corriger is caught by the Ethiopian warriors, they may think he is Italian because he is white and likely will kill him. The famous Corriger does not care for either possibility. Voilà! Robinson! Some fool must have recommended you very highly. It would appear you are considered the best pilot in Ethiopia . . . besides Corriger, of course. "

"To the front? I'll fly the emperor to the front?"

"Bien sur, mon ami. He is a warrior, too. He will want to see everything for himself and be seen by his soldiers."

"He shouldn't risk getting in an airplane with the sky full of Italians. They could be here over Addis Ababa any month now, any week. We don't have a single plane that can outrun them. God Almighty! What if I get him killed?"

No one answered.

When they arrived back at the Akaki airfield, John looked out at the pilots and ground crew milling about the planes. He had to smile. Half of them were barefooted. The Ethiopian ground crew and even some of the pilots absolutely refused to wear shoes. They all said the same thing: Shoes were uncomfortable, they could run faster without them, and shoes would trip them up on uneven, rough ground. *The soles of their feet must be as tough as my boots.*

"Okay," Robinson said. "Call 'em over here. I've got a new schedule. It sure ain't gonna be much fun."

In the days and weeks that followed, John and his pilots continued to fly orders to the northern front and reports to the capital while Mulu Asha and his group covered the southern front where General Graziani still held a defensive position along the border of Italian Somaliland. To the north, out of the town of Bedda on the eastern edge of the Danakil region, Ethiopia lost its first plane and pilot. More were to follow.

The only encouraging news John had was that his efforts to promote black aviation were beginning to be recognized as the war in Ethiopia gained a following in the American press. A letter from his mother told him that the prominent NBC radio network broadcaster Lowell Thomas had picked up on the Brown Condor and mentioned him from time to time during his evening news program. She said the Gulfport-Biloxi newspaper the *Daily Herald* was printing stories about him, too.

After moving out from Adowa and taking the town of Adigrat, General De Bono received a direct order from Mussolini to attack Makale. General De Bono objected, pointing out that to do so would leave the entire left flank of his army uncovered. But the order stood and De Bono obeyed. Makale fell, but at a heavy cost to the Italian troops on the left flank.

Taking into account reports of large Ethiopian troops gathering south of him on a line between Dabat and Bedda, De Bono was determined not to follow such unsound orders again. He stopped to once again consolidate his forces. Robinson and the pilots assigned to the northern front kept Selassie's staff abreast of the fact.

The general stressed caution in his communications with Il Duce, emphasizing the very rugged terrain that made slow work of bringing up his trucks, tanks, and artillery while affording the enemy opportunities for ambush. Ignoring De Bono's reports, messages from Rome impatiently requested resumption of the Italian advance. When a direct order from Mussolini arrived demanding that De Bono immediately resume the march without delay, the general balked, indicating in his reply that to resume the advance without consolidating his forces and supplies could lead to disaster. Six days later De Bono was informed that he was being relieved of his duties. He would be replaced by General Badoglio.

It was not a marked difference in competence that was to greatly alter the nature of the war in Ethiopia. It was a difference of character. De Bono was a capable warrior who saw his role more as a pacifier of the Ethiopian people than as a ruthless conqueror. Badoglio, like Mussolini, considered Ethiopians "savages in need of civilizing." Badoglio's single aim was to quickly destroy Ethiopian resistance by any and all means available.

Haile Selassie had no pool of trained generals from which to choose his leaders. A few young Ethiopian officers had received training at Saint-Cyr, the French military academy, and a few others at Sandhurst in England, but none of Selassie's generals had formal military training or experience in the traditional sense. He had to choose from among the rases of his country whose followers comprised the army. That presented a problem. Selassie was aware that Italian agents had been in his country for a long time. He suspected, and in many cases confirmed, that some Ethiopians were in their pay: Rases, especially the Galla, were disgruntled from losing some of their power to Ethiopia's new constitution. There were others in the government hungry for power. Because of the danger of internal revolt, Selassie was forced to choose his generals based upon one qualification: loyalty.

But there was another problem: greed. Informants and some Ethiopian military leaders were won over by Italian bribes—the Black Eagle, Hubert Julian, appointed commander of an infantry unit, had been forced to leave the country under such suspicion.

Badoglio arrived on November 20, 1935, only to recognize, as had De Bono, that a consolidation of men, equipment, and supplies was indeed essential before launching the next stage of campaign. The reason? The Italian army on the northern front was under attack.

Selassie had chosen his generals well. In late 1935, Ras Seyoum Mangasha's force of thirty thousand, Ras Kassa's forty thousand, the thirty-thousand-man force of Ras Mulugeta, and Ras Imru with another forty thousand men not only held the northern Italian army, they began to push the Italians back from the Takkaze River.

The Ethiopians quickly learned to move by night, attack at dawn, and then fade away to hiding. These tactics avoided air attacks and murderous artillery fire. They used the night to infiltrate the Italian lines, engaging the enemy with rifles and bloody hand-to-hand battle. Wave after wave of warriors assaulted the Italian fortifications in this manner.

John was flying back and forth to the front daily. For a time, the reports he brought to the capitol were encouraging. One battle in particular greatly raised Ethiopian morale, though at a high price. Ras Imru's forces attacked a group comprised of Italian and Eritrean troops supported by CV3/35 tanks. The two-man tanks were armed with twin 8mm machine guns.

The Ethiopians, some armed only with spears, attacked the Italian forces and cut off their escape route. The Italians turned their twelve tanks against the Ethiopian line, blocking their escape across a ridge at Amba Asar. The Ethiopians immediately broke ranks, not to retreat but to attack in the face of deadly crossfire from the tanks. Running in mass, the Ethiopians engulfed the steel machines by sheer weight of human flesh, killing the crews by shooting point blank through the drivers' and gunners' vision slits. By sundown, the Italian force had lost half its troops.

The Ethiopians pushed back the Italians all along the Takkaze River, exposing the Italian flank. Ras Imru now began to hammer away at it. Simultaneously, Rases Seyoum and Kassa engaged in a siege against the Italians at Warieu Pass. Ras Mulugeta pushed against the Italian third corps and began to encircle the town of Makale, threatening to retake it. If Badoglio was forced to withdraw, it would mean moving seventy thousand men, fourteen thousand mules, and some three hundred artillery pieces down a single road. To do so would open their columns to attack on both flanks.

The Ethiopians accomplished gains against the superior Italian force in spite of being under air attack, something the warriors had never before experienced. They had few automatic antiaircraft guns. To make up for the lack of proper antiaircraft protection, Selassie's warriors were trained to kneel and fire their rifles in mass at attacking planes. The training was effective. After Regia Aeronautica Italiana suffered the loss of 110 crewmen killed and 150 wounded, they learned not to fly low. As a result, their bombing and strafing was less accurate.

John, flying as close to the front as he dared, not only delivered reports confirming the Ethiopians were pushing the Italians back, but saw the Italian lines retreating northward himself. Though Ethiopian losses were great, spirits ran high.

The Italians on the northern front had moved forward less than fifty miles in a month of fighting. Despite Mussolini's badgering, Badoglio was no more willing to resume the drive toward Addis Ababa, nearly four hundred miles to the south, than De Bono had been. After two months, facing the real possibility of an embarrassing retreat, Badoglio sent a message to Rome requesting permission to use "special" weapons. De Bono had refused to use such weapons. Badoglio had no such qualms even if they were illegal according to the Geneva Protocol of 1928, which outlawed "the use in war of asphyxiating, poisonous, or other gases and of all analogous liquids, materials, or devices." By 1935 thirty-nine nations had signed the protocol including both Italy and Ethiopia. But Mussolini not only personally authorized the use of poisonous gases, but he also encouraged their use. Large stores of a variety of 'special' weapons were shipped and brought up to the front. On January 20, 1936, Badoglio was at last ready to resume the initiative.

From the sky fell a "terrible yellow rain." The weapon was Yperite: mustard gas delivered in artillery shells and bombs and sprayed from specially equipped tri-motor bombers. The Ethiopian warriors could not understand "rain that burned and killed," had never faced anything like it. Though terrified, they tried to fight, but in just four days of such brutal attacks, the battle of Tembien Province was over. By the January 24, 1936, the Ethiopian warriors who had fought so bravely against impossible odds could no longer stand up to the deadly clouds of mustard gas that blistered their skin and lungs and blinded their eyes.

John Robinson had seen the terrible price the Ethiopians had paid. From the air, one battlefield looked as if it was spotted with patches of snow, the snow being piles of dead warriors clad in their white garments, thousands of them. Mussolini's sons Vittorio and Bruno and son-in-law Count Ciano all flew Caproni aircraft for the Regia Aeronautica—Vittorio would later record his experiences in his book *Flight Over the Ambas*. In one passage, Vittorio describes how much fun it was making great "white blossoms" on the ground below. The "flowers" he described were composed of the white-clad bodies of Ethiopian warriors blown high in the air as Vittorio's bombs exploded among them.

Meanwhile, the Italians had suffered less than two thousand casualties. Still, they were shaken. Only the use of poisonous gas had stopped the Ethiopian attack.

John increasingly flew closer to the fighting to guide larger planes carrying medical supplies to forward aid stations, some run by the Egyptian Red Crescent others by the Swedish Red Cross. Count von Rosen of Sweden flew his own plane, which he had outfitted as a flying ambulance. All the medical planes were painted white and marked with large red crosses, as were the field hospital tents.

Though never enough, there were medical volunteers aiding Ethiopia. American born soldier of fortune Hilaire du Berrier arrived and offered himself as a pilot, but when the United States and England canceled the military planes Ethiopia had on order, there was no aircraft for him to fly, and instead Du Berrier volunteered to help by working with the medical services. (He would ultimately be captured by the Italians. Undaunted, Du Berrier in 1936 flew in the Spanish Civil War. During WWII he fought with the OSS in China and survived it all.) An impressive list of volunteer doctors from all over the world included Robert Hockman of America, George Dassios of Greece, Shuppler of Austria, Hooper of America, and Balau of Poland. The British furnished an ambulance service commanded by John Melly (who was killed late in the war). Field hospitals and medical teams were sent by Sweden, Finland, Greece, Norway, and America.

After the battle of Tembien, those Ethiopians still able-bodied melted away in small groups. Counting on there being little need for Italian air support in the area, John thought it was safe for him to make a quick reconnaissance of any new Italian movements. It was a mistake. The Italian pilots, no longer needed in coordinated mass attacks, had been set loose on their own. They were out hunting for sport, shooting at remnants of retreating Ethiopians. They found it fun.

As Robinson finished his run and turned for home, he caught movement out of the corner of his eye. He swiveled his head to see two dots in the sky to the north. As he watched, the specks grew larger. John was a very good pilot, but had no combat experience. He had never been shot at in the air. His plane was unarmed. A chill climbed up his spine.

Come on, you rabbit. This ain't no game. Those dogs are after your hide.

John pushed the throttle forward to the stop. At sea level, his engine was rated at 450 horsepower. In the thin air at twelve thousand feet, the engine wouldn't produce near its rated horsepower. The two Italian planes slowly gaining on him were new IMAM RO 37 bis—biplanes of the Italian 103 Squadron equipped with 560-horsepower engines and armed with machine guns. They could reach speeds of 180 miles per hour.

There was no question that they would catch the 450-horsepower Potez with a top speed of only 130 miles per hour.

As he flew southward, John knew his only hope was to trade the danger of being shot down for the danger of flying into the clouds that lay hovering over and among the low mountaintops ahead. He flew directly for them. He had to reach the clouds.

Robinson looked back and saw the two Imams now only about a mile behind. The next time he looked, he saw they were much closer, maybe eight hundred yards. Orange flashes were coming from both planes. *Those bastards are firing at me.* John fought to stave off panic. *You panic, you die.* Fighting to overcome a big knot of clawing fear in the pit of his stomach, he remembered what the man on the ship crossing the Atlantic had told him. *If they get behind you, use your rudder to skid the plane back and forth. They'll think you are turning. It will throw their shots off, they'll aim too far ahead of you.*

The Italians were too anxious. They were flying abreast, shooting at too great a distance, each interfering with the aim of the other. But they continued to close the distance to within a few hundred yards. John felt bullets popping through the fabric of his plane. Panic was rising—he could taste its foulness in his mouth. *Snyder help me.* He remembered a trick his instructor had used one playful afternoon in Chicago returning from a lesson in aerobatics. A fellow instructor in a faster plane had gotten on their tail in mock dogfight. In spite of his combat experience, Snyder was having trouble shaking him off until he pulled a stunt to force the other pilot to overfly him. John hoped the old Potez would hold together. He took more hits as the Italians got closer. Then he chopped the throttle, yanked back hard on the stick, and slammed full left rudder. The Potez slowed suddenly and whipped into a snap roll. The horizon spun violently. The glass gauges on his instrument panel shattered and he felt a hot burning across his forearm. The plane had pitched up into the line of fire of one of the Imams. At the same moment, the two Imams flew past the Potez, maneuvering violently to avoid ramming it, nearly having a midair collision with each other. The Italians, suddenly in front of the Ethiopian plane, thought they were now the targets. They both racked into steep turns. Seeing John flying straight ahead, the Imams continued their turns to get back into shooting position behind the Potez. John, nearing the cloud dead ahead, looked down, desperate to recognize some terrain feature to orient himself. There below he was sure he recognized the Takkaze River. If it was the Takkaze, he knew it led through a narrow pass in the mountains. He quickly aligned himself with it, noted the compass course, and plunged into cloud.

The Italians were not willing to be so foolish. They stayed in the clear, chasing up and down the line of clouds believing no pilot in his right mind would long stay in clouds clinging to the mountains. Surely he would circle back out. They would be waiting for him.

Inside the cool, turbulent air of the cloud, John broke out in a sweat. He felt no relief. The hard knot of near-panic was swelling up in his gut again. His mouth was dry. Thank God his compass had not been shot away. He had no choice now but to try and hold the course as steady as he could, the course of the Takkaze. But was it the Takkaze?

He had no instrument to tell if his wings were level. The altimeter and airspeed indicator had been shot away. He could not tell if he was climbing or descending. He could only hold the stick in a frozen position. If the compass moved, he tried to stop it with a little rudder. He strained to see through the gray fluff that surrounded him. He knew about vertigo and how easily it could trap a pilot into believing he was turning or climbing or descending or spinning when he wasn't, or make him think he was flying straight and level when he was doing any or all those other things. He had escaped the Italians, but unless he broke out of the clouds and soon, he would lose either to vertigo or the side of a mountain—or both.

The dark gray of the cloud began to lighten, then brighten. Suddenly the Potez broke into sunlight. John was startled to find he was descending in a slight turn with the rocky slope of a mountain ridge directly ahead. He banked away sharply, brushing the edge of another cloud. He continued banking left and right in large arcs across the sky to avoid both cloud and rock until he could at last orient himself and set course for home.

The clouds became more scattered as he flew southward. He could only judge his altitude by rough comparison to the mountains. He constantly checked behind him. The Italians were gone. His knees were shaking. His face and limbs were numb with cold. He was short of breath, light-headed, tiny stars winked across his vision, sure signs of hypoxia. *I'm too high*. He began a descent. As altitude decreased, his lungs gathered more oxygen. His vision sharpened and the numbness of the cold began to wear off. He became aware of a throbbing pain in his lower left arm. He could not move his left hand from the throttle. He looked down. The palm and fingers of his glove were stuck to the throttle control with clotted blood. By the time he landed an hour later, the pain in his left arm was acute. He felt weak from loss of blood. When he didn't get out of the cockpit, his ground crew climbed up on the wing to help. They wanted to carry him, but he walked to a waiting car, the only one on the field, and was driven to the hospital.

The doctor who dressed his arm told him a bullet had passed through the flesh of his forearm but not broken a bone. John mumbled something to himself. The doctor made out the word "rabbit."

"What's that about a rabbit?"

"I said it's gonna be embarrassing to tell my men 'bout a dumb rabbit that got his self caught by a couple of dogs."

It was the second of three wounds John would sustain.

Chapter 19

A Lonely War

BY LATE 1935, IT WAS CLEAR THAT NOT A SINGLE MEMBER OF THE League of Nations would move to stop the invasion of Ethiopia and the slaughter of its people. Though no governing body of any nation would act to aid Ethiopia, there were demonstrations of support by citizens of many countries. In England, three thousand young men offered to volunteer to fight for Ethiopia. In America, there was a rally of ten thousand people, both black and white, at Madison Square Garden. Blacks in many communities of the United States staged boycotts of Italian-owned businesses. In Cairo, Egypt, the faithful prayed to Allah to spare Ethiopia.

Some support came unexpectedly. In Fascist Berlin, a film entitled *Ethiopia 1935* carried an anti-Italian theme. Germany secretly wanted the Ethiopian war to continue. It would keep Italy from interfering with Hitler's plan to annex Austria, an ally of Italy. Toward that goal, Germany clandestinely supplied thousands of Mauser rifles and ammunition to Ethiopia (likely smuggled across the border from Anglo-Egyptian Sudan).

There were statesmen throughout the west who intuitively realized the Fascist invasion of Ethiopia foreshadowed universal conflict, yet all met passive resistance that prevented any organized effective means of stopping Mussolini's aggression. France did the most to hinder Ethiopia by barring shipment of any war materials through their colonial port of Djibouti. They didn't want to antagonize their Fascist neighbor Italy. As long as Italy was bogged down in Africa, it wouldn't be a threat to France.

As early as October 1935, Haile Selassie acknowledged that his loyal followers had but two choices. They could either submit to becoming an Italian colony after more than two thousand years of self-rule or continue to resist Fascist aggression alone with no hope of aid. It was an agonizing choice. The battle of Tembien had shown the terrible price in loss of lives continued resistance would cost. His council of chiefs, supported by the fierce pride of the people, left him but one choice: to lead his people as long as they had the will to defend their land.

Haile Selassie was not blind to what lay ahead for his nation. The only hope was that Ethiopia could buy time, time in which the Western world might say "enough" and pressure Italy to cease its imperial brutality against a people that never threatened it or meant it harm.

To boost his warriors' morale, Selassie determined that he should be seen among them at the front. It was a decision that placed a heavy burden on John Robinson of safeguarding the life of the emperor of Ethiopia while in the air.

American newspapers carried a small feature among the articles concerning the Italian-Ethiopian war stating, "Piloted by John C. Robinson, a Negro from Chicago, Emperor Haile Selassie made his first plane flight in several years to inspect Ethiopian defenses." It was the first of many flights the emperor would take, his life dependent upon the flying skills of a black aviator from Mississippi.

A civilian Beechcraft plane finally arrived in Addis Ababa. The wings, fuselage, engine, and other various parts were carefully removed from their shipping crates and assembled by Corriger, Demeaux, and Robinson. When finished, they all thought it was the most beautiful aircraft they had ever seen. (To this day, many pilots would agree.) It was a cabin biplane called a Staggerwing because its wings were inversely staggered, the lower wing set slightly ahead of the upper wing. The fuselage tapered smoothly from the streamlined engine cowling over the cabin gracefully back to the tail. It had clean lines and an added feature which helped increase its speed: retractable landing gear. It also was equipped with the latest gyro-driven instruments, which allowed it to be flown safely in the clouds and at night without outside references. The plane was officially called the Beechcraft B17 and had been ordered with a 420-horsepower Wright engine. The interior was finished in leather and could carry up to five people including the pilot. As soon as it was assembled, it was painted the same green color used on the other Ethiopian aircraft and decorated with the Ethiopian roundel as well as the symbolic insignia the Lion of Judah, in deference to the fact that it was the emperor's personal plane.

John immediately began test-flying the Beechcraft and found it a delight to fly. It could perform decent aerobatics, and what's more it could reach a speed of 200 miles per hour in comparison to the old Potez which could barely make 130 miles per hour. John's confidence in the Beechcraft grew with every test flight. *With this plane I can keep the emperor safe.*

Both John and Mulu Asha were flying reconnaissance and courier missions daily under constant danger from attack by the aircraft of the Regia Aeronautica. The loss of pilots and planes had only served to increase their flying to the point of exhaustion. In a letter to his friend and former student, Harold Hurd, John told of flying conditions at the front:

> *The only thing I can say for myself is that I am trying to do my best in whatever mission or duty I have. We are having a hard fight over here with our limited amount of modern war equipment. Every man, woman, and child is doing their part to help, and I am sure with God's help and our courage we will come out okay in the end. Sometimes I have to fly almost constantly. I went two weeks without pulling my boots off during what little time I have to sleep. This is when I am along the northern front. I am glad to do my part, but these conditions might help to finish my flying career . . .*

Mulu Asha brought back reports from the southern front indicating increased activity. During the early stages of the conflict, the Italians had established a defensive line running from the Kenyan border to British

Somaliland parallel with the border of Italian Somaliland. The defensive role did not please an ambitious Italian commander, chaffed at the fact that on the northern front, Badoglio, having been given ten divisions, was getting all the "glory" while he had been given but one division and ordered to sit. His name was General Rodolfo Graziani.

The general finally had enough of doing nothing. He set out to change his defensive role. He expanded port facilities at Mogadishu and opened new supply roads. He motorized his division by buying hundreds of motor vehicles supplied mainly by American manufactures via British automobile dealers in Mombasa and Dar es Salaam. He then communicated his desire for action to Mussolini who, because of successes on the northern front, was at last willing to listen.

While all this was taking place, Mulu brought promising reports from the southern front. The two Ethiopian armies of the south had very different leaders than those of the north. One army was under the command of Ras Desta Damtu, the other under Ras Nasibu, who had traveled extensively abroad. Both were young, progressive, and loyal. There was also Ethiopia's only female general, Weizero Asegedech, who led the thirty thousand warriors of her late grandfather, Ras Tassama. Her warriors were armed with modern rifles and machine guns she had bought for them herself.

With the aid of an old but knowledgeable Turkish officer named Mehmet Wahib Pasha, perhaps better known as Wahib Pasha, the troops of the southern armies were better trained and equipped than those of the north. The officer, who had been exiled by Turkey's dictator Mustafa Kemal Atatürk, insisted on wearing his Ottoman fez and gray-green uniform from the Great War. He had commanded Turkish troops at Gallipoli after which he was given command of the Turkish 2nd Army. It was said that he came to the aid of Ethiopia because he absolutely loathed Mussolini.

In the early battles, the Ethiopians on the southern front held their own against Italian probes, knocking out many of their light tanks upon which the Italian infantry depended for supporting fire, but the

Ethiopians found they could not attack in force. They were under constant surveillance by Graziani's reconnaissance aircraft and if caught on the move would be subjected to incessant bombing and strafing by the Regia Aeronautica.

Increasingly, Mulu's reports grew less encouraging. The Ethiopians were faltering under constant air attacks. The reports also indicated the effects that poor rations, malaria, and dysentery had on the Ethiopian troops. The only good news was that deep behind the southern front, the fortifications of the cities of Harar and Ogaden, all organized by Wahib Pasha, were complete and manned by Ras Nasibu's army of thirty thousand.

On the first day of January 1936, John, Paul, and Mulu were all together in Addis Ababa for the first time in a month. In celebration, they managed to gather the fixings for a small feast at a time when rations were becoming lean in the capital that was now subject to occasional bombing raids. A lamb was prepared for dinner. Corriger supplied choice French wine from his seemingly endless supply.

The three sat on cushions around a low table, talking not of war but of the good times they had spent together before the fighting began. They ate, drank, and spoke of the beauty of the landscape to which they had introduced John during his early days of Ethiopian flying.

"It's so different from what I expected," John admitted. "I thought it would be all desert, brown and rocky. A lot of it is raw and primitive, but I've seen the green valleys, snowcapped mountains, and rivers like the Omo cutting its way through jungle on its way to Kenya. It's beautiful. I wish my momma could fly with me to Lake Tana and follow the Blue Nile, see the waterfalls and rainbows and watch the sun light up the clouds that rest on the mountaintops."

"I believe, mon ami," replied Corriger, "that you have the romantic soul of a Frenchman."

"What I believe is that you two have been deep into French wine," said Mulu, with a smile. "Which reminds me, Corriger, I hope you have your wine cellar well hidden so the Italians won't find it."

"Hell," said John, "if you haven't found it with me sending him off on errands just so you can look for it, the Italians damn well won't find it."

"So that is what you two do when Paul Corriger is away. You are untrustworthy friends and terrible flyers, but this is war. What can one expect? So! I will share my secret even though you are undeserving. I get the wine from a British friend, Gerald Burgoyne, in charge of transporting medical supplies. He somehow manages to get me a case of French wine now and then mixed in with medical supplies shipped up from Djibouti."

"Oh, hell."

"What, John?"

"You didn't hear? Burgoyne was killed up north in an Italian bombing. The damn Italians are bombing and gassing field hospitals and ambulance planes. Count Rosen's plane, painted white with huge red crosses on the wings, was destroyed on the ground last week at Quoram. I know damn well their pilots can see the red crosses in the centers of the big white circles painted on hospital tents and air ambulances. That's one target they fly low over 'cause they know they are all unarmed."

Paul spoke up. "Tonight we agreed not to speak of such things. Our bellies are full, the wine is from another and better year, and we are together for the moment. Let's drink to that."

On the southern border near Kenya where the Ganale Doria River crosses into Italian Somaliland, General Graziani had assembled supplies and strengthened his one Italian division by bringing up several divisions of Eritrean Askaris. At dawn on January 12, Graziani's artillery opened fire on the Ethiopians, beginning a battle that would become known as the Massacre of Ganale Doria.

Mulu Asha had landed behind a quiet section of the Ethiopian line at sundown the day before. He was at the message center to pick up reports to deliver to Addis Ababa when Graziani's artillery opened the battle. He took the dispatch case and ran to his plane hidden under brush just off a tiny cleared landing strip. He had managed to get the plane uncovered when the first wave of Marchetti SM 81 tri-motor bombers roared overhead. The tops of their wings were painted in large red sunburst patterns designed to make them easier for search and rescue planes to spot should any be forced down in the semi-desert terrain. Mulu and his helpers rushed for cover. As they ran, a bomb exploded fifty yards ahead of them. Mulu did not remember hearing the blast. When he awoke, the cool air of dawn had been replaced by midmorning heat. Sounds of fighting and rifle fire drifted faintly from a distance.

Something was wrong. He fought nausea as his mind cruelly regained consciousness. He felt pain, pain he had never felt before. His left eye was not working. His face felt like it was on fire. His throat and lungs were burning. He could not get enough air. Trying to get up, he crawled over the body of one of his ground crewmen before staggering to his feet. Through his right eye he saw the smoldering wreck of his plane. Mulu tore at his canteen and poured water down his burning throat. Then he tried to wash a foul-smelling liquid from his face and arms.

"What's happening?" he asked hoarsely of a passing Ethiopian rifleman.

"Move. We have order to move back. We can't hold. The yellow rain," he said by way of explanation. The rifleman looked at Mulu a moment. "Take that and move." He pointed Mulu to the canteen of the dead crewman, and then he joined the retreating riflemen.

Mulu took the canteen and followed them.

Graziani had given the Regia Aeronautica special orders that morning. The Marchetti SM 81 tri-motor bombers carried no ordinary bombs. The ones dropped that morning were filled with mustard gas, which is not a gas at all but a sticky liquid aspirated into droplets small enough to be breathed, or sometimes, depending on the device used, thrown out in blobs erupting from imperfectly exploding casings. In addition to delivering mustard gas in bombs and artillery shells, numbers of Italian planes, equipped with spray booms and pumps, laid down "yellow rain." The spray planes flew in-trail so that a continuous "rain" of mustard gas would saturate a targeted enemy position or troops on the move. The Ethiopians did not understand the "yellow rain" and were terrified by it. The Italians gassed villages of unarmed civilians as part of their new "terror" strategy.

Mustard gas on contact blisters human skin. If breathed in, it blisters the lungs. Wherever it touches skin, it burns horribly. If the lungs are severely coated, pulmonary edema follows causing death by asphyxiation. The victim literally drowns as the lungs fill up with liquid. Agonizing death comes sometimes in hours, sometimes in days. It is a horrible way to die.

Ethiopia had no gas masks when gas was first used on the northern front. They appealed to the International Red Cross Committee (ICRC) in Geneva to send gas masks. Italy was trying to hide the fact that they were using gas. Under Italian, French, and Swiss influence, the members of the ICRC refused to send the masks on the basis that the appeal for gas masks by Ethiopia "did not state for what purpose they intended to use them." If the ICRC approved the shipment of gas masks, they would have to explain to the media why they were doing so. Italy did not want such an explanation given; it would be embarrassing.

The wife of the British consul in Addis Ababa, Lady Barton, organized the manufacture of gauze bandages impregnated with soda. Ethiopian soldiers wrapped them over their mouths and noses. Though primitive, breathing through soda gauze during gas attacks helped. When they ran out of the soda bandages, the troops were told to tear off pieces of their uniforms or shammas, urinate on them, and breath through them during attacks to help neutralize the gas. It was all they had.

Using motorized columns, the Italians on the southern front outflanked the retreating Ethiopians. They rounded up and shot dispersed remnants of Ras Desta's army. Others fleeing on foot across burning desert sand were often strafed by Italian planes. The few wells that lay along the path of retreat were poisoned by Graziani's mechanized scouts.

On the second day, Mulu ran out of water, as did all the retreating Ethiopians. Most had no food. Those who could keep walking did so. Those who could not were left behind.

Mulu had been splashed by mustard gas. His arms and face were masses of raw blisters. His blind left eye had become infected. Pink, foamy spume leaked from his nose and lips. As he staggered on, he breathed with audible moans. Whether in the blazing heat of day or cool of night, there was no relief from pain. Only raw determination kept him going.

On the fourth day, he was part of a large group that had managed to reach the Genale Doria River—the cool, blessed river. Crazed with pain, Mulu attempted to run toward the river. He stumbled and fell. Fighting for breath, he staggered up and tried to run again, but his damaged lungs would not support such effort. Struggling, stumbling, falling, he finally crawled to the river's edge. The water waited there for him just down the slope of the riverbank.

Machine gunfire erupted from across the river. To Mulu's left and right, cries rang out all along the bank. Mulu crawled on, the pain in his eye unbearable. Almost to the water's edge, Mulu felt a sharp pain tear through him. Pain! He *was* pain. His legs were no longer working. He pulled himself along with his raw, blistered hands until he could lower his face into the muddy, bloody river. He dropped his head, took a single sip. For one brief moment he felt blessed cool water soothe his poor face. Then . . .

Mulu Asha was dead. They were all dead, all of them.

Italian mechanized scouts, guided by air reconnaissance, had reached the river first. Setting up their machine guns on the far bank, they waited. They knew what was left of Desta's army was staggering, thirst-crazed to the river.

Three young Italian soldiers manning one of the water-cooled machine guns saw the dark-skinned hoard crest over the far bank like stampeding animals. Down poured the first wave to prostrate themselves at water's edge, row upon row waiting their turn behind, bodies so densely pressed together not a grain of earth lay uncovered.

On command, the young Italians opened fire. One of them fired the gun, swinging the barrel back and forth, the trigger pressed. The second one fed the ammunition belt into the breach, his hands growing raw from fast-moving cartridges coursing over his fingers. The third boy ran back and forth from their supply point carrying boxes of belted ammunition, lest they run out. It seemed to them it took forever before they were given the order of cease-fire.

Steam rose from the overheated barrel of the water-cooled machine gun. There was not a sound save the ringing in their ears. The three baby-faced young Italian soldiers sat stunned. From the other side . . . not a cry, not a moan, silence. The far riverbank was covered with bodies piled on bodies, hundreds of them, many face down in water stained red by rivulets of blood streaming into the sluggish current.

The road to Neghelli, capital of the southern Galla Borana district, now lay open to General Graziani. Just to make sure, he ordered forty tons of bombs to be dropped on the town. On January 20, 1936, Graziani occupied Neghelli for the glory of Fascist Rome.

Chapter 20

Sportsmen and Warriors

JOHN AND PAUL NEVER KNEW THE FATE OF THEIR FRIEND AND FELLOW pilot. Mulu Asha had not returned from his last mission to the southern front. After news of the defeat of Desta's army reached them, their hopes that Mulu would turn up among the survivors of the battle of Ganale Doria faded as weeks passed. John had lost other friends and pilots, but after the loss of Mulu, he sank into depression. He was physically and mentally weary. He could not understand a seemingly uncaring world that did nothing to stop Mussolini.

Tired or not, Robinson continued flying unarmed planes between Addis Ababa and the front. He was often the only link carrying information between the emperor and his staff. The one bright spot was the Beechcraft. He loved the Staggerwing. It was fast enough to keep the Italian pursuit planes from catching him if he had a few minutes head start. The Staggerwing was rugged. Its vacuum-operated flaps allowed a low landing speed that got him in and out of hastily prepared, short landing strips. He no longer had to endure the cold flying at 12,000-foot altitudes. In the Beechcraft, five people could fly in the comfort of a heated cabin. It was true that a Staggerwing was quick to reward a gear or wing-bending ground loop to a pilot who let his attention drift during landing, but in the air it would do anything a pilot asked of it. John demanded everything it could deliver.

The emperor took special interest in the beautiful new plane and was reassured by John's praise of it. John flew him to and from the front lines. The few times he could not stay ahead of the Italians, he easily lost them in the almost ever-present clouds, flying with confidence on instruments. The rabbit had turned into a fox able to throw the dogs off the scent. His one fear was the plane being caught on the ground. Though he had suffered a mild mustard gas attack on the ground (which affected his breathing for some time), he did not give the Italians another chance to shoot up his plane.

John C. Robinson was becoming somewhat of a hero in the United States, particularly in the Associated Negro Press (ANP). The African Methodist Episcopal Church (AME) and other groups raised funds to aid Ethiopia. Such groups considered John their representative. The *Daily Herald* newspaper in his hometown of Gulfport published articles about Robinson. His family was openly proud of him but privately deeply feared for his safety.

Like all mothers, Celeste Cobb could read between the lines of her son's letters. Sometimes, when she was alone in her kitchen reading a newly arrived letter (four to six weeks old), she could feel the sadness she knew must lie in her Johnny's heart. Too proud to show her fear, she would quickly dry her eyes with her cotton apron and busy herself with household chores. She tried especially hard not to cry in front of Charles Cobb. She knew how worried he was about his boy, and she did her best to put up a brave front.

Because of the press coverage he received in the United States, which was forwarded to Generals Badoglio and Graziani via Rome, John Robinson garnered special attention from the Regia Aeronautica. It was rumored that a price had been put on Robinson's head payable to any Italian pilot who brought him down. Through skill, luck, and prayers, John continued somehow to get through.

To many members of the Regia Aeronautica's squadrons, the war had turned to sport. They were unopposed. The sky belonged to them. Searching for targets of opportunity, they made a sport of shooting small groups of "savages in need of civilizing" wherever they caught them in the open. It was good target practice, but not totally without hazard.

Two young Italian sportsmen decided to go hunting one afternoon. They each took off in the latest Italian plane to arrive in Ethiopia, the IMAM RO 37, a two-place reconnaissance biplane. Normally they carried an observer-gunner in the rear cockpit, but this day the two machine guns mounted in the nose would be sufficient for their sporting purposes. They would each fly solo.

Not too far in front of the Italian lines, they spotted a group of warriors wearing traditional white shammas. They caught them late in the day on open flat ground and began to take turns making low strafing runs on the retreating Ethiopians. The warriors were tired and hungry. There was nowhere for them to hide and they could run no more. They had lost everything except courage.

One of the young Italian pilots, swooping in low for his gun run, noticed that the Ethiopians had stopped and turned to face him. He saw orange flashes. They were all kneeling, firing their rifles at him. He pulled up and banked steeply away to watch his wingman make a run. His wingman did not pull up in a turn but continued a slow climb toward the Italian lines. Something was wrong.

The first pilot followed his fellow airman. As he easily closed on him, he could see a trail of vapor streaming from the aircraft. It had to be fuel. A few moments later, the stricken aircraft's propeller stopped turning. With a dead engine, the pilot had no choice but to put the IMAM down. He picked a reasonably flat area of scrub brush and made a successful landing. The second IMAM circled low overhead and rocked his wings when the pilot of the downed aircraft stepped from his cockpit and waved.

It was late in the day. The pilot of the second plane knew the sun set rapidly near the equator. There was no way a rescue team could find the downed airman before dark. He pulled up and flew an expanding circle around the area. Maybe he could find and alert an Italian scouting party.

About three miles away, he saw not an Italian scouting party but a group of about thirty Ethiopian soldiers on a hilltop. It seems he had not been the only one to see his friend go down. As he watched, the warriors began leaving the hill in the direction of the downed plane. Pulling up in a tight turn, the pilot leveled his wings, lined up on them, and fired. They quickly dispersed and tried to take cover behind scrub bush. The Italian hit many of them before he ran out of ammunition. He continued to make passes hoping to slow them or turn them back, but when he did not fire, they knew he was bluffing, that he was out of ammunition. Fifteen or so of them stood up and began moving again.

The sun would be down in less than thirty minutes. The young flyer had plenty of fuel and time enough to reach a landing field behind his lines before darkness, but he felt compelled to take a gamble. He would not leave his comrade there alone. After all, he reasoned, if his friend had made a successful landing without damage to his crippled aircraft, he could do the same. His friend could jump in the rear cockpit and they would be home in time for supper.

Flying low over the site, he surveyed the landing path of the downed plane. It looked chancy but he would do it. He swung around to line up for the landing. He throttled back. Slowing his plane to just above stalling speed, he dragged onto the landing site with just a little power so he could touch down at the lowest possible speed to shorten the landing roll. His wheels touched. The plane bounced along the rugged ground, the lower wings scraping over scrub bushes, the propeller chopping through a few of them. The pilot could see his friend running toward him.

Without warning, the right wheel slammed down into a hole. The jolt bottomed out the landing strut with such force it was torn loose. The plane careened violently to the right, dropped the lower wingtip into the dirt, and swung. Turning the plane around, it kicked up a huge cloud of dust. It came to a stop resting on the left gear and right wingtip. The idling wooden propeller struck the ground and tore itself to pieces. Fearful of fire, the pilot leaped from the cockpit. The only fire was that in the setting African sun.

"Mother of God! You should have left me. In the morning you could have brought help to find me."

"I'm afraid that would have been too late, my friend. There are others who have already found you. Now they will find us both. They are coming from that far little hill over there . . . maybe twenty of them, maybe less. I cut their numbers down some.

"We can't fight them off until morning. If we run now, maybe we can lose them in the dark.

"They'll know we'll travel toward our lines which must be thirty or forty miles to the north. We can try. Do you have a canteen? We'll need water in this godforsaken desert."

"It really doesn't matter." As he spoke, the Italian pilot drew his pistol and crouched beside the wreckage of his plane. "It seems your friends, some of them at least, have arrived in record time."

"Where? I can't see in this fading light."

"Just there to the left about two hundred meters. I see only one."

A rifle shot rang out. Then a second shot. Young Ethiopian runners had been launched ahead of the main party to quickly reach the plane wreck and pin down any survivors. The Italian hunters had become the prey. Firing occasional shots, two of them held the flyers at bay as the last gleam of dusk faded into darkness.

The two young pilots sat back-to-back, pistols drawn, waiting to be rushed from any or all sides.

"I've heard they are good night fighters."

"Save the last bullet for yourself. You know what they did to the last flyers they caught."

"I saw the report. It seems we should have paid more attention."

A report was circulated to all Italian pilots about two airmen who had been downed at Daggah Bur. They had been found beheaded, their bodies mutilated.

While the Italians waited in darkness, the Ethiopians, masters of the art of night infiltration, drew straws for the honor of using their knives.

"I'm sorry to have caused all of this. I was foolish to have flown so low. We've been warned about that. You were crazy to try to pick me up, but I want you to know I am grateful to you, my friend."

"I, too, am sorry, but you would have done the same for me. With a little luck we would have made it. Now we finish it together."

As the light of dawn crept over the desert, a pair of hyenas cautiously approached the site of the wrecked planes. Overhead, vultures circled. The two pilots stared up at them with glazed, unseeing eyes. The men's feet were bare, their flying boots and leather jackets missing. Just below their chins, black flies covered their gapping throats like living, squirming beards. Slit from ear to ear, the flyers had bled out onto the sand in great dark pools, the now clotted blood a feast to beetles and ants. The vultures flapped down near the bodies and begin a rude debate with the hyenas over how to divide the spoils of war.

Badoglio's army of the north cautiously pressed on toward the capital. His continued deployment of gas was not limited to the battlefield. Civilians were also targeted in his attempt to terrorize the local population. From low flying, tri-motor planes, gas was repeatedly sprayed like insecticide over villages as well as Red Cross and Red Crescent camps and ambulances. A second gas, phosgene, was introduced. It had the pleasant odor of fresh mown hay and could be breathed in or absorbed through the skin. Once introduced to the body in sufficient quantity, phosgene, like mustard gas, attacked lung cells, preventing the passage of oxygen into the blood thus causing its victims to suffocate slowly, agonizingly for days after exposure. (Records show Mussolini himself authorized the use of the weapons.)

One by one, the Ethiopian armies were destroyed. Ras Mulugeta was killed at Amba Aradam. The armies of Ras Seyoum and Ras Kassa had been blown to pieces by the Regia Aeronautica which rotated its aircraft in such a way as to keep at least a dozen planes over the battlefield at all times during daylight hours.

Only Ras Imru's forces remained stubbornly undefeated. Badoglio halted once again to prepare a new drive against Ras Imru. He ordered forty-eight thousand artillery shells, seven million rounds of small arms ammunition, and hundreds of tons of bombs. Ras Imru had no supply depots, no reserve troops. As they ran out of ammunition, they attacked at night with swords and clubs.

Haile Selassie had reason to be proud of his troops. The Italians recorded the interrogation of a mortally wounded Ethiopian officer. When asked who he was, the man replied, "I am the commander of a thousand men." When asked why he did not lie down on the stretcher they had provided, he told them he preferred to die on his feet. He said, "We swore to the negus that we would hold against you or die. We have not won but we have kept our promise." He pointed to the valley below. It was littered with nearly nine thousand dead Ethiopians. He joined them before nightfall.

To the south, General Graziani was having a more difficult time. He had run into the "Hindenburg Wall," named after the German line of defenses of the same name built during the Great War, a defense line designed and set up by Wahib Pasha, advisor to Ras Nasibu. And as April 1936 arrived, the beginning of the rainy season added to Graziani's problems. The earth turned to mud and the rain-swollen creeks and rivers became difficult to cross. The Ethiopians dug in at the Jerar River. Besides being firmly lodged in caves and hollows, they dug trench positions.

When Graziani suffered heavy losses and was stopped at the line, he brought up another of his "special" weapons. His troops employed flamethrowers. Not only were there flamethrowers carried by troops, there were also CV 3/35 tankettes that had been converted to flamethrower tanks, their fuel carried in special armored trailers pulled behind and connected by hoses. Using motorized infantry, aircraft, bombs, artillery, tanks, flamethrowers, and poison gas, it still took Graziani ten days of fierce fighting to finally break the "Hindenburg Wall."

Unlike so many of the foreign volunteers who drifted away as the situation grew steadily worse, John was determined to serve as long as he was needed. He was called to fly the emperor once more. With only one forty-thousand-man army left, the negus was determined to lead the last battle himself. When the emperor arrived at the field, John was shocked to see how worn and weary the small, dignified ruler appeared. He and a small staff boarded the Staggerwing and sat in silence. They all knew John was flying them to the last battle.

When they landed, Haile Selassie turned to John. "Colonel Robinson, you have served me and my people faithfully and well. You have endangered yourself unselfishly. You have done everything asked of you. Now you must go home and tell your nation what you have seen. I failed to convince the League of Nations to understand that it is not just my country that is at stake. If they refuse to act in the future as they refused to stop Fascist aggression in Ethiopia, then what you have seen here is not the end. It is only the beginning."

John could say nothing. He bowed his head in respect.

Haile Selassie looked up at John. "Take my hand, friend." The emperor extended his hand. John, with tears in his eyes, grasped it. "Thank you, John Robinson. May God keep you. I pray we meet again."

John returned to Addis Ababa. By this time, the capital suffered bombing raids daily. There was finally a use for the captured 1896 Italian cannons. They were used around the city for air-raid warnings: one shot for air-raid warning, two shots for all clear. Robinson refueled the plane, hid it in a remote corner of the field, and waited, hoping to receive a call to fetch the emperor from the field of battle.

Across a lush green valley near Mai Ceu, thirty-one thousand Ethiopian soldiers plus the imperial guard faced forty thousand well-equipped Italian and Eritrean troops. Another forty thousand Italians held in reserve were deployed between the Belago and Alagi passes, poised to fill any gaps in the Italian line or take advantage of any breech in the Ethiopian defense.

Haile Selassie sent a message to his wife describing the battle: *From five in the morning until seven in the evening, our troops attacked the enemy's strong positions, fighting without pause. We also took part in the action and by the grace of God remain unharmed. Our chiefs and trusted soldiers are dead and wounded.*

With only twenty thousand men left, the emperor ordered his troops to retreat. Because the few Red Cross and Red Crescent hospitals had been bombed out of existence, the Ethiopians could do nothing for their wounded but carry them. The retreating army was under constant air attack as they moved toward Lake Ashangi. Italian planes dropped seventy tons of explosives on the exhausted Ethiopians. Men and pack animals were blasted to pieces. The Italian planes faded away, only to refuel and rearm, this time with mustard gas. They returned to contaminate the waters along the shore of Lake Ashangi with the poison. Many of the thirst-crazed troops who drank from the lake died.

The emperor later described the scene: "It was no longer a war for the Italian airmen. It was a game, a massacre."

John did get the call and returned Selassie to Addis Ababa. There the emperor conferred with Sir Sidney Barton, the British foreign minister, and Monsieur Albert Bodard, the French ambassador. He informed them that his imperial council had beseeched him not join Ras Imru, as he wished, to organize a guerilla war from the gorges of the Blue Nile. His council had convinced him he should try to escape in order to maintain Ethiopian rule in exile until such time as his government could return. By that act, Ethiopia could, at least symbolically, refuse to accept defeat. His council advised that as long as "Haile Selassie was free and unbowed, Italian rule in Ethiopia could have no legitimacy." To do otherwise, they said, would end futilely in capture, public humiliation, death, and the end of thousands of years of Ethiopian self-rule.

The British foreign minister arranged for the gold from Ethiopia's treasury to be deposited in Barclay's Bank in Jerusalem. Barton also promised that if the emperor could reach the port of Djibouti in French Somaliland, a British warship would meet him and transport his party to safety.

On May 2, 1936, at four o'clock in the morning, the last train left Addis Ababa. Because of the number of foreign citizens, the diplomatic corps, and members of the world press that were aboard the train, Mussolini refused to approve his commander's persistent requests to bomb it. It was, after all, a French train. On that train, Haile Selassie and his government in exile made it to Djibouti. Two days later, on May 4, the day before Italian troops marched into Addis Ababa, Emperor Haile Selassie and his staff departed Djibouti aboard the British cruiser HMS *Enterprise.*

In the chaos of Addis Ababa, some were fleeing the Italians while others took advantage of the pandemonium to loot businesses and homes, especially those belonging to foreigners. Mixed among them were Azebu and Galla tribesmen who had sided with the Italians. General Bono had cleverly sent them into Addis Ababa ahead of his army. Their job was to create chaos. If that meant taking revenge against Selassie's followers and looting as they pleased, so be it.

For John it was past time to leave. Robinson found his paymaster had fled and the banks all closed. The consulates scattered through the city were all barricaded and under siege. He thought, *I should have left two weeks ago with Corriger and Demeaux.*

Perhaps the Regia Aeronautica were distracted by the celebrations of victory that had already begun at the airstrips, for John was able to retrieve Staggerwing from hiding, get it off the ground, and fly unmolested to French Djibouti. He landed the morning of May 4 just as HMS *Enterprise* got under way. At the field, French officials impounded the sleek biplane bearing the colors and insignia of Ethiopia.[3]

The French weren't quite sure what to do with an American citizen wearing the uniform of an Ethiopian colonel and possessing passports of both countries. After a day of interrogation, they impounded his sidearm

---

3 This Beechcraft Staggerwing aircraft was destined for a long and fascinating history. Records indicate that this particular Staggerwing was given the French registration, F-APFD. It took part in the Spanish Civil War flown by the French pilot, Lebaud, for the Basque government 1936–1939. Lucky again, it survived to cross the Spanish border into France. In November of 1942, it was captured by the Germans at Briscous, a town on the French side of the Pyrenees. Dismantled, it was taken to Paris for display at a Luftwaffe exhibition. Sometime after World War II, this same Staggerwing somehow wound up in the United States and was refurbished and registered as NC 15811.

and released him. John had escaped with a few possessions stuffed in a suitcase and very little money. His only option was to catch a freighter bound for Marseille and try to get home as best he could.

On May 5, Badoglio's armies marched into Addis Ababa. Although Ethiopia never surrendered, the Italo-Ethiopian war was over. The kingdom of Italy annexed the Ethiopian empire on May 7, and on May 9 in Rome, Mussolini proclaimed King Victor Emmanuel III emperor of Ethiopia. Italy merged Italian Eritrea, Ethiopia, and Italian Somaliland into a single colony known as Italian East Africa.

Chapter 21

Stranger to Peace

Robinson arrived at the port of Marseille early in the morning and was able to catch a train to Paris that same day. It was a long 450-mile ride in third class. He managed to buy a loaf of bread, some cheese, and cheap wine. Upon arrival at the railroad station in Paris, he went to the information booth where he found an elderly woman who spoke English. John told her he had limited funds, some French francs but most in English pounds sterling. He asked if she could recommend an inexpensive hotel. She remarked that the few American Negroes she had seen in Paris all seemed to be musicians, and he was the first she had seen in uniform since the Great War. She told him which bus to catch—that a taxi would be expensive. The hotel was small, old, but clean. It was located not far from the Seine on La Rive Gauche, the left bank. Bone-tired, Robinson fell into bed and slept for twelve hours.

His main concern was how to get home with so little money in his pocket. The Ethiopian government, he knew, was fleeing into exile. He had no idea how to contact them to obtain the back pay and transportation to America he had been promised.

Haile Selassie had briefly put into port at Haifa to visit Jerusalem, his first choice as a location to establish his government in exile, but an Arab revolt against Jewish emigration made the city too dangerous. Arabs and Jews, both armed, were fighting in the streets of the holy city and the British were hard put to stop it. The emperor proceeded aboard HMS *Enterprise* to England where he established residence in exile.

John's only choice was to swallow his pride and send a telegram via the Atlantic cable asking his former partner, Cornelius Coffey, for help.

While he waited for an answer, John took in the sights of Paris, spending as little as possible. He toured the Louvre, Notre Dame, walked along the Seine and down the Champs Elysées. He marveled at the Eiffel tower. He searched out small neighborhood restaurants where he could eat inexpensively. He loved the sidewalk cafés but could afford only coffee. Paris was an expensive city. He passed several clubs that advertized American Negro Jazz Orchestras, but he could not afford them.

Generally ignored by the French, John felt lonely in crowded Paris. He was relieved to be safely away from the senseless slaughter in Ethiopia, but felt uneasy surrounded by the bustling day-to-day activity of people engaged in ordinary life. The French seemed unconcerned about the war their neighbor Italy had waged on Ethiopia. There was little to nothing about it in the news. The war in Africa was over, no longer of interest. News of an impending civil war in Spain had chased "that Abyssinian business" off the front page. Some nights, John awoke in a cold sweat wondering if he had cried out in his sleep or only in his dreams, dreams of Italian planes surrounding him, of running for cover from bombs and shells, of hearing the screams of terrified wounded and dying people.

One evening while eating at a small restaurant, an old Frenchman, curious about the black man at the next table who had trouble ordering because he spoke little French, struck up a conversation with John. He said he had learned to speak English from American soldiers during the Great War. After discovering John had fought in "that African war" against Italy, he shrugged and said, "What can that Abyssinian business teach us about war? Italy is no threat to France. I was in the Great War. I already know all about such things. It will never happen here again. We are building the Maginot Line."

When his food arrived, John excused himself from the conversation. "Sir, unlike you Frenchmen, it seems I am a stranger to peace."

On the way to his hotel, John picked up a copy of the *Herald Tribune*, the English-language newspaper published in Paris. Contrary to what the old Frenchman had said, it appeared that the French government was mildly apprehensive about new German claims to territory occupied by France since the Great War. The newspaper claimed that Hitler was moving troops disguised as civil policemen into the Rhineland. It seemed to Robinson there was plenty of other news that should have concerned France, America, and the rest of the world. The paper claimed that civil war between the communist-leaning Republican government (*republicanos*) and the Fascist-leaning nationalist movement (*nacionales*) in Spain appeared certain. Japan was engaged in aggression against China. John read about one American who he thought had things right. A general named MacArthur, quoted saying, "If another great conflict ever should occur it will not be fought from trenches as was the Great War. Troops will be highly mobilized, fighting mostly in the open with fast units using tanks and trucks. Aircraft will play a great part in any conflict." John folded the paper and tossed it aside.

I've just been witness to the truth of that, but who will listen to me?

It was 1936 and America was still in the depth of the Great Depression. Business, especially the aviation business, was suffering. When Cornelius Coffey received John's telegram, he was struggling to keep the flying school open. He had few students and little cash. What he did have was a Great Lakes Trainer biplane he had bought wrecked and painstakingly restored to like-new condition over the past year. When he received word of his best friend's predicament, he didn't hesitate. He sold the Great Lakes for five hundred dollars and sent all of it to John in Paris.

A few years later when Coffey applied for his air transport and instrument ratings, the Commerce Department flight examiner recognized

Coffey. The examiner was the man who had purchased the Great Lakes and learned to fly in it. Needless to say, Coffey was awarded his air transport and instrument ratings.

In Cherbourg, France, a young black man who felt very old and tired for his thirty-one years boarded the North German Lloyd Lines passenger ship *Europa* bound for New York. The money Coffey had sent him allowed John to pay his Paris debts and book passage home. John sent a wire to Coffey thanking him and giving him the name of his ship and date scheduled for arrival at New York.

Because of Germany's promotion of the forthcoming 1936 Olympics in Berlin, Lloyd Lines advertised cheap fares to lure Americans to the games. A round-trip, first-class ticket from New York to Bremen via Southampton and Cherbourg could be had for $212. The cheap fares did not apply to one-way passage from France to New York. John booked second-class passage, Cherbourg to New York. It would not be as luxurious a voyage as his first-class trip over, but it was a ticket home. John found there was an advantage to second-class: dinner was only semi-formal. His uniform would do. He had lost his black tie and tuxedo when his hotel was bombed.

As *Europa* sliced its way across the Atlantic, the tension of the past year began to ebb from him like ice melting in the warmth of spring. John admitted to himself how tired he was and how glad he was to be going home. He splurged sixty-five cents to rent a deck chair and blanket for the duration of the trip.

Each morning, printed in German, French, and English, the ship provided news highlights obtained over the wireless the night before. After breakfast, John liked to sit in his deck chair and read the ship's newspaper. He found many items of interest. Germany had launched the giant zeppelin Hindenburg. It would be put into service between Germany and America. In England, the grand new ocean liner *Queen Mary* was preparing for her maiden voyage to the United States. The new United States aircraft carrier *Yorktown* was christened by Eleanor Roosevelt. It was equipped by the navy's first-line fighter, the Grumman F3F biplane.

John couldn't believe it. He had read that Germany had a sleek new fighter called a Messerschmitt and England had unveiled the beautiful Spitfire. They were both monoplanes and reported to be much faster than any fighter the United States had at the time.

The atmosphere onboard the ship was light. Most conversations Robinson overheard were about fashion, sports, or business. When the subjects of conflict in China or Germany rearming were brought up, they were often dismissed with the statement, "Well, yes, war seems inevitable," stated as if the speaker had the impression that the "inevitable war" would be somehow remote from his own nation. "After all," one gentleman said, "we have the Locarno Treaty under which Germany, France, and Belgium promised not to attack each other. England and Italy have been charged with enforcing the treaty should one of the signatories violate the terms." John couldn't believe his ears.

These fools still believe in treaties and the League of Nations.

In a new edition of the ship's little paper, there was a piece of news about students in the United States staging demonstrations pledging not to support the United States in any war. President Roosevelt, speaking during his campaign for re-election, said the United States would not increase its arms and intended to stay out of war. There was a blurb about Charles Lindbergh returning from a personal tour of the new German air force. He said America and the rest of the world had nothing to compare with it.

What was crystal clear to Robinson was that the whole world seemed headed where he had just been: to war.

If a black child from Mississippi can see it, why the hell can't high-falutin' white folks see it? John lost his appetite for news. He borrowed a book from the ship's library: a translation of *Night Flight* by the French flyer Antoine de Saint Exupéry.

John had not slept well for months, often waking from dreams of bombings, of flying lost in clouds, of animals eating the unburied dead, of fogs of poison gas, of lost friends. In the mornings he would get up feeling tired and sick.

Robinson knew he was a curiosity among his fellow passengers. He was black and he was returning from "that Italian thing in Africa." Walking past a group of young Americans one day, he overheard one say, "No joke. That's that nigger aviator, I swear to God." The comment was followed by laughter. John kept walking. *I reckon some things are never gonna change.*

At his assigned table in the second-class dining salon, everyone was stiffly polite. Once in a while, someone would ask his opinion on an issue being discussed, but usually he remained silent.

About mid-Atlantic, John was in his deck chair when two young Germans approached and introduced themselves. They said they were members of the advance party for the Zeppelin Hindenburg and asked if he would join them for a drink. "We would be most interested in hearing about the flying and bombing tactics used by the Italians in Ethiopia," one of them said.

John stood up. "Both you boys Nazis?"

The Germans looked at each other.

"What would that Hitler fellow think if he found out a couple of his boys could learn a thing or two from a black man? Might ruin that whole Aryan race thing I been reading 'bout."

One of the Germans replied, "Why be so rude? We are just flyers and offered you a drink to talk about flying."

"I've been bombed, gassed, and shot at by Italian Fascists for the last year. You boys will have to excuse me if I'm not ready to sit down and drink with German Fascists just yet."

John turned and walked away. The encounter made him wonder how many Nazis there were among North German Lloyd's crews and how much they learned about France, England, and America when they were in port.

Later that afternoon, an Englishman approached Johnny. "Look here," he said, "I hope you don't think me rude, but I couldn't help but overhear what you said to those two German fellows this afternoon. You're the American chap that flew Emperor Selassie, aren't you?"

"I was over there."

"I admire the way you gave those fellows what for. I thought perhaps you might consider having a drink or two with me and a couple of your countrymen. Would you care to join us this evening in the first-class bar? I'm afraid I told them about this afternoon and your German friends, but they won't embarrass you with any questions if you don't want to talk about it. You might be interested that my business in England and their business in America concerns building aircraft."

John paused a moment to think it over. "To tell the truth, it's been a lonely trip. I think I would like to join you."

"Right! How about seven o'clock? I'll introduce you around and we'll fetch a drink. Don't worry about a formal dinner in first class. We'll order something in the bar from the grill."

The Englishman was true to his word. No questions were asked unless John mentioned something about the war first, which he did occasionally during the evening. John learned the two Americans, one from Texas and the other from Massachusetts, worked for a fledgling aircraft company in California named North American Aviation. The Englishman was with the British Air Purchasing Commission. That's all John learned about them. As they talked into the night, they exchanged flying stories, particularly humorous ones. John found he could still laugh and was glad for the company, the refreshments, and the stories.

Robinson slept well that night for the first time in many months. He awoke to find himself feeling fit and hungry. He had finally come to a realization. *God knows where the world is headed, but I'm going home.*

Chapter 22

Reluctant Hero

O N A MORNING IN LATE MAY 1936, THE SHORELINE OF THE United States was clearly visible over the bow of *Europa*. It was a bright morning. A cool breeze was blowing off the Atlantic. John showered, shaved, put on a pair of slacks, a shirt, and his leather flying jacket with the Royal Lion of Judah insignia woven in gold thread on the left breast. On deck, he walked forward to watch the New York shoreline slide toward him.

Europa slowed to take on a harbor pilot and quarantine inspector before passing from Lower Bay through the Narrows. It was not unusual for an eager news reporter or two to ride the pilot boat out to an incoming liner to sniff out a story about some movie star, socialite, or other important passenger and get the scoop ahead of any news hounds waiting at the dock, but on this morning, more than a dozen journalists scrambled aboard behind the pilot and quarantine official. They were all interested in only one passenger. As *Europa* crossed Upper Bay, the gang of reporters thronged into the public rooms and passageways in search of a thirty-one year old black man they called the Brown Condor of Ethiopia. When they didn't find him, they paid several stewards a dollar a piece to scour the ship in search of Colonel John C. Robinson.

Far forward, a solitary figure was leaning against the ship's rail gazing at the towering skyline of Manhattan. He turned to look curiously at a noisy crowd rushing down the deck toward him. Several had cameras while others carried notepads in their hands. John was startled when the group surrounded him.

"Your name Robinson?"

When he admitted he was, individuals vying for attention identified themselves as representatives for various news services. Those with notepads shouted questions at him while the cameramen fired flashbulbs in his face.

By the time *Europa* entered the Hudson River, John had been asked dozens of questions. At first embarrassed by the attention, John reminded himself that this was what had taken him to Ethiopia in the first place: the chance for a black flyer to gain favorable publicity to help open the door to the field of aviation for Negroes. Quiet by nature, he tried his best to answer every question. English composition and public speaking had not been his best subjects at Tuskegee, but this day he silently thanked his teachers. He might not have lost his southern accent completely, but he could speak clearly and correctly.

The interview ended when *Europa* arrived at its berth at the North German Lloyd dock. The reporters, anxious to get ashore to file their stories, were the first in line when the gangway to the passenger terminal was secured

John returned to his cabin, gathered his one piece of luggage, and joined the line of passengers waiting to disembark. He was surprised when the ship's purser approached to lead him past the lines of passengers to the gangway. "It seems there is a crowd waiting for you, Colonel Robinson. The demonstration has interrupted the processing of passengers and baggage. We can't handle all our passengers until you and your fans clear the terminal."

John couldn't imagine what the purser was talking about until he started down the gangway. Someone shouted out his name and a roar erupted from a large crowd waiting just beyond the customs fence. A forest of little American and Ethiopian flags began to wave. A group of young officers and staff members from the Ethiopian embassy burst into a patriotic song barely audible above the cheers.

Thomas B. Terhune, in charge of the customs inspectors, gave orders that Colonel Robinson be cleared as soon as possible. That way, he figured, the hundreds waiting to greet him would clear the area so the rest of the passengers and their baggage could be processed. The customs inspector assigned to Robinson asked a few perfunctory questions, smiled, said, "Glad to see you back, Colonel," and shook the flyer's hand. It was ironic that the bewildered porter trailing behind John with his suitcase was a recently immigrated Italian.

As John cleared customs, he was met by a distinguished gentleman in a dark suite that introduced himself as Dr. P. M. W. Savory, chairman of New York's United Aid for Ethiopia. When John and Dr. Savory stepped into the large terminal waiting area, the crowd fell silent. "They are waiting for a speech, Colonel," Savory said. Someone put a microphone in front of Robinson. John was still in shock over the reception, but managed to make a brief, modest talk in which he thanked the crowd for their rousing welcome.

Nothing would do but for John, suitcase and all, to be lifted onto the shoulders of the crowd and carried down to the street level where pandemonium again broke out: people shouting, car and taxi horns blowing. A totally overwhelmed Robinson could do little but smile and wave at the mobs of people around him.

Dr. Savory and several members of his committee helped rescue John from the throng and pushed him into a waiting limousine while the chauffeur retrieved his baggage and put it in the trunk. Safely seated in the black sedan, they pulled away from the curb and left the cheering crowd behind.

John, completely exhausted, sank back into the seat and took a deep breath. "Man, that was scary."

"Well, Colonel," Dr. Savory said, "I'm afraid you had better get accustomed to a little of that. You are somewhat of a national hero. For a while, at least, you'll receive a lot of attention. Tonight, for example, there will be a banquet given in your honor." John looked uneasy. "But right now," Savory continued, "I know you need a little peace and quiet. We'll drop you off at your hotel. You'll find a room full of messages and invitations, but you can deal with them tomorrow."

John was embarrassed to admit, "I hope the hotel is not too expensive. I'm a little low on funds."

What Savory had not yet told John was that a few community and business leaders had already discovered his lack of finances and set about to correct the situation, but now was not the time to discuss business matters.

As the La Salle limousine made its way through New York traffic toward Harlem, a thousand thoughts raced through John's mind. *What am I into now? These people want speeches. How am I gonna get through that? When am I ever gonna get home to see Momma and Daddy Cobb? What in the world am I gonna do for money? I gotta pay Coffey back.* With the excitement of the welcome from the crowds, Dr. Savory, and his committee, it was hard for John to organize any answers. He stopped trying and looked out the window at the busy streets of New York. *Leaving a war behind is gonna take a little gettin' used to.*

They drove past the famous Theresa Hotel at 125th Street and 7th Avenue in Harlem. Dr. Savory's group couldn't put John up there. Although there was no official segregation in the North, the Theresa Hotel and many other places were simply closed to blacks.

The La Salle pulled in at a small Harlem apartment hotel. John found he didn't have just a room, but a suite. Dr. Savory noticed the worried look on John's face, told him not to worry about a thing, that the committee would cover all expenses, and that they would pick him up at seven in the evening for the banquet. Robinson, still in shock from the reception he had received, lamely thanked the reception committee and closed the door.

The suite was filled with flowers, baskets of fruit, messages, and bottles of champagne. John stood there for a moment, a little bewildered. Ignoring the iced champagne, he reached for a bottle of bourbon sitting among the gifts. Although John was not much of a drinker, this night he poured a measure into a glass, sat heavily on an overstuffed chair, and took a couple of sips of the dark liquid. After a few minutes, he put down the unfinished drink, undressed, went into the bath, and filled the tub with hot water. He lowered his aching body, bruised from having been carried, pulled, and tossed about by the crowd, into the tub, leaned back, and gratefully let the wonderful steaming water drive tension from his body and confusion from his mind.

That was a damned frightful experience. What in the world am I supposed to do now?

John didn't know it, but the ride was only beginning. The journalists who had scooped the Brown Condor on board *Europa* launched a news blitz about John Robinson. Newspapers throughout the country carried stories about Robinson under such headlines as "All New York Greets Pilot on Arrival;" "Newsmen Get Lowdown on African War from Colonel John C. Robinson;" "Pioneered Aviation in Chicago—Started Air School;" "Colonel Robinson, Brown Condor, Returns Home;" "Gangway for the Brown Condor;" "Crowds Wait on War Hero."

Radio wasn't about to be outdone by print media. The enormously popular commentator Lowell Thomas started a deluge of radio accounts on Robinson and the part he played in the Italo-Ethiopian War. Trans-Radio Press, the Mutual Broadcasting System, and the Press Radio News all jumped on Robinson's story. Bulletins were sent out over the Blue Network and the Red Network, the only two nationwide radio networks in the United States at the time.

Somewhere far away, a telephone rang. John stirred, then awoke with a start, not sure where he was. The phone rang again, this time loud, no longer far away, right next to him on the bedside table. The room was dark. Through the open window, he could hear the noise of street traffic below. He fumbled for the receiver.

"Hello."

"Hello, is this Colonel Robinson?"

"I'm Colonel Robinson."

"This is Dr. Savory. I'm down in the lobby. We have your car waiting."

John sat up and found the bedside lamp and switched it on. He was naked except for a towel tucked around his waist.

"I'm just getting dressed, Doctor. To tell you the truth, the phone woke me up. I can be down in twenty minutes. I'm sorry. Will that make us late?"

"Not at all. There's plenty of time. By the way, how do you plan to dress?"

"I bought a dark suit in Paris."

"I wonder if you would mind wearing your uniform. It's what the people will expect to see. You are their hero. I think they would like to see the colonel in uniform."

John was embarrassed. "I'm not a hero, Doctor. I just tried to prove a Negro can be a good pilot." The phone remained silent, Dr. Savory waiting. "If you think wearing my uniform will help, I'm obliged to wear it. It's a little wrinkled." John paused. "Doctor, I'm a little nervous about tonight. I mean, I don't have a speech or even any notes."

He heard Dr. Savory laugh. "You sure beat all, Colonel. You go halfway around the world to fly for an emperor, get shot at and make world headlines, then you come home and get nervous over accepting credit from your people. Everything will be fine. You won't need a speech. They just want to hear a few words from you and thank you for what you have done. Take your time. I'll be in the lobby. It's your night, Colonel Robinson."

John hung up the phone.

Momma, you ought to see your boy now.

He started to get up, stopped, picked up the phone, and asked to be connected to Western Union. "I want to send a telegram to Mr. and Mrs. C. C. Cobb please, at 1905 Thirty-First Avenue in Gulfport, Mississippi." The message told his folks that he was fine, that he had several meetings in New York, and would let them know when he could get home and not to worry. Then he shaved, got dressed, and checked himself in the mirror. *Well here you go, Johnny, ready or not.*

In the car, Dr. Savory explained that he and a group of businessmen were arranging a speaking tour and that John would be paid well from his share of ticket sales to the events. "We'll raise enough money so you won't have to worry about starting a new school of aviation back in Chicago."

John didn't know what to say. He felt enormous relief. "I'll be able to pay back my partner. He sent the money to get me home. I owe him five hundred dollars."

"Yes, we learned about that. Coffey is waiting to meet you in Chicago. You'll have more than enough to get started again. People are willing to pay to hear you. You'll see. There'll be plenty for you after we take out expenses."

The car pulled up to a side entrance to Rockland Palace. The enormous hall was filled with five thousand enthusiastic supporters. It was the largest room full of people John had ever seen. He was led by Dr. Savory to the head table where he was greeted by Dr. William Jay Schieffelin, chairman of the board of trustees of Tuskegee Institute, and Claude A. Barnett, director of the American Negro Press and leader of a large delegation from Chicago, the city that had adopted John Robinson as its own.

The only one at the table John knew besides Dr. Savory was Claude Barnett. It had been Barnett that had arranged for the first meeting between Robinson and Malaku Bayen that resulted in John volunteering to go to Ethiopia. John was introduced to other civic and business leaders, both black and white, that were also seated at the head table. Several of them made speeches, noting that John had been the commander of the Imperial Ethiopian Air Corps, that he had been Haile Selassie's personal pilot, flying him to and from the front lines, and that John had been wounded in the air by Italian fighters. The speeches, one reporter would write, "paid tribute to Colonel John Robinson's great contribution to Negro America."

I wonder if they gonna leave anything for me to say.

When at last asked to speak, John thanked the audience for giving him such a welcome and told them that he was both humbled and honored. He then gave a brief account of the war, calling the Italian invasion, mass slaughter of Ethiopians, a disgrace to civilization and the League of Nations. He talked about the courage of the Ethiopian soldiers. He said that all but two of the Ethiopian aircraft had been shot down or destroyed on the ground, but did not speak of himself or the role he had played. He described how the government staff and army chiefs had to persuade Haile Selassie not to stay and fight to the last. How they had to convince him to take the Ethiopian government into exile and, by doing so, continue Ethiopia's long history of unbowed self-rule. He said Ethiopia had not and never would surrender. When he finished, the audience gave him a fifteen-minute standing ovation.

During the ride back to the hotel, Dr. Savory informed John that Claude Barnett would call for him in the morning. "You and Claude are flying to Chicago tomorrow where another reception has been arranged for you."

What in the world have they gotten me into?

John nodded his head. "Yes, sir. What time should I be ready?"

If John thought nothing could compare with the welcome he received at New York, he was in for a surprise. Barnett and Robinson landed in Chicago on Sunday aboard a brand new Transcontinental and Western Airline (TWA) Douglas DC-3, which at the time was the newest and most modern airliner in the world. When Robinson appeared at the doorway, an enthusiastic crowd of three thousand cheering supporters were there to meet him. Hundreds broke through police lines to surround the plane. Janet Waterford Bragg, Willa Brown, and other female members of the Challenger Air Pilots Association John had founded in 1932 presented him with flowers as he stepped off the plane. Officers of the Eighth Infantry of the Illinois National Guard, members of the United Aid for Ethiopia, dignitaries including Robert Abbott, editor of the *Chicago Defender*, and former representatives Oscar de Priest and W. T. Brown took part in

Chicago's welcoming party. John saw his old friends, Cornelius Coffey, Harold Hurd, and Grover Nash in the crowd, and although he waved he hardly had time to say hello before he was whisked away to a limousine that led a parade of five hundred automobiles from the airport to the south side of Chicago. It was estimated that as many as twenty thousand people lined the route. From the balcony of the Grand Hotel, John Robinson addressed a crowd of eight thousand people standing shoulder to shoulder in front of the hotel and completely filling the intersection of Fiftieth and South Park Avenue.

The *Chicago Defender* newspaper stated, "There has never been such a demonstration as was accorded the thirty-one-year-old Chicago aviator who left the United States thirteen months ago and literally covered himself in glory trying to preserve the independence of the last African empire. There are reports that he will be joining the faculty of Tuskegee Institute to teach aviation." Three thousand newspapers throughout the country carried stories and printed pictures about the Brown Condor's return.

There was a huge banquet held in his honor similar to the one in New York. Again speeches were given and he was asked to speak. It was just the beginning of a pre-arranged tour that would raise money for John . . . and for the more than a dozen sponsoring organizations.

In spite of all the attention, John retained his quiet, almost shy manner. He smiled often, traveled to cities, and made talks wherever he was asked. He truly felt honored, but he was tired even before the whirlwind speaking engagements began. John found himself saying the same things over and over. His audiences wanted to hear about the war, but he knew, as every man who has seen war knows, they didn't want the true reality of it, the horror. They wanted to hear a story about a great adventure, the flying, how he escaped the Italian fighters, but these were the things he wanted to talk about the least. His audiences wanted to hear only about the war—it's what they'd paid to hear—but what John wanted to talk about was the continued need for creating opportunities for blacks in aviation.

The more questions he was asked, the more he realized there is no way to convey to those who have not experience war what it is like.

How could I tell them about the fear; how it feels to be shot at, what it's like to duck into a cloud and suddenly see a rock wall just in time to avoid it, or not, the relief that comes with surviving another day, the restless nights knowing you would go up the next morning and do it all over again. How, after landing, you put on an act as if there's nothing to it and laugh at being alive even if you are shaking so much, you need help to get out of the cockpit. How you discover that a simple hot meal cooked over a small fire under a straw roof in the rain is the best tasting meal you can remember. How you react when news comes that another friend hasn't returned and never will— how at first you hardly acknowledge the message, you act too busy to dwell on it, and maybe you are too busy. It has happened before, it is happening all around, maybe you're next. And then later, maybe days later, you have to face what it really means, that you will never share the gift of your friend's unique company, his smile, voice, handshake, the simple treasures of his fellowship. You walk off to be alone, so heavily alone, but only for a moment for there is another flight to make.

How am I supposed to explain all that to all those folks in the audience? How do I tell them that I faced every flight in dreadful anticipation, but that during the flight things happen too fast to think of anything but the flying, that it's only later that fear catches up and you think about what could have happened but didn't . . . this time. How do you explain what it's like to pick up a fallen child from the street while you are running for your life only to find, when the bombing is over and you are safe, that the child has bled to death while you were running with it in your arms? How do you describe the smell of burning flesh?

No, the audience doesn't really want to hear 'bout that. They couldn't understand unless they lived it. Maybe that's why wars keep happening, why some new leader can talk a new generation into war. They don't forget what the last war was like—they can't, 'cause they never knew it in the first place.

Colonel Robinson was grateful when the banquets and parades and speeches were over. He had refused no invitation, but he had been uncomfortable. "I'm no hero. I just did what I could to help and somehow survived," he repeated often.

News John didn't want to hear filtered in, news about Ethiopia. He knew it would all be bad, and it was. Information arrived in bits and pieces, bits and pieces Italy didn't want released. Ras Desta was fighting an effective guerrilla war from the hills. The Italians had hunted down his sons and executed them. Three sons of Ras Kassa were executed after surrendering. Mussolini had given Marshall Graziani the title of viceroy of Ethiopia. John learned that prior to Ethiopia, Graziani had been dubbed the Hyena of Libya for his cruelty.

The new viceroy ordered all captured rebels shot and had the head of the Coptic Church executed. Then came news that was even worse. After an attempt on his life, Graziani allowed his soldiers and Libyan askaris to embark on a systematic massacre, setting native houses on fire with gasoline and then shooting the inhabitants as they fled the flames. During the following weeks, it is estimated that thirty thousand Ethiopians, including half the younger educated population, were executed in retaliation.

John tried many times, but was never able to contact or learn the fate of his weisero—the widow he had befriended.

The Brown Condor was welcomed home to national attention in mid-May. An event in July 1936 wiped both John Robinson and the plight of Ethiopia from the pages of newspapers and news broadcasts on national radio. In Spain on the May 10, 1936 the conservative Niceto Alcala Zamora was ousted as president of Spain and replaced by left-wing Manuel Azaña backed by a consortium of socialists and communists to form what was called the Second Republic of Spain. As a result, a group of Nationalist Spanish Army officers, including Emilio Mola, Francisco Franco, Juan Yague, Gonalo Queipo de Llano, and Josè Sanjurjo attempted a coup d'état. The result was the outbreak of the Spanish Civil War on July 17, 1936. The tragedy and suffering of Ethiopia and the exploits of John Charles Robinson were suddenly old news.

Chapter 23

Toward Home

JOHN DIDN'T MISS THE ATTENTION. FREE OF THE SPOTLIGHT, HE could get on with his life. With funds raised during his speaking tour, John, with his old partner, Cornelius Coffey, put his flying school back in business. A new economical trainer was on the market. It was called the J-2 Cub and cost $1,470. It was underpowered with an engine with only 37 horsepower, but would do fine for primary flight training. The partners paid $668 down and were in business again. The little plane cost them $1.98 an hour to operate including gas, oil, hangar rent, and insurance. They paid off the balance in six months.

At last, John's personal business was in order. His obligations to the many groups who had sponsored him, or whose causes his appearances had aided, were complete. At long last he could go home to visit his parents. Home! Once again he would sleep in the house in which he had grown up, take in the wonderful aroma of his mother's kitchen, go fishing with Daddy Cobb, visit the Mississippi town of his boyhood, the things he dreamed of while far away at war.

John would go home in style. He had enough money left over to make a down payment on a new 1936 gull-wing Stinson SR 8 B Reliant, registered NC 16161. It was a five-place, high wing, cabin monoplane, expensive but reliable and fast—165 miles per hour cruise with its 250-horsepower Lycoming R680B6, nine cylinder, radial engine. The Stinson Reliant and the Beechcraft Stagerwing were the executive planes of their day. The Stinson, painted a beautiful blue with silver-gray trim, had graceful elliptical wings. Robinson had chosen the Stinson because it could perform so many roles. It could carry pilot and four paying passengers in comfortable leather seats and had a heated cabin. With the seats removed he could carry cargo. It had an electrical starter, carried seventy-six gallons of fuel and could fly up to six hundred miles without refueling. It was a stable, easy-to-fly plane that would draw students to his school for advanced flight training. John was rightly proud of it.

Lake Michigan and the sprawling metropolis of Chicago slipped behind him as he lifted into the cool air of early morning and pointed the Stinson southward. He was where he most loved to be: alone in the sky with all the earth spread out before him. He felt happy and relaxed. Scanning the sky out of habit, his reverie was interrupted. In the distance he spotted a formation of five planes, little more than dots off his right wing. For a moment, the chill of war raised the hair on the back of his neck. Keeping his eyes on the formation, his palms began to sweat.

What's the matter with you? There are no enemy aircraft in the peaceful skies of America. His instinctive, instant assessment had been correct. The biplanes were military fighters, but they continued on their way, crossing his path well behind him. *Just a training flight. You best settle down there, Colonel. You home now.*

He relaxed, surrounded by the throaty rhythmic sounds of the Lycoming radial engine and the sweet smell of the new leather interior of his aircraft's cabin.

Having landed many times in Addis Ababa with near empty fuel tanks, John was determined not to ever worry about running short of fuel again. His first stop was Cairo where the states of Illinois, Kentucky, and Missouri meet at the junction of the Ohio and Mississippi rivers.

After supervising the fueling of his plane, a habit learned in Ethiopia, he bought a root beer and a package of Ritz crackers for a nickel each. It was a classic pilot's lunch.

From Cairo, John followed the mighty Mississippi. The cornfields gave way to cotton fields as he followed "Big Muddy" southward toward Memphis. The paved highways of Illinois gave way to Tennessee's highways whose paved sections were broken by long stretches of gravel roads. Over Memphis, he turned southeastward toward Birmingham for fuel. From there he would fly on to Tuskegee where he was expected to make a talk and spend the night.

After he landed at Roberts Field in Birmingham, he couldn't help but notice the looks on the faces of a small group of men who came out of the line shack when he taxied up to the lone fuel pump. He knew well what had caused their surprised expressions. It wasn't the plane, though the group had seen the new Stinson land and come out to have a closer look. No, the real surprise came when John opened the cabin door and climbed down. He overheard one of the group say, "I'll be damned. I ain't never see a nigger flyer before." Another man wearing a worn leather flying jacket stepped forward. "That's a fine looking plane. Do you mind if I have a closer look at it?"

John asked, "Can I get the tanks topped?"

The man in the jacket turned and hollered, "Henry, top her off!"

A young black man, barefooted and wearing oil-stained coveralls stepped forward. "Yes sir, Mr. Hayes," and moved over to the pump marked Phillips 66. He pulled enough hose off the reel to stretch out to the plane and then got a stepladder so he could reach the wing tanks.

Hayes turned to John. "Your name happen to be Robinson?"

"That's right."

"You the one was in Ethiopia in that Italian war?"

"I was there."

"I've read about you." The man offered his hand to John, a gesture not common in the South at the time: a white offering to shake a black hand. "I'm Hayes. This is my flight operation. Could you use a cup of coffee?"

"That would be mighty fine," John replied. He looked back at the plane. Henry had a ladder and was climbing up to the wing with the fuel hose over his shoulder, careful of the finish on the wing. Satisfied that the line boy knew what he was doing, John followed Hayes past the onlookers toward the small frame building twenty yards behind the pump.

A cup of coffee later, John paid his bill and walked out to the plane where onlookers were still gathered. "It's a beautiful ship you got there," one of them said.

"Thank you. It's a good flying plane." He answered a few other questions about the Stinson while he climbed up to check the fuel caps. They were secure. The line boy removed the ladder and John climbed into the cockpit. He called out "Clear!" Hayes nodded. John cranked the engine and taxied out.

The group stood outside to watch the blue Stinson lift off and turn to the southeast, and then they filed into the line shack. "Well, that was something," one of them said. Another walked over to the coffee-pot. Two cups from the rack of mugs sat on the desk with a little coffee left in them. "Dammit, Hayes, did you let that nigger drink out of my cup?"

Hayes looked at him. "No. I knew you would whine. I used your cup. He drank out of mine. I'll tell you something else since you brought it up. That 'nigger,' as you put it, was Haile Selassie's personal pilot. He's just been through a war in Africa and from what I've read in the news and heard on the radio, I'd lay money he could fly rings around your dumb ass."

The rest of the group thought that was funny.

Hayes walked out of the office and saw the young black line boy still looking toward the sky where John's plane was just a tiny speck. "Henry," called Hayes, "you been doing a good job around here. I guess maybe you've earned yourself a plane ride. You want one?"

The young man broke into a wide grin. "Yes, sir! Mr. Hayes, I been wantin' one since the first day I come out here."

"Well, go climb up in front of that WACO. We'll take her around the field a couple of times."

Henry ran out to the biplane. "I told my daddy I'd get a ride, but he didn't believe it."

"If you can find your house from up there, we'll fly over it and you can wave at him. He ought to be home from work by now." Hayes stood on the lower wing and helped fasten the safety harness of a very happy, young black man.

In the late afternoon sunlight, John's graceful Stinson circled the campus at Tuskegee and then settled gently on a freshly mowed field nearby. Shortly after the plane came to rest near the fence, several automobiles pulled to a stop beside the Stinson where John was standing. From the first car, two men got out and walked over to him. The first was John's old friend, Captain A. J. Neely, the college registrar. Close behind him was Dr. F. D. Patterson, president of Tuskegee.

Patterson offered his hand. "Welcome home, Colonel Robinson. We are very proud to have you with us again."

"Thank you, sir."

"We plan to have supper at my home. After supper the teachers and staff would love to meet you. Tomorrow we thought you could address the students at the summer session. Then the folks at Meridian and Jackson want us to call and let them know when you will be there. You can see we have a lot planned for you, Colonel. I hope you don't mind too much."

John smiled. "I've kinda gotten used to it. But I tell you what. Supper sounds fine. All I had for lunch was a root beer and peanut butter crackers."

"Well, John, we didn't plan anything fancy. We thought you might want a little southern cooking. How does fried chicken, field peas, candied yams, and apple pie with ice cream sound?"

"President Patterson, those Italians must have killed me after all, 'cause it sounds like I've died and gone to heaven. Now if you tell me I can have hot biscuits and buttered grits with breakfast in the morning, I'll know it's true."

They laughed and started for the car.

The *Tuskegee Messenger* in town reported at great length about the visit of "one of the boys enrolled at Tuskegee in the early twenties" who now returned a celebrity. Recounting John's appearance before the student body, the newspaper stated, "In presenting Colonel Robinson, President Patterson referred with pride to the fine record of this Tuskegee graduate in blazing the trail for Negro youth in the field of aviation and proving to the world beyond doubt the Negro's capacity for accuracy, endurance, skill, and courage." The article ended by saying, "A course of instruction in aeronautics is being planned by the Department of Mechanical Industries at Tuskegee and Mr. Robinson is scheduled to return as instructor of the course."

John knew things were not going to be quite that simple. He held long discussions with school officials during which he explained the requirements of setting up a school of aeronautics. He realized such a program was still a long way off. The school simply did not have the finances available. What did happen as a result of the meeting was a firm commitment by Tuskegee to continue to work toward the establishment of such a school.

After his address to the students, John was short of time and went directly to the plane. He had two stops to make before flying home to Gulfport. He was expected to make talks at Meridian and Jackson Mississippi. He checked the plane, thanked Patterson and Neeley, cranked up the engine, waved to the students lining the fence, and took off. Flying almost due west he passed Montgomery and followed the Alabama River until it turned south at Selma. He was happy. It was a pilot's day: sunshine, clean air, and a sky decorated with white fluffs of fair-weather clouds.

By the time he passed Demopolis where the Black Warrior and Tombigbee rivers join to flow southward to Mobile Bay, John knew he'd had one coffee too many at breakfast. He had been in such a hurry to leave he skipped the usual trip to the restroom before the flight. Now he was sorry as the urgency of nature got his attention. To solve the problem, he needed to make an unscheduled stop. Some miles west of Demopolis he spotted what appeared to be a clear, freshly mown field near a gravel highway. The field was just behind what looked like a country store. He made a low pass over the area. The field was clear and level, no electric or phone wires. No sweat. He banked around, lined up on the field, and put the Stinson down gently. Halfway through the landing roll, he felt a bump followed by a strong pull toward the right. He was rolling too slow for the rudder to be effective so he applied hard left brake to keep the plane from ground looping.

Once stopped, he cut the engine and climbed down, already knowing what he would find. He squatted down beside the right wheel. "Damn. Flat as hell." What was worse, the sidewall was badly cut, there would be no fixing the tire and tube.

John stood up and looked around. No traffic on the road and no human as far as he could see. He relieved himself—which had been the reason for landing. When finished, he walked down the track the right wheel had made through the short grass. It didn't take long to find the cause of his cut tire. Lying a foot to the side of the track was the dirt-encrusted, jagged top half of a broken gallon jug. *Hell of a place to throw an empty jug.* He reckoned the mowing tractor had broken it. John took off his uniform blouse (he had worn his uniform for his appearance at Meridian), slung it over the pilot's seat in the plane, walked across the field to the fence, climbed over it, and started down the road toward the store.

Most of the barn-red paint had weathered off the pine board siding of the building. A wide porch ran across the width of the storefront covered by a tin hip roof that extended out over a single gasoline pump. Across the facade above the hip roof were the words, painted in faded, foot-high letters, "Feed, Groceries, Hardware, Dry Goods." Several signs were nailed to the wall under the hip roof. The largest read "Coca-Cola 5¢." A poster in the window had a border made up of pictures of airplanes. In the center it advertised Wings Cigarettes. There was a handmade sign on a piece of cardboard that read "For sale, 22 Model-T, Runs, $25."

John walked up the well-worn, wooden steps and opened the screen door. Inside, three naked light bulbs hanging by their cords from the ceiling were spaced evenly down the center of the room. There were no windows in the side of the building, just long shelves of merchandise. A large attic fan, installed through a hole cut in the ceiling, labored noisily. An elderly man dressed in khaki pants and shirt and a white bib apron was sitting on a stool behind the counter working on a ledger. He looked up and eyed John walking through the screen door.

"I didn't hear you drive up. What you want?"

"I don't have a car. I need to use a telephone. Do you have one?"

"Yep. We got one." he motioned at a wooden telephone box hanging on the wall behind him. "I ain't seen you 'round here before. You say you walked clear out here?"

"Well, I didn't walk here, exactly. I flew."

The man looked up at John. "You trying to fool with me, boy?"

"My plane is in the field just back of here."

"The hell you say! You mean to tell me you landed an airplane right out there behind my store?"

"You can see it from the edge of the front porch," John said. "Come on and I'll show you."

The man came out from behind the counter and followed John outside. "Well I'll be damned. You flew that thing here by yourself? How far you come?"

"Started in Chicago. Landed here to take a rest on my way to Meridian. I cut a tire. I need to call the Meridian airport to see if they can get me a new one."

"Chicago! Well I reckon it'll be alright to make your call," the man said, walking back in the store, "but the operator will have to tell me what it's gonna cost. I'll have to charge you." He walked behind the counter to the phone box fixed to the wall, picked up the receiver, and listened a moment then spoke into the mouthpiece protruding from the phone box. "Say, Mrs. Hinton, this is Duley Perkins, that's right, at the store. I wonder if ya'll would mind lettin' me have this line for an important call, long distance. That's right, long distance. I got a fellow here who landed an airplane. He's a colored fellow, too. That's right, a colored fellow. Well, you might never heard of such, but he done it. Yes, ma'am. I sure will." He paused, turned to John. "We got a five party line on this thing." He turned the crank on the side of the phone box. "Operator? That you Pearl? This is Duley. Yeah, at the store. Listen, I got a fellow here wants to call Meridian. When he gets through stay on the line to tell me how much to charge for the call. That's right. Here I'll let you talk to him." He turned to John. "Here you are. Come around the counter here. Just tell her who you want."

"Hello, ma'am, I'd like to speak to someone at the flying service in Meridian. Yes, ma'am at the airport."

A short while later a distant sounding voice came on the line. "Key Brothers Flying Service."

"This is John Robinson, I'm over here just west of Demopolis."

"I'm Al Key. Can you speak a little louder? You say you're west of Demopolis?"

"Yes, sir. I blew a tire on a Stinson and I wonder if someone over there can get me some help. I'll need a new tire and tube and tools to change it out."

"You the Robinson that flew in Ethiopia? Supposed to make some kind of speech here today."

"Yes, sir, I am. Are you one of the Key brothers that set the world endurance record?"

"That's right. Look here, there must be a thousand colored folks at the field already. I'll come over and get you myself before we have a riot or something out here. If you can get the wheel off your plane, we'll bring it back here with you. We got a tire and tube to fit it. My boys can mount 'em while you talk to these people. Then we'll get you and the wheel back to your plane. That sound alright?"

"Mr. Key, that would be mighty fine of you. I'll pay for the service. Hang on just a minute and I'll get Mr. Perkins here to tell you exactly where we are."

"Just tell him you're at Perkins' store on Highway 80, four miles west of the Tombigbee Bridge."

John relayed the location to Al Key. Then he paid for the phone call, borrowed a screw type automobile jack and a toolbox from the store-keeper, and returned to the plane where he jacked up the right gear strut and removed the wheel. Afterwards he returned to the store and bought a quart of milk, a tin of sardines, and a box of crackers for lunch. He sat out on the porch talking with Mr. Perkins. They heard the sound of an aircraft directly overhead. By the time they walked out to the pasture, Al Key was waiting for them beside his plane, a Curtiss Robin.

A year earlier, Al Key and his brother Fred had set a world endurance record flying a high- wing Curtiss Robin monoplane modified with an in-flight refueling system of their own design. The plane also had a platform attached, which allowed them to walk out and add oil to the engine while flying. A second plane lowered a fuel line several times every day and night. Food and water was lowered to them on a rope through a hatch in the cabin top. They remained airborne in the vicinity of Meridian for twenty-seven days, a record that was only broken by astronauts living in the International Space Station.

The two Mississippi pilots stood for a moment looking at one another.

"Mr. Key, I'm John Robinson. I sure thank you for taking the time to help me. I would be in a mess without you."

"Well, come on. We got to get you and that tire to Meridian. I think every black from the town and surrounding parts must be waiting for you at the airport. Never seen anything like it."

John thanked Mr. Perkins and told him if he could leave the plane on the jack he would pay him for the use of his tools.

Al Key with Robinson approached the airfield at Meridian. It had just been named Key Field in honor of the two brothers.

Years later, Al Key described their arrival: "We circled over the field and could see the crowd waiting on the ramp. There must have been about three thousand people down there, all looking up at us. In those days we weren't so concerned about regulations. I checked the area and saw no other traffic. Robinson gave me a questioning look and I just smiled and pointed at the crowd. Then I gave it full throttle and put the plane in a shallow dive to pick up lots of speed. We flew down between the terminal building and the hangar just over the heads of all those folks. They were looking up wide-eyed at us with their mouths open. I pulled the Curtiss right up and over into an Immelmann turn. Later one of the boys on the ground swore to me that the whole crowd went wild and that one old colored man standing near him hollered out, 'God Almighty! Look at that nigger fly!'

"After I had done that Immelmann, Robinson looked over at me and laughed, shaking his head, but he didn't say anything. In any case, when we came in and landed, I let Robinson get out and I sort of stayed hidden in the plane. Later, after he had made his speech, he paid me and we took the new tire mounted on his wheel and flew back to pick up his plane. He told me that all the blacks thought he had done that crazy stunt. I told him we would leave it that way. He grinned, thanked me again, and we shook hands. I liked him. Yes, he was all right."

Chapter 24

Gulfport, 1936

JOHN TURNED WEST CLIMBING OUT OF THE FIELD BY PERKINS'
STORE to follow Highway 80, part of the ten-year-old designated
United States highway system. He followed it west to Jackson where he
landed at Hawkins Airfield (originally called Davis Airfield) and made
a brief talk at Jackson College, founded in Natchez in 1877; the black
college was moved to Jackson in 1882. Late in the afternoon John took
off from Jackson for the 150-mile flight home to Gulfport. He picked up
US Highway 49 south. The highway was mostly sandy-clay and gravel
with a few new stretches of paving. The last seventy-five-mile stretch from
Hattiesburg to Gulfport seemed the longest. The late afternoon sun cast a
yellowish hue on the earth below where a young forest was struggling to
cover the scars left by the clear-cutting practices that sadly had, with no
thought given to conservation, destroyed the vast stands of virgin long-
leaf yellow pine. Some miles south of Hattiesburg on the east side of the
road, he saw the abandoned, deteriorating buildings and overgrown acre-
age known as Camp Shelby. It was federal land that had been set aside as
a training camp for the army during the Great War.

Flying at five thousand feet fifteen miles south of the little lumber mill town of Wiggins, John saw a distant, clear, unbroken horizon that made his heart beat faster. The clean line stretching beyond the flat coastal plain was the Gulf of Mexico. The sight filled him with the happy-tired feeling that comes at journey's end—a journey home from halfway around the world.

The Stinson let down to a thousand feet to circle over Gulfport. Black smoke poured from the tall smokestack of the town's power plant situated on the beach at the foot of Thirtieth Avenue. The port wasn't as busy as he remembered. There was but one steamship in the harbor. John looked down at the stately 200-room Great Southern Hotel made entirely from fine, Mississippi long-leaf pine timber. People playing tennis on the hotel's court looked up as he banked over the town. Along the shore, the concrete steps of a seawall, begun in 1927, now stretched east and west from the harbor paralleled by a two-lane road that had been designated US Highway 90 in 1925. The coast locals still called it Beach Drive. Most of it was paved, replacing the old oyster-shell road. The streetcar tracks along the beach were gone and the tracks in town sadly no longer used. Several broad streets in Gulfport had center dividers planted with palm trees and flowers. *It's a pretty town,* John thought to himself, *but it sure seems smaller.*

He circled over the shimmering water to look down at East Pier and saw it was still a popular fishing spot. Men, women, and children, black and white, sat or stood along the end of the earth-filled pier trying their luck. *I guess in these hard times, all those folks are trying to catch their supper.* Several people waved as he flew overhead.

John turned eastward down the shoreline toward Biloxi. The hotels were mostly vacant since the crash of 1929. The beautiful Edgewater Hotel with its grand, oak-shaded lawn and eighteen-hole golf course cast a lonely shadow in the setting sun. In the 20s, whole trainloads of tourists used to come down from Chicago every winter to stop at Edgewater's own station. The White House Hotel, the lovely Buena Vista, and the elegant Markham Hotel in Gulfport were all suffering. Cannery Row in Biloxi was still in operation. Huge piles of oyster shells stood witness to that. Canned oysters were shipped as far as Chicago and New York. The shells supplied material for roads, driveways, and parking lots all over the coast. Biloxi still called itself the seafood capital of the world, but, like the country, the industry was struggling.

Turning offshore back toward Gulfport, Robinson could see the barrier islands, Horn, Ship, and Cat. Looking down on East Beach near the harbor, he picked out the spot where he saw his first airplane, Moisant's Curtiss Pusher. *Seems like a long time and a million miles ago.*

Over the port, he picked up the northbound Gulf & Ship Island Railway tracks and followed them across the L&N Railroad toward Gulfport's grass airfield located west of the tracks and north of 33rd Street. Out his left window, he could see the Big Quarter and was able to pick out the two-story house on Thirty-First Avenue where he grew up. He wondered if his sister Bertha would get home during his visit. Bertha had married a fellow school teacher, H. L. Stokes. They were teaching school in Arkansas.

At eight hundred feet, John flew a left downwind pattern, lowered the vacuum-operated flaps, and turned base. Letting down to four hundred feet, he did a final turn and crabbed into a crosswind from the southeast. He set the plane down and taxied to the flight line where four planes of various makes were tied down in front of the one hangar on the field.

The hangar doors were open. John could see a man working on a WACO biplane. His name was Arthur Hughes. Arthur had been running the airport since 1934. There was barely enough local and transient business to keep the field going. The only regular flight into Gulfport was a mail plane, since airmail service had begun in 1928. Hughes got by selling fuel, working on aircraft engines and airframes, and giving flying lessons to the few students who could afford them.

Mr. Hughes saw the Stinson taxi up. He climbed down from the WACO. Cleaning the oil off his hands with a rag, he walked out to meet the pilot. When he saw John step down from the Stinson, he knew right away who he was. He had read all about him in the local *Daily Herald* newspaper. Hughes introduced himself and helped tie the Stinson down for the night. It was quittin' time and he offered to drive John to his mother's house. John thanked him. "That would be mighty nice of you, Mr. Hughes." Johnny was surprised at the courtesy.

In answer to the knock on her front door, Celeste Cobb came from the back of the house wiping her hands on her apron. All she could distinguish through the screen door in the failing light of dusk was the silhouette of a tall man.

"Hi, Momma."

The small, stout woman held both hands to her lips. "Johnny! Oh! Praise Jesus!" She threw open the door and put her arms around his neck. He picked her up off the floor and swung her around on the front porch.

"Oh, Johnny! Daddy Cobb and me prayed so hard for you. We so proud. Everybody's been waitin' for you. Now you put me down! I got work in the kitchen to do." John set his mother down, picked up his suitcase, and followed her into the house. "Your old room is ready upstairs, fresh, clean sheets and bath towels. We all ready for you." She walked down the hall toward the kitchen wiping joyful tears from her eyes with her apron. "My baby's home!"

John and his mother were sitting in the kitchen when they heard the front door open and the distinct step of a person walking with a limp. Celeste motioned for John to be quiet. "I'm in the kitchen, darlin'. Did you bring home the fresh shrimp for the gumbo?"

Mr. Cobb, walking down the hallway answered, "Yes, honey, I got shrimp, fresh okra, and I also bought a basket of peaches and some fine pork chops." He rounded the kitchen doorway.

"That boy gonna need lots of your cookin' when he gets . . ."

John stood up and grinned at the gray-haired man standing in the doorway. "Hi, Daddy."

Charles Cobb came in and set the groceries on the kitchen table. "Let me look at you, boy. Don't you look fine, just fine, son." The older man fought the tears welling up in the corners of his eyes. He stepped forward and wrapped his arms around Johnny. "I'm so thankful you're home, son."

To John, Daddy Cobb looked much older than he remembered and the limp had grown more pronounced. "You lookin' mighty fine yourself." For a moment longer, John held tight to the gentle man he loved.

The word that Johnny Robinson was home spread rapidly. That evening, the Cobb home filled with friends and neighbors of all ages. Many brought food and drink turning the homecoming into a neighborhood party that spilled out on the front yard and into street. To his surprise, Janette Sullivan brought him a chocolate cake just like she used to when he came home from Tuskegee. She was one of several women who paid a great deal of attention to John.

Everyone wanted to hear about the war, about Emperor Selassie, the world travels, his battles with the Italians. John answered many questions, but passed lightly over as many as he could. He tried to hide the embarrassment he felt from all the attention.

Some wondered if the war had changed John, but in an interview in 1974, Bernadette Barabino (Graham) remembered, "When he came home, he was the same old sweet Johnny. Women were crazy about him. He was a gentleman everybody loved."

Celeste introduced her son to leaders from the AME and the Bethel Baptist Church. They said they hoped he didn't mind that they had arranged a big day of events for him on Sunday. First, they said, there would be a picnic at the airport where they hoped he wouldn't mind giving airplane rides. They would raffle off chances for the rides.

Now John understood why Mr. Hughes had been so nice to him. All the doings at the airport on Sunday would be good for business. He glanced at his beaming mother and knew he was trapped. He smiled at her and told the church people, "I'll be happy to do it."

"That's just wonderful. Several city officials including Mayor Milner will be out at the airport, and afterwards there'll be a big reception at Bethel Baptist Church. And don't you forget, the *Daily Herald* called and asked if you will go in to see 'em tomorrow. They want to do a story on you and the doings at the airport."

"That sounds mighty fine," John said without much enthusiasm. "I can tell ya'll put a lot of work into all this."

When the last guest left, John let out an audible sigh and slumped into an overstuffed chair in the living room. Charles Cobb returned from the kitchen with two bottles of Dixie beer. For a while both men sat quietly and sipped their beers.

"You seem a little uneasy, son. I guess we making too much fuss over you. Everyone 'round here heard you was coming and wanted to see you. There was folks here tonight I ain't never seen myself."

"Well, Daddy, it's nice to get all the attention, but after a while it gets a little heavy to carry." John easily picked up the familiar speech of his youth. "Folks keep wantin' to hear 'bout the war, but they don't want to hear 'bout it, I mean what it's really like. I can't tell 'em anyway. Don't want to talk 'bout it, not to them, not to the newspaper. I'm sick to death of it. I don't even want to think about it." John paused a long minute. "You know it's gonna happen again, war I mean. Hitler and Mussolini and all their Fascist thugs are gonna set fire to Europe if the rest of 'em don't do something to stop 'em pretty soon. I heard people talking 'bout it on the ship. They sittin' round waiting for the League of Nations to help. It ain't gonna be no help—didn't help Ethiopia. Talk ain't gonna stop 'em. Proved that already. It's gonna happen, Daddy, but I'm through with it. I'm gonna go back to my flying school and teach pilots. We gonna need pilots and lots of 'em. Some of 'em gonna be black if I have anything to do with it."

John paused, then shook his head.

"We mighty glad you're home, son. Wish you would stay."

"I wish I could, but there's no place for me down here. You know, more than half my students in Chicago are white. They got more money up there. Mr. Hughes told me he had only two students. Those two and a few young ladies from Gulf Park College are all that can afford lessons on the whole coast. Seems there's a Dr. Cox from the college teaches the

Gulf Park girls in his own plane. I know you and Momma do alright down here. Most white folks here on the coast treat blacks fair . . . long as they don't get too ambitious. Things are different up North. Sure there are whites up there who don't like colored folks, places where coloreds aren't allowed same as down here, but there's more opportunity. I have a business in Chicago I can't walk out on. I'm making good money. I have a place in the community."

"Son, I understand. This has been a good place for your mother and me. Not everything's right for colored folks, I don't mean that, but I doubt we would be happy anyplace else. We know you're used to a different way and you got things to do. I reckon Chicago is more home to you now."

"Ya'll worked so hard to send me and Bertha to school. Ya'll are part of everything we do."

Mr. Cobb got up and put his hand on John's shoulder. "Come on, son. I reckon we've worn you plumb out." As the two got up from their chairs, Mr. Cobb said, "I've got tomorrow off. How long since you been fishing?"

"Lord, I don't remember."

"I got two poles and a bucket. The tide'll be changing late afternoon."

"Sounds good to me, Daddy. "

John woke up late feeling rested. Celeste Cobb came into his room carrying his uniform she had brushed and pressed.

"Good morning, sleepyhead. It's nine o'clock. I'll have you some breakfast by the time you get dressed. You're supposed to be at the newspaper by ten-thirty."

"Momma, I thought I could be out of that uniform now that I'm home."

"Well, you can't. You gonna wear it to the newspaper. They'll want a picture I bet and you gonna wear it for the goings-on this Sunday at the airport too. Besides, I took your suit to the cleaners and the rest of your stuff I'm washing and ironing."

"Momma, you haven't changed a bit. You still boss around here." John laughed.

"That's right. You may be an emperor's pilot and a big hero, but 'round here, I'm queen."

"Yes, ma'am."

By the time John had cleaned up and finished dressing, the wonderful blended aroma of brewed coffee, baking biscuits, and frying bacon drifted up from the kitchen. He put on his tie, buffed his shoes, and went downstairs to a morning feast. Celeste fussed over him, glowing with the joy of having her boy home. She served up hot coffee to start things off. Then came two eggs over light, crisp bacon, steaming buttered grits, and biscuits with homemade scuppernong jelly.

Finishing his last cup of coffee, John protested, "I think after all this breakfast I'm gonna have to go back upstairs and take a little nap."

"You get yourself out of this house and down to the paper. Walking to town oughta work off a few of those biscuits you helped yourself to."

John walked down Thirty-First Avenue and turned left on Thirteenth Street. There was a new service station on the corner of Thirtieth and Thirteenth. Like most of the gas stations in the South, it had two gas pumps and three toilets, one on the side marked Women, one marked Men, and the third in back marked Colored. The station attendant looked a little perplexed. He had never seen a Negro man in an officer's uniform before.

John crossed the G&SI tracks and turned north on Twenty-Seventh Avenue toward the train station. "Johnny! Johnny Robinson," called a large man pulling to the curb in a new four-door Dodge D2 sedan. John recognized the well-dressed white man wearing a seersucker suit, white shirt, tie, suspenders, and a sailor straw hat. John had worked for him after school, weekends, and summers as a teenager.

"Hello, Mr. Simpson. How have you been?"

"Just fine, Johnny. Mrs. Simpson's maid told her this morning that you got home yesterday. You have really done yourself proud. We kept up with you in the papers and from Lowell Thomas on the radio. Several men including the mayor were talking about you this morning at coffee. Do you need a ride somewhere?"

"Thank you, Mr. Simpson, I appreciate the offer but I've just got a few blocks to go and sorta want to look the town over. It's been a while since I was here."

"All right, Johnny, just want you to know we think a lot of you."

At the train station, where the GS&I tracks running north from the port crossed the east-west L&N tracks, things did not look as busy as when he was a boy. The waiting room was still divided between white and colored, but the hustle and bustle was gone. The buildings across the brick paved street were beginning to look a little shabby, especially the small hotel.

John walked around to the Railway Express freight door. A stout black man was loading cartons onto a baggage wagon. He was wearing railroad bib overalls and a seasoned Railway Express cap. A watch chain hung down from one pocket, while from the small center pocket of the bib the drawstring of a tobacco pouch suggested he was a roll-your-own smoker.

"Can you tell me when the next train leaves for New Orleans?"

The man looked up at John. He put down the package he was lifting and broke into a wide grin. "Johnny! Hot damn, if you don't look like something! I mean, you lookin' good!" He shook John's hand and slapped him on the shoulder. "Come on, I want you to meet everybody. I been telling 'em about you and the fun we used to have. You know, I remember when you gave me a model airplane you made from an apple crate. Come on and meet some folks."

"I only have time to say hello, Marcus. I've got to get down to the newspaper. I'll look you up later."

"Well just let me introduce you to the stationmaster and my bossman."

Marcus led John to the office window where a telegraph operator sat working his key. After he had been introduced to all the railroad men in sight, John excused himself by inviting them all to the airport on Sunday. Marcus, his boss, and the stationmaster were promised a flight.

It was already ten o'clock. John quickened his step. He passed the theater with its side ticket window for blacks who had to climb an outside staircase and enter the balcony to see the moving pictures. It was the only theater in town that allowed Negroes at all. It, the Anderson Theater, and the larger Paramount Theater were the only buildings in town cooled with "refrigerated air."

Turning east down Fourteenth Street, he walked past merchants celebrating Trade Day. Elmer's department store had a sale on men's seersucker suits at $3.98. Pants and shirts were on sale for $1.00 each and Panama straw hats were seventy-nine cents. Nearer the paper was the Hill Grocery Store where signs in the window advertised steak at twenty-three cents a pound and lettuce at five cents a head. A package of five bars of Octagon soap was priced at ten cents.

John passed the Markham Hotel. On the opposite corner was the *Daily Herald* office. He knew that if he had been a white celebrity, the paper would have sent a reporter out to his house, but he had grown up with such differences and rarely let it bother him. *It's not so different in the North; they just don't call it segregation. I reckon one day maybe this country will get over all that, but I got too much to do to worry 'bout it.*

He entered the *Daily Herald* office and was invited into the newsroom which was separated by little more than a counter from the rest of the interior. In the back the presses could be heard running while the *click-click* of the linotype machines joined the pecking of typewriters, ringing telephones, and people talking over the noise—or at least trying to. Windows were open and the air was circulated by numerous oscillating fans, some mounted on walls, some sitting on the floor, but it was still hot and humid inside. The men all worked with their coats off, their ties left on, and their sleeves rolled up to their forearms. The ladies all wore light cotton summer dresses. The editor, Mr. Eugene Wilkes, invited John into his small office, which had windows on three sides through which he could observe the entire operation. In the office, John met Mr. Glen Rutledge who introduced himself and offered John a chair and the interview began. The two newsmen were genuinely interested in John's story. All in all, John thought the interview was a well-spent hour. *I bet maybe it was the first interview ever with a black man sitting down in the editor's office.*

The story made the front page of the afternoon paper under the head-line, "Gulfport Negro Who Piloted Emperor Haile Selassie Visits Home; Relates His Experiences In Wartime Flying."

The article dated June 26, 1936 began: "J. C. Robinson, Negro aviator who gained worldwide fame as Emperor Haile Selassie's official pilot and who was in charge of the entire Ethiopian Air Force, is in Gulfport visit-ing his stepfather and mother, C. C. Cobb and wife, who reside at 1905 Thirty-First Avenue. Robinson called at the *Herald* office this morning wearing the Ethiopian army official uniform. His rank is colonel and his uniform carries the official emblem of the emperor, the Lion of Judah, worked in gold thread mined from the gold mines of Ethiopia from which King Solomon was supposed to have secured much of the gold for his famous temple at Jerusalem.

"He was employed by C. A. Simpson in Gulfport at one time and went from Gulfport to Chicago, where he worked for six years with the Curtiss Flying Service.

"Ethiopia had twenty-four airplanes during the war, he said, and all but three of them were shot down.

"During his thirteen month's service in the Imperial Ethiopian Air Ser-vice, he was wounded three times and gassed twice."

The article went on to describe the situation in Ethiopia and the emper-or's escape. It concluded by announcing that Robinson would make an appearance at the Gulfport airport sponsored by church groups before returning to Chicago.

Celeste Cobb carefully clipped the article from the front page and placed it in the scrapbook with all the others she had collected. Then she put the scrapbook back on the table beside her Bible.

The following Sunday, Gulfport Airfield was overflowing. The mostly black crowd was salted with white officials, aviation enthusiasts, and curi-ous onlookers. Children ran among the crowd, paying little attention to their mother's warnings not to get their Sunday-go-to-meeting clothes dirty. Arthur Hughes patrolled the hangar and ramp warning, "You young'uns stay off those airplanes! Don't touch the propellers!" There were five planes on the field and Hughes had his hands full protecting them, not just from children but from curious adults as well. "Don't touch the airplanes!" It was the largest crowd ever gathered at the airfield.

Booths had been set up by church groups to sell sandwiches, cookies, cakes, ice tea and soft drinks. Mr. Hughes was to get ten percent of the proceeds. Several churchwomen walked through the crowd selling chances for a plane ride with Colonel Robinson.

Chairs had been set up on the flat bed of a truck decorated with red, white, and blue bunting. Charles and Celeste Cobb were introduced and seated there with various dignitaries who took turns making short speeches and announcements. Among the white citizens seated were Gulfport Mayor, J. W. Milner, and Dr. Cox, president of Gulf Park College who also taught flying at the all-girl school. John, uncomfortable in his uniform, was seated beside Mayor Milner.

Speaking last, John made a short speech thanking those present for honoring him with such a homecoming. There was much applause. It was then time for the drawing for the airplane rides.

A lady from the AME church climbed up the steps to the platform and held out a large hat box filled to the brim with tickets. John reached into the box and pulled out a ticket for the first ride. When he read the number there was a squeal from the crowd as a young woman ran forward holding the matching number ticket tightly in her hand. The crowd applauded and then roared with laughter when a man at the edge of the platform recognized the winner and called out, "My goodness, Colonel Robinson, you be careful! That's my daughter."

John smiled down at the man. "I certainly will, Mr. Gaston."

The crowd standing around the blue and silver-gray Stinson parted to allow John and his passenger through. They watched with intense interest as the colonel made a last inspection of the craft before helping a very excited Julia Gaston into the plane, securing her seat belt and closing the passenger door. He asked the onlookers to move away from the plane, climbed into the pilot's seat, and closed the door. Checking to make sure the area was clear, he primed the engine and engaged the starter. The propeller turned several revolutions before the engine roared to life exhaling a cloud of blue smoke from oil accumulated in the lower cylinders of the radial engine. The blast from the propeller scattered those standing behind the plane as it began to taxi. Miss Gaston waved frantically at her friends. The crowd moved to the edge of the grass runway and grew silent as John wheeled the plane into the wind. The engine thundered as the plane began its takeoff roll. Several young boys ran chasing after the graceful ship. The Stinson lifted into the air, the people all waving and clapping their hands. Standing on the speaker's platform, tightly clutching the arm of Charles Cobb, Celeste felt both immense pride and trembling fear as her son's plane roared past.

John carried his passenger south over the shore then circled the town. A few minutes later he was back over the field. Before landing he made a long, fast, low pass down the field to the great approval of those gathered below. He then brought the Stinson around on final approach, lowered the flaps and made a graceful landing. Slowing quickly, he taxied back to the parking area.

For a dollar and a half a piece, John flew eager passengers, four at a time, all that afternoon, including Mayor Milner, Dr. Cox, and a slightly reluctant Mr. Gaston. Finally, he took his quietly terrified momma and his proud and thrilled daddy for a gentle flight at sunset, giving them their first aerial view of the beautiful coastline. John pointed out their house and the G&SI railroad shop where his daddy worked. His momma closed her eyes for the landing.

Those who were there that day remembered it as a grand occasion, outdone, perhaps, only by the brief stop that year of the presidential train. During his short appearance and speech, given from the observation platform of the club car, Franklin Roosevelt, campaigning for re-election, assured the crowd gathered at the Gulfport Railroad Station that the nation's dreadful economic problems were being solved by government spending and that America would never become involved in another war in Europe should one occur.

Chapter 25

Hard Choices

BY LATE 1936, JOHN, ALONG WITH HIS PARTNER CORNELIUS COFFEE, moved the John Robinson National Air College to Poro College in Chicago. The move was made at the invitation of Annie Turnbo Malone, one of the most successful businesswomen in America. She had started the first cosmetics company devoted exclusively to the development, manufacture, and sale of beauty products designed for Negro women. She moved the original Poro College from St. Louis to Chicago because of the larger Negro population there. The huge main Poro College building served not only as the cosmetics development and manufacturing plant, but as a business school to train young Negro women in the management and sale of her products. Annie Malone, then a woman of "a certain age," was a pioneer in the field of black entrepreneurship and recognized in John Robinson his achievements in aviation and his ability to set an example for others. It is not unreasonable to say that she, like women of all ages who met him, was charmed by his sometimes daring yet always gracious manner.

The separate building on the Poro College campus where the Robinson aviation school was located was a two-story stone building that faced South Parkway. Entrance was gained through an iron gate. As you entered, John had a large office to the left. His secretary, Rosie Morgan, had a small adjoining office. Classrooms occupied the rest of the first floor and the entire second floor. The school taught both flying and mechanics. Actual flying instruction was carried out at Harlem field located south of Chicago Municipal Airport. The school had about fifty students and six instructors. Most did double duty as classroom and flight instructors. Coffey oversaw the aviation mechanics classes on the second floor where students practiced on actual aircraft engines. It was an impressive operation especially considering the country was still in the grip of the Great Depression.

In the summer of 1937, John, flying the Stinson, and Coffey, piloting one of the school's new J-3 Cubs, went on barnstorming tours to promote their aviation school. While Coffey flew the J-3 training plane to the smaller towns surrounding Chicago, John flew a recruiting tour in the Stinson. At their stop at Kansas City, the Kansas City newspaper described the flight under the headline, "Colonel John C. Robinson Lands at Local Airport." The article continues:

"Ambitious to make American Negro youth air-minded, Col. Robinson, chief of Haile Selassie's air forces during the Italo-Ethiopian war, landed his five-passenger monoplane at the Kansas City municipal airport Sunday morning, July 4, to spend a few hours before continuing to Topeka where he spoke Sunday and Monday nights. The blue and silver-gray Stinson monoplane, NC 1616, hit the runway of the airport at exactly 11:50 AM on Sunday.

"Flying with the colonel were his two copilots, Frank Browning and Joe Muldrew, both of Chicago. His passengers were Mrs. Annie Malone, head of the Poro College of Chicago, and Miss Yutha Tolson, Kansas Citian, who has been in Chicago several weeks taking a special course at the Poro College.

"Robinson and his copilots are making a tour in the interest of Colonel Robinson's school of aviation in Chicago in which fifty students already are enrolled, forty white and ten Negro. Colonel Robinson believes that aviation is a field with a great future for young Negroes well trained in aeronautics.

"At his school on the Poro College grounds in Chicago, established in September 1936, half a dozen instructors are busy teaching youths flying from the bottom up.

"The Brown Condor will be in Mound Bayou, Mississippi, for the fiftieth anniversary celebration July 12–17."

They continued on to stops at Paducah, Kentucky, and Cairo, Illinois, where John made a speech at Sumner High School. It was a well-planned tour, the expense of which was shared by Mrs. Malone who promoted Poro College and her products at each stop while Robinson promoted his school of aviation.

While John spent 1937 successfully promoting his flying school, including performing stunt flying in Dallas at the Pan American Exposition (on Negro participation day), it was a disastrous year for aviation. In one terrible month, five planes serving America's struggling airlines were lost at a cost of forty-five lives. Amelia Earhart and navigator Fred Noonan were lost on a flight from Lae, New Guinea, to Howland Island, and the German Zeppelin Hindenburg was destroyed by fire while landing at Lakehurst Naval Air Station in New Jersey. There was also talk of "mystery rays that could see planes and ships miles away even in fog." Three years later, the "mystery rays" were instrumental in saving England during the Battle of Britain. The name of the applied technology was "radio direction and ranging," more commonly known as radar.

Robinson continued to build a profitable business in the risky field of aviation at a time when the nation was struggling to find a way out of the Great Depression. Re-elected, Roosevelt continued his New Deal programs, spending massive amounts of money in an attempt to create jobs and gaining from Congress more power than any president in history.

Across oceans, Hitler, Mussolini, and the military leadership of Japan were also creating jobs but they were doing it by expanding their military might. An article that appeared in several major newspapers described a Chinese warlord who controlled the entire northeast of China. His name was Mao Tse-tung. "In the West," the article stated, "his growing Communist army is viewed with curiosity." The newly created *LIFE* magazine published photographs of German aviation students being trained in bombing techniques, while in Spain, bombs were falling on civilians from German and Italian planes supplied to the Fascist Nationalists and from Russian planes supplied to the Marxist Republicans.

In America, the focus was on problems at home. In 1937, unemployment remained stubbornly high. On Broadway, Erskine Caldwell's play *Tobacco Road* depicted the plight of the struggling poor to sellout audiences. Then, the disastrous flood of 1937 saw the Ohio and Mississippi rivers overflow their banks, forcing nearly a million refugees in eight affected states to flee their homes. Although Memphis, Tennessee, did not flood, it had to deal with an estimated fifty thousand refugees that fled to the city. John Robinson, with the sponsorship of the *Chicago Defender* newspaper, made repeated flights from Chicago to Memphis transporting donated clothing and supplies to flood victims.

John had never been blind to the problems of segregation and prejudice. In his home state, more than one white politician used racial fear to get elected. One such politician, elected to the US Senate, was a white supremacist, a defender of segregation, and a member of the Ku Klux Klan who filibustered the US Senate in an attempt to block an anti-lynching law. His name was Theodore Gilmore Bilbo.

All his life determined to succeed, Robinson found ways to work around such prejudice. He saw some of the same sort of men in the North, but he had no time to worry about racists and bigots. He never let such things distract him from his goals. "Nothing worth a damn ever comes easy." Like Booker T. Washington, Tuskegee founder, John believed the best way to help the advancement of his people was to teach them knowledge and skills that were in demand. It had worked for him. Now he was certain that war was coming and that men with flying skills, white or black, would be needed. Yet, he found that even in his own school there were more whites than blacks learning to fly. He felt he was not accomplishing enough alone. But John Robinson was not alone.

A fresh graduate of West Point, class of 1936, was Benjamin O. Davis, Jr. He got to West Point because his father, Benjamin Davis, Sr. was the first Negro to be promoted to the rank of general in the United States Armed Services. Even so, for four years the cadets at West Point refused to speak to cadet Davis except in circumstances prescribed by official school duties.

When Benjamin Jr. graduated from the academy, he applied for flight training. In reply to his application, he received a letter signed by the army chief of staff stating flatly that no Negroes were in the Army Air Corps and there weren't going to be any.

Tuskegee had never given up on John's idea of gaining a school of aviation. The college was ever struggling to find the financial means to establish such a school. Then in 1939, an event occurred that changed the playing field. A former corporal named Hitler invaded Poland.

President Roosevelt realized the United States needed to find a way to greatly increase the number of pilots he was sure would be needed to defend America. In 1937, the Army Air Corps had less than two thousand pilots and an inventory of less than nine hundred obsolete aircraft. Politically, Roosevelt wanted a way to increase the number of American pilots without alarming voters. The answer was the creation of the Civilian Pilot Training Program (CPTP). Airport operators badly in need of business and colleges all over the country applied for the program.

Cornelius Coffee was among the first flying instructors to apply for a grant to establish a new school under the Civilian Pilot Training Program, and left the John Robinson National Air College in preparation to start his own flight school. His application was turned down, as were those from black colleges across the country including Tuskegee.

A group of black pilots, Coffee among them, organized a flight to Washington to seek help for inclusion in the CPTP from Senator Harry

Truman. Truman played a significant role in the passage of the Civil Aeronautics Act of 1938 which created the Civil Aviation Administration (CAA). But Senator Harry Truman had the common prejudiced opinion of the time: He didn't believe Negroes had the inherent aptitude necessary to learn to fly. Confronting the contingent, he casually asked how the group had traveled to Washington. He was more than a little surprised to learn that they had all flown themselves there. Truman changed his mindset and began to support aviation training for blacks. As a result, Coffee got a CPTP certificate and started the Coffee School of Aviation, and Tuskegee finally received a government grant to establish its own Civilian Pilot Training Program. By 1940, six years after John Robinson had convinced them of the need for a school of aviation, Tuskegee was ready to open the program.

Thirty-seven-year-old John Robinson was immediately notified by Tuskegee officials. They estimated the school would be ready for operation by late 1940. He was overjoyed that the school could finally establish an aviation department. He was also saddened that he could not accept the offer made to him by the college. Robinson's school, which was well-established and had a majority of white students, had just been requisitioned under the government pilot training program as part of the Works Project Administration (WPA). Besides monetary compensation, Robinson was appointed to the position of director of the Chicago National Youth Administration, another of Roosevelt's WPA projects. When the offer from Tuskegee was weighed against his obligations, he felt compelled to turn down the offer to head the Tuskegee aeronautics school, which he had inspired. There was another factor that influenced his decision. The government of Ethiopia in exile had maintained contact with him. There was hope that Britain, now engaged in war with both Germany and Italy, would drive the Italians from Ethiopia to protect their interests in Sudan and Kenya, both bordering Ethiopia, as well as ensuring the operation of the vital Suez Canal. If the British were successful, John had obligated himself to once again volunteer his services should the emperor need him.

With John Robinson unavailable, the man selected to head the school at Tuskegee Institute was another serious young black flyer, C. Alfred Anderson. Years earlier he had saved his money and bought a small, 65-horsepower used airplane. Because there was no instructor available to him, he taught himself to fly it, not an unusual occurrence at the time. On one occasion Anderson made a forced landing in a field where he sustained a nasty head injury. Afterwards he had to keep finding new places to hide his repaired plane because his mother started carrying an ax in her car and searching the countryside for it. She said if she found the plane she would "chop it up" to keep her crazy son from killing himself.

Later, Anderson with his friend Dr. Forsythe bought a new 90-horsepower Lambert Monocoupe, named it The Spirit of Booker T. Washington, and flew it island-hopping across the West Indies all the way to South America. Anderson was recruited by Tuskegee through his affiliation with the Howard University Civilian Pilot Training Program.

Anderson's first order from Tuskegee was two-fold. First, he was to pick up a new WACO UP-F-7 biplane from the factory at Troy, Ohio. Second, he was instructed to fly the new WACO to Chicago and take advanced training from John C. Robinson, including aerobatics, in preparation for the Civil Aeronautics Authority (CAA) commercial certification as a flight instructor. While in Chicago, Anderson stayed with Robinson as a guest in his apartment. The two became fast friends.

The following fall, "Chief" Anderson (as he was fondly called the remainder of his life) set up Tuskegee's flying school at a small grass strip just off the Union Springs Highway. A short time later, Tuskegee purchased land for a new field nearer the college. It was named Moton Field in honor of Dr. Robert R. Moton, a former president of the school (1915–1935) and the man John Robinson had convinced of the need for a school of aviation during his flying visit to the institution in 1934.

By 1941 Germany and Italy controlled virtually all of Western Europe. Only Great Britain remained unoccupied, standing alone against Hitler at a terrible price. In the United States, though the public was still in an isolationist mindset, the Roosevelt Administration ordered thousands of new aircraft while the Army Air Corps was establishing new training bases as quickly as possible. Judge William Hastie, an aide to Secretary of War Henry Stimpson, fought, begged, and fought some more for the establishment of a particular Army Air Corps training base. He finally got it. Judge Hastie was black and the base he had fought for was built at Tuskegee, Alabama, in 1941. It was located ten miles from Tuskegee Institute's Moton Field and named Tuskegee Army Airfield. After graduating from primary flight school at the Tuskegee School of Aeronautics under Chief Anderson, volunteer students were sent to the Army Airfield for advanced training in AT-6 and BT-13 aircraft.

The Air Corps sent Major Noel F. Parrish to Tuskegee Field as director of operations to replace Colonel Fredrick Kimble. Kimble was a strict segregationist who had ordered the white officers not to go to the base theater because they might have to sit next to a black and put twin water fountains around the base marked "white only" and "colored only." Major Parrish, a pilot, was white, as were all the staff officers and flying instructors there. He was a Southerner who had graduated from high school in Cullman, Alabama. He had been brought up under segregation but was raised by his minister father to treat all people with dignity. The first thing he did was do away with the humiliating water fountain signs. He found there was little recreation for the black troops so he arranged to bring in entertainers like Joe Louis, Louis Armstrong, and Lena Horne. He formed a football team. The morale of the Tuskegee Airman soared.

Parrish's primary assignment was to turn young black men into fighter pilots. Many members of the Army Air Corps didn't give him very good odds for success. He suffered a lot of jokes from fellow officers. High-ranking members of the Army Air Corps in Washington had tried their best to prevent the establishment of the program. His friends generally thought he had drawn an assignment that would dead-end his career. (They were wrong. Noel Francis Parrish would reach the rank of Brigadier General.)

Parrish related an incident that happened shortly after his arrival at Tuskegee: "A black pilot landed his own plane at the field. His name was John Robinson. I had heard of his flying in Ethiopia. He introduced himself and conveyed to me how proud he was to see the new Army Air Corps program at Tuskegee. He was sharp. I was very favorably impressed by his quiet, sincere manner. He was a no-nonsense, skilled pilot. Robinson set the bar. He erased any doubts I had. I got on with my assignment with confidence."

Eight months later, the first five graduates of the Advanced Flying School at Tuskegee Army Airfield received their wings. One of them was Benjamin Davis, Jr. By the end of World War II, more than six hundred pilots had graduated from the school. The segregated 99th and 79th Pursuit Squadrons were combined into the all-black 332nd Fighter Squadron and took part in the invasion of Sicily and the battle for Anzio. Once in Italy, they escorted bombers on missions reaching all the way to Berlin. It turned out that the bomber crews they protected didn't care what color the pilots of the 332nd Squadron were. "They could fly like hell and shoot straight." They were so good, bomber outfits started requesting the Red Tails, so called because the tails of the 332nd aircraft were painted bright red. Eighty-three pilots of the 332nd earned the Distinguished Flying Cross. Two of them were later awarded the rank of general, Benjamin Davis, Jr. and Daniel James, Jr. Daniel "Chappy" James went on to become the first four-star black officer in United States history when he was appointed Commander, North American Aerospace Defense Command (NORAD). None of the members of the 332nd fighter group knew the debt they owed John Robinson without whom there would have been no Tuskegee Airmen. John was to play another unsung role in the development of the Tuskegee Airmen.

John Robinson did not stand idly by after the Japanese attack on Pearl Harbor and the German declaration of war against the United States. He immediately volunteered his services to the Army Air Corps. The AAC told Robinson he was too old to fly combat, but at least someone in the war department in Washington had sense enough to interview Robinson for his knowledge of the effects of strategic air tactics. After all, he was the first American to encounter the deliberate terror-bombing of civilians by modern aircraft, the first to be on the receiving end of up close blitzkrieg warfare used by Mussolini in Ethiopia prior to Hitler's invasion of Poland.

John wanted to contribute more than just talk of his war experiences. When told that at thirty-eight he was too old for the Air Corps, Robinson told them he could still help the war effort. "I can tear down an aircraft engine and put it back together blindfolded. I taught aircraft mechanics at Curtiss-Wright and at my own school of aviation." He had CAA Aircraft and Engine Mechanics certificates to prove it.

The Air Corps needed more aircraft mechanics than pilots. Thousands of aircraft were on order, hundreds waiting for delivery. They would need mechanics to keep them flying. The Army Air Corps realized they needed Robinson and others like him for a very special reason. The armed services were segregated. Because the black squadrons were to be strictly segregated, it followed that the aviation mechanics and ground support troops assigned to maintain their planes must also be black. (Segregation was carried to the point that even their flight surgeons had to be black.) This presented a problem. Where would they get qualified black instructors to train them?

John Robinson recommended many black previously trained aviation mechanics. Based upon his recommendations, they were immediately hired as civilian aviation mechanics instructors and assigned to Chanute Army Airfield in Illinois. They were to train the first two hundred fifty black aviation mechanics in the Army Air Corps to support the Tuskegee airmen. Upon arrival, Robinson and his group were introduced to the Army Air Corps aviation mechanics curriculum and indoctrinated in the army methods of training. They quickly gained the reputation of knowing what they were doing. They settled down to train the mechanics that would keep the Tuskegee airmen flying. Once again John Robinson was playing a direct part in the development and support of Tuskegee airmen.

New army airfields were being constructed throughout the country. One was Keesler Army Airfield at Biloxi, Mississippi. The demand for

Negro mechanics and other segregated squadron support troops grew quickly. Robinson accepted an assignment as a civilian instructor at Keesler Field where he could be close to his home. (By the end of the World War II, some seven thousand black troops had been trained at Keesler Field.) John was put in charge of twelve other black aviation mechanics and instructors transferred from Chanute to Keesler.

John arrived home to Mississippi in his usual inimitable style, driving a 1941 Cadillac convertible, one of the last pre-war automobiles built. The US auto industry would stop making automobiles for the duration, turning out trucks, jeeps, tanks, and aircraft instead.

Following the establishment of Keesler Field in Biloxi, the Gulfport Army Air Field was quickly built twelve miles west of Keesler. At Gulfport Field there was a need for training mechanics on the radial engines of C-47 transport planes, as well as B-25 and B-17 Bombers. Because of a critical shortage of aviation mechanics instructors, John was asked to pick a couple of instructors and transfer to Gulfport Army Air Field. He was happy to do so. He and several other black aviation mechanics and instructors were already living at his mother's boarding house in Gulfport. One of the men John selected to instruct at Gulfport Field was his close friend, six-foot, six-inch tall Jim Cheeks, a pilot and aviation mechanic who had come down with him from Chanute.

Upon arrival at Gulfport Army Air Field, they were a little surprised to find they would be teaching white students.

Jim Cheeks recounted, "Segregation was the rule, not just in the South, but in the armed services overall. We had no trouble teaching young white air corps men aviation mechanics. They and the maintenance school officers found we knew what we were doing and respected our ability. We were turning out damn good mechanics. But in the mess hall where we ate, they built a six-foot-high white wooden lattice screen around a table where John and I ate. We could see all the white soldiers in the mess hall through the screen and they could see us, but I guess that met the rule of segregation. In town we couldn't go but to one movie house and had to sit in the balcony of that one. Restaurants were closed to us except for the

Negro restaurants like Pal's Café and Happy Jack's Café in the Big Quarter and clubs in north Gulfport. None of that bothered John. He paid no attention. He had been raised there and thought little of it, didn't let it get to him. He knew the girls in town and we had fun, lots of fun, and I sure remember John's momma's cooking, but that segregation setup bothered me. As it turned out, we weren't in Gulfport for too long. Seems somehow it got to Washington, to a US Senator from Mississippi named Bilbo, that down there in his state Negroes were teaching white boys. At least that's what we were told by our supervisor who said he was not happy to see us go. We received orders to transfer to Offutt Army Air Field in Nebraska. Damn if I didn't miss Gulfport."

Chapter 26

Once More to Africa

D ISTANT EVENTS WERE TAKING PLACE THAT WOULD AFFECT BOTH
John Robinson and Jim Cheeks. On June 13, 1940, a certain
"Mr. Strong" had been taken aboard a Short Sunderland flying boat
that took off from Poole Harbor, England, and landed in the harbor at
Alexandria, Egypt. There, a certain "Mr. Smith" disembarked the flying
boat, boarded a Royal Air Force plane, and was flown to Khartoum,
Sudan. Haile Selassie was back in Africa. He was there to encourage his
people, fighting as guerrilla warriors, to join the British and Allied forces
and drive the Italians out of Ethiopia. On January 18, 1941, Emperor
Selassie crossed the Sudan border into Ethiopia near the village of Um
Iddla, four hundred and fifty miles northwest of Addis Ababa. There
began a hard march that saw him enter his capital of Addis Ababa on
May 5, 1941, five years to the day after he had been driven from his
country.

Six months later, November 1941, allied forces comprised of troops
of the British Army, British Commonwealth Nations of India, Sudan,
East Africa, and South Africa, a small commando outfit from the British
Mandate Palestine, Free French and Free Belgian units, and Ethiopian

irregular forces under Haile Selassie forced the surrender of most of the two hundred fifty thousand Italian soldiers in Ethiopia—most, but not all. About forty thousand Italian troops with various native Italian East African Askaris troops retired to mountain strongholds and began scattered but effective guerrilla warfare against the British and Ethiopians that would not end until October 1943.

A short time after that, John Robinson received a communiqué from Haile Selassie asking if he would assemble a small cadre of pilots and mechanics and return to Ethiopia to set about building a new Ethiopian Air Corps. It was a message John had been waiting for. He knew that the flying school business at home would never be what it had been when thousands of trained pilots returned home after the war. He accepted the emperor's offer. The question was how to carry it out.

Robinson arranged for five black pilots, all of whom were also aircraft mechanics, to travel with him under contract to Ethiopia. Their names were James (Jim) W. Cheeks, Andrew Hester, Edward Jones, Haile Hill, and Joe Muldrew. The group knew that starting an air force from scratch and teaching flying and aviation mechanics in Ethiopia would not be easy, but they had no idea that just getting there would be a great adventure in itself.

In December 1943, war raged across Europe and the Mediterranean. In May the Germans and Italians under Rommel had been defeated in North Africa and Italy had surrendered to the Allies on September 8, 1943. The Italians may have surrendered Italy, but the Germans had not. Hitler sent troops into the country to contain the Allies. German aircraft out of southern France and northern Italy were still a threat over the Mediterranean, as were U-boats.

The first task Robinson faced was to find a way to get his group to Ethiopia. There would be no luxury ocean liner to take the group merrily across the Atlantic, into the Mediterranean, through the Suez, and down the Red Sea to French Djibouti the way John had traveled pre-war in 1934. John first tried the Army Air Force transport and ferry service (AAFBU) that had established a South Atlantic route to fly aircraft and supplies via Recife, Brazil, to African and Eurasian continents, but every pound of freight and every cubic foot of space was precious. None was available for Selassie's intrepid black American aviators and their heavy load of tools and equipment.

Room was finally found for John and his entourage aboard a British merchant ship in one of the many convoys streaming across the North Atlantic with cargos to supply England for the planned invasion of Europe. The happy group was not particularly comforted to hear that although the U-boat threat had been greatly reduced, it had not been totally eliminated. One might think that John, Jim, and the rest, being pilots, would not suffer from seasickness, but they did. Blazing through the ocean at the breakneck speed of nine, sometimes ten knots, the long, stormy, cold voyage across the North Atlantic was miserable enough in itself, not to mention the terrible food, or that the convoy twice received U-boat warnings mid-Atlantic.

Upon their safe arrival in England, there was hardly time to tour London, much less the British Isles. Selassie had made arrangements with his British ally for the immediate transport of Robinson's team. They and their load of tools and equipment were quickly put aboard a British C-47 Dakota dressed in civil aviation livery. (They would have to refuel in neutral countries that did not allow military aircraft.) The twin-engine workhorse took off from a field in southwest England for an eight-hundred-mile flight to Lisbon in neutral Portugal. After refueling and spending the night they took off on the second leg, another eight hundred miles to Algiers. From Algiers it was nearly one thousand miles to Benghazi, Libya. The next leg was eight hundred miles to Cairo, Egypt. The last leg was the longest and stretched the range of the C-47 to the maximum: Cairo to Khartoum, Sudan.

Along the way, the RAF crew allowed John to fly as copilot, glad to get some relief. When John was not asking incessant questions about the plane, he was reading the operating handbook. John was allowed to spend at least ten of the thirty plus hours of flying in the cockpit. By the time they landed at Khartoum, the British crew told him they were confident of his ability to fly a Douglas DC3/C47. John found the type handled much like the Ford tri-motors, or the Farman or Fokker multi-engine planes he had flown in the thirties except that it was more comfortable and faster.

Once on the ground in Khartoum, the real journey began. The intrepid flyers were given an old Chevrolet stake-bed truck with a canvas cover, a guide, fuel and water, stored in five-gallon tins, and canned food supplies. Spare wheels and tires hung on both sides of the truck. Thus equipped, they loaded their tools and equipment and set out for Addis Ababa some four hundred and fifty miles away along a road marked on an English army map as "passable in fair weather."

Jim Cheeks described the highlights of the trip: "We put the guide in the cab between two of us, one driving, one riding in the cab, while three of us had to ride in back with the gear. We would switch out every four hours. It's a wonder we made it. We breathed tons of dust and had our kidneys rattled on the worst road I've ever been on. The map said passable in fair weather and I learned what that meant. Any rain and we struggled from one mud bog to another slipping and sliding in-between. Man, that was a trip. I think that truck must have been one left over from the British commandos in North Africa, you know, the Desert Rats. I heard they used the same Chevrolet trucks.[4] It's a good thing we were mechanics. We must have taken apart the carburetor and cleaned it and the spark plugs about every fifty or sixty miles. The fuel we carried was dirty. The brakes weren't too good either. It was rough country. We barely made it up some of the steep passes and going downhill was a thrill. Besides our baggage, tools and equipment, we had to carry fuel, oil, water, and food. On the best twelve hour-day, we made less than fifty miles. We didn't know where the hell we were. The guide, who spoke a little broken English, had to assure us about ten times a day that we were headed for Addis Ababa. Sometimes we could get cooked food at a village, but we had to

---

4 One is on display at the Imperial War Museum in London.

cook most of our meals. After seeing a snake or two, nobody wanted to sleep on the ground.

"We had tracked southeastward from Khartoum until we reached what our guide said was the border between Sudan and Ethiopia. It was unmarked and meandered generally southward. Then late one day near sundown, we came to a military outpost surrounded by barbed wire and sandbags and manned by black troops. We all thought the fighting in the area was over and suddenly here were armed troops. We were more than a little concerned. We didn't even know exactly which country we were in, which side of the border we were on. Then a white British officer came out of a tent and walked to the gate. This white guy asked if we had been attacked or seen any armed men. We hadn't. He said we had been lucky and then asked if we could shoot a rifle. I asked him if that meant we would have to shoot black men, 'cause if it did, I explained, we weren't going to do it. He said, 'Look around you. These black men will bloody well shoot them if they attack this camp.' The officer said, 'I'm talking about holdouts from the guerilla war on the Italian side, Selassie's tribal enemies. They are now mostly raiding bandits. If they attack, it will be at night and I can assure you that if they get through the wire they will try to kill everyone here and it won't be pretty.' I looked at John, he looked at the British officer. 'I believe we'll take those rifles,' he said. We had a good meal of some kind of wild meat . . . didn't ask what it was, exactly. We kept the rifles close and didn't sleep much. No attack came. We thanked the officer and his troops and left the next morning wishing maybe we had brought along our own rifles.

"We finally made it into Addis Ababa to a huge welcome. Seems the people remembered John Robinson. A week later we were welcomed by the emperor at the palace and then got to work. I'll add this: John was saddened by what the Italians had done. We didn't know too much about it, I mean the way he remembered things. He didn't talk to us about it much, but we could see that he was kind of down a little till we got to work."

John was devastated by what he found upon his arrival in Addis Ababa. He learned the Italians had executed thirty thousand Ethiopians, virtually every educated and technically skilled Ethiopian they could catch, as revenge for a failed attempt on the life of General Graziani. It would take a generation or more to replace them.

One of the few educators to survive was Mrs. Mignon Inniss Ford who had moved from the United States to Ethiopia in 1931. She had opened the Princess Sanabe School, the only private girl's school in the country. Her family had close ties with the emperor. She first met John Robinson during the war while he was in the hospital recovering from wounds he had received in combat. During the Italian occupation she hid in the outskirts of the capital, supporting her small children by making clothes.

When Haile Selassie returned after the war, he placed the highest emphasis on schools and lines of communication throughout his country. Mrs. Ford helped reopen the schools. The emperor once again turned to John Robinson to help re-establish lines of communication. Selassie determined that Ethiopia must become an essentially air-minded nation. The terrain demanded it. Modern roads were terribly expensive to build due to the rugged terrain in much of the country. The Italians had built a few roads linking some of the towns but much of the coffee crop, the most important export product of Ethiopia, could take four weeks by donkey to reach the railroad station in the capital for shipment to the sea and international markets. By air, it would take only hours to transport the same coffee. Ethiopia needed John Robinson. Besides rebuilding the Ethiopian Air Corps, he was asked to lay the foundation for an Ethiopian airline.

Jim Cheeks said of the start-up training, "At first we stayed in a hotel. Then John was given a large villa some Italian general had built. We all lived there. It was very nice and we had a cook and two servants to take care of us, do our laundry, clean. The living was good.

"We went out to set up the flying school at what was called Lideta airport. We found the first class of eighteen students waiting. They more or less spoke English. It was a requirement for qualifying for the program. The problem was that at the time, there was only one aircraft to use for training. It was not a plane considered a primary trainer. Ethiopia had somehow gotten hold of a US surplus Cessna UC78. It had been used by the Allies for training navigators and graduate pilots in multi-engine aircraft. It was used overseas for liaison and utility duty. The Americans dubbed it the bamboo bomber because the wings and tail were made of fabric-covered wood. I think the civilian models were called the Bobcat. The fuselage was steel tubing with wood fairings and the whole thing fabric-covered. It had two 245-horsepower Jacobs radial engines. I mean, who starts a student out in a twin?

"All of us flew the thing. It was easy to fly, but we had to convince ourselves that we could take an Ethiopian kid who had never been off the ground and teach him to fly in this five-seat, twin-prop plane without killing them and ourselves. As far as I know, that had never been done since the Wright brothers. We decided to start with a mechanics course so we could rebuild the engines. After that we started teaching flying. Now you have to realize that teaching someone that's never been in an airplane is difficult enough in a simple single-engine 65-horsepower cub. We started the first class of students at Addis Ababa in that twin Cessna with two 245-horsepower Jacobs radial engines. Most of them had never driven a car. Hell, we had a hard time making 'em wear shoes. But they were smart and proud and wanted to learn. They had gone through a lot just to be selected for training.

"There was another thing about the UC78. The plane did not have feathering propellers. It is bad enough to lose an engine with fethering props. The plane wants to yaw toward the dead engine. But if you lose an engine you can't feather, the prop on the dead engine just kept windmilling which produces even more drag. It had barely enough rudder to hold course with one engine windmilling like that. It didn't have a steerable tail wheel. You kept it straight on takeoff and landing by tapping on the brakes, right or left as necessary. Cessna claimed the plane had a ceiling of twenty-two thousand feet but would hold only three thousand feet on one engine. That's not too comforting when you remember that Addis Ababa is seven thousand feet above sea level. Practicing engine-out proce-dures was some kind of fun I'm here to tell you. You can believe we took real good care of those engines. If we ever were to actually lose one in flight, the remaining good engine would rapidly get us all the way to the crash site. Anyway, we did it, and we did it without killin' anybody. We were proud of the fact that we trained the first class of Ethiopian aviation cadets in that Cessna bamboo bomber. I don't know of any other group of instructors or students who participated in such a program. We did it because we didn't have a choice at the time. We took a bunch of kids that had never been in a plane, had never been off the ground, and taught them to fly in a twin-engine plane because it was all we had. John said we could do it, so we did. It wasn't long before we got war-surplus light single-engine training planes from the United States and the British. But I tell you, I was proud of that first class.

"By the time our contract was up, we five instructors had trained more than three hundred pilots and mechanics. Many of those students became the leaders of the new Ethiopian Air Force—several of them eventually made general. No one was prouder of those students than John Robinson.

"When our contract was over, most of us chose to go home. The war was over, and compared to our hardship getting to Ethiopia, it was a lot easier getting home. Flying had come a long way during World War II and transatlantic flight was common. John accepted the offer to stay and continue to head up the new, growing air force. Ethiopia had, I believe, become John's home. It was a tough decision for me to make. Johnny Robinson was my best friend. We had been through a lot together. He was a great guy. But it was time for me to go home. There were other things I wanted to do. I tell you this, it was a time, place, and experience I will never forget." Jim Cheeks went on to retire after a full career with Lockheed Aircraft.

In 1946 John helped the Ethiopian government reach an agreement with TWA Airlines to furnish technical personnel and aircrews to fly a small fleet of DC-3 aircraft. After this agreement was implemented, John turned his full attention back to training Ethiopia's small but growing air force.

In order to accelerate the rebuilding of his country, Haile Selassie arranged for scholarship programs at US colleges for Ethiopian students. The emperor knew he would need someone to help prepare these students for the cultural shock they would experience when they left Ethiopia for the first time to travel to the most modern country in the world. Again John helped. He suggested that Janet Waterford Bragg, a nurse, and a pilot in her own right, be contacted. Janet Waterford Bragg was the perfect choice. Bragg organized a sort of receiving depot for arriving young Ethiopian students. She would become affectionately known as "Mom" to hundreds of them. Many of them would arrive in the United States carrying notes to her from John Robinson. Years later, she recalled, "Some of the notes from Johnny had grease smudges on them, the mark of the ever-busy hands-on aviation instructor, head of the air force or not."

John *was* busy. He was teaching, he was flying, he was administering the creation of a new air force, monitoring the TWA-operated Ethiopian Air Line, and he was happy. He personally taught Prince Makonnen, Duke of Harar, to fly. They became the best of friends, often flying together. John also gave lessons to Mrs. Ford's son, Yosef Ford. (Yosef Ford would later move to Washington D.C. and become a professor of anthropology at the Center for Ethiopia.)

Then an incident occurred that brought home the reality of prejudice and politics to an admired and loved black man living in the oldest black-ruled nation in the world. In 1948 Swedish Count Gustaf von Rosen, who had flown an ambulance plane during the Italo-Ethiopian War, flew a new Swedish Sapphire single-engine training plane from Sweden to Addis Ababa setting an aviation record. Von Rosen made an offer on behalf of Sweden to supply several of the Sapphire planes as trainers for the Ethiopian Air Force. The emperor accepted the offer and commissioned von Rosen as a major in the Ethiopian Air Force.

Von Rosen had an extensive reputation as a pilot adventurer. After flying a Swedish ambulance plane in Ethiopia (which was destroyed on the ground by Italian bombers), he went to the Netherlands and was hired by Royal Dutch Airlines (KLM). He met and married a Dutch woman. Against the wishes of his wife, he joined the Finish Air Force in the Winter War against the invading Soviet Union in 1939. When Germany occupied the Netherlands, von Rosen went to England leaving his wife behind in Holland. (She joined the Dutch underground and worked bravely until captured and killed by the Nazis.) In England, Von Rosen applied for the RAF but was turned down, in part because his aunt, Baroness Karin von Kantzow, had married Herman Goring, head of the Luftwaffe, and the fact that he had flown for Finland, which was allied with Germany at the time. Instead, von Rosen continued flying for KLM on the route between London and Lisbon. It seems that von Rosen, who was from a wealthy family in neutral Sweden, preferred the adventurous life of a mercenary pilot to family obligations or other pursuits in life. Some who knew him said that he wanted to live the noble life of helping the cause of the underdog. Others said that he did it to feed his enormous ego. Perhaps it was for both reasons.

In any case, when once again in Ethiopia, Count von Rosen let it be known among the diplomatic community in Addis Ababa that he was not pleased to be outranked by Colonel Robinson, a black American, and not happy serving under his command. It appears that his ego and aristocratic sensibilities rebelled against taking orders from any black man under the rank of emperor. Perhaps he was jealous of John Robinson's reputation as a pilot and the acclaim he received from the emperor and Ethiopian people.

John was aware of the count's attitude. Friends in the diplomatic community had informed him of von Rosen's complaints. Nonetheless, Robinson persevered in building up Ethiopia's new fledgling air force. He intended to do it with or without a jealous count's cooperation.

Trouble boiled to the surface when Ethiopia was given a surplus American C-47/DC-3 twin-engine transport, which had to be picked up and delivered to Addis Ababa. (The pickup point is not known, but may have been at Djibouti or somewhere in Sudan or Kenya.) A C-47 normally requires a pilot and copilot. John recognized that he and Gustaf von Rosen were the most qualified pilots in Ethiopia. Their differences aside, John picked the count as his copilot to help deliver the plane to Addis Ababa. Von Rosen, curiously, insisted on flying his own plane to the pickup point rather than flying with John. The reason would become clear. Both men flew in separate planes, each carrying a pilot to return their planes to Addis Ababa.

According to witnesses, von Rosen refused Robinson's order to fly in the right seat as copilot of the C-47, saying something to the effect that John should fly copilot because he, von Rosen, wasn't about to fly second seat to an American nigger. Evidently von Rosen had insisted on flying himself to the pickup point for that reason.

John reined in his temper, putting the mission ahead of his personal feelings. Over the count's vociferous protest, John climbed into the C-47 alone, closed the door, started the engines, and flew the large aircraft to Addis Ababa. During flight he was required to reach across the cockpit to perform a copilot's duties of, among others, raising and lowering the landing gear and flaps, operating the radio, managing fuel, navigating and cross-checking the engine instruments, etc. while flying the plane. John landed in Addis Ababa ahead of the count.

When von Rosen landed, he marched into Robinson's office and launched into a tirade that ended in a fight that was over almost before it started. Robinson broke von Rosen's jaw and evidently the pride of Sweden. Von Rosen, after having his jaw set at the hospital, saw to it that a formal complaint was filed by the Swedish consul to the Ethiopian government.

Robinson was put under house arrest for two days. He was visited by Prince Makonnen, Mrs. Ford, Yosef Ford, and several friends including members of the diplomatic corps. Mrs. Ford recalled that John was perhaps more hurt than angry.

It seemed that more was at stake than a count's broken jaw. The emperor sent an emissary to try and explain to John what the situation involved. Shortly after the war, John's group of instructors received a few training planes through military aid to Ethiopia from the United States and United Kingdom. By 1948 neither the United Kingdom nor the United States were interested in providing further assistance. However, Sweden had a long missionary history with Ethiopia and since the end of World War II had established support, providing planes, parts, educational and medical facilities, and business interests. Ethiopia, it was explained to Col. Robinson, simply could not afford to lose Sweden's support. Sweden had promised to provide more Sapphire trainers, Saab B-17 single-engine light bombers, and acquire more C-47 transport aircraft from the United States. Apparently Count Gustaf von Rosen had become the key to continued Swedish support.

It was obvious to John that this was no longer a personal matter. He could handle a case of insubordination in his command, but he could not compete with Swedish foreign policy and aid. John Robinson submitted his resignation from the Ethiopian Air Corps. Von Rosen was put in charge of the new Ethiopian Air Force John Robinson had built.

The emperor sent a personal communiqué to John asking him to remain in Ethiopia and continue development of the new Ethiopian Airlines. John was allowed to keep the villa he had occupied since 1944. His salary was to continue. He also remained an advisor to the Ministry of War.

John joined Prince Makonnen, Duke of Harar, in an import/export business and accepted a royal appointment to head the Duke's new aviation school. John and the duke became inseparable friends. The incident with von Rosen remained a bitter memory, but John was still flying, the ladies still loved him, his friends stood by him, his income was more than satisfactory—life for John Robinson was good once again. But at home in the United States, Robinson and all he had accomplished was forgotten by all except for his mother and a few friends in Gulfport, Mississippi, and Chicago.

Six years later, on March 14 1954, an L-5 Stinson, returning from a mercy flight, radioed Lideta Airport with the most dreaded words in aviation, "Mayday! Mayday!" followed by the aircraft identifier and position.

On the outskirts of Addis Ababa there was a flaming crash. One of the volunteers, copilot Biachi Bruno, an Italian engineer, was killed outright. The mission command pilot somehow managed to crawl out of the flames before collapsing in excruciating pain. How John Robinson was able to extricate himself from the flaming wreckage can only be attributed to the strong will and determination that had carried him so far during his lifetime.

The staff of the American consulate donated blood to him. An emperor visited his hospital bedside. For two weeks the doctors and nurses did all in their power to save him. It was not to be.

On March 28, 1954, at age fifty-one, the Brown Condor, this remarkable hero, folded his wings. The brotherhood of pilots never say that a fellow pilot has died; they say that their friend has simply gone west into the setting sun.

The people of Ethiopia loved him. His funeral cortege stretched for more than a mile through a city whose population lined the streets to say farewell. John Robinson was buried with ceremony at Holy Trinity Church, Addis Ababa.

Ten thousand miles away in the town of Gulfport, Mississippi, in a house darkened by closed curtains, a proud, heartbroken black woman clutched a telegram. With her hands she laid the paper on her apron-clad thigh and smoothed the wrinkles from the crumpled yellow page as if by doing so she could rub away the terrible words. With trembling fingers, she placed the message on the last page of a thick, worn scrapbook, closed the cover and, holding it close to her heart, wept with the pain only a mother can know.

Another loved, lost airman, Antoine De Saint-Exupéry, once wrote of flying and cited the words of his fellow pilot and friend Mermez: "This landscape was still laved in golden sunlight, but already something was evaporating out of it. I know nothing, nothing in the world, equal to the wonder of nightfall in the air. Those who have been enthralled by the witchery of flying will know what I mean . . . those who fly professionally and have sacrificed much to their craft. Mermez said once, 'It's worth it, it's worth the final smash-up.'"

And so it must have been for John Charles Robinson, 1903–1954.

EPILOGUE

Haile Selassie and Ethiopia

Ethiopian Losses from the Italian invasion and occupation

Ethiopia listed the following losses from 1936 to 1941:

275,000 Killed in action

17,800 Women, children, and civilians killed by bombings

78,500 Patriots (guerrilla fighters) killed during the occupation 1936–1942

30,000 Massacre of February 1937

35,000 Persons who died in concentration camps

24,000 Patriots executed by Summary Courts

300,000 Persons who died of privations due to the destruction of their villages

760,300 TOTAL

In addition to human loss, Ethiopia claimed the loss of 2,000 churches, 525,000 houses, and the slaughter and/or confiscation of 6,000,000 beef cattle; 7,000,000 sheep and goats; 1,000,000 horses and mules; and 700,000 camels.

Haile Selassie

As was the case with so many small countries, Ethiopia was caught up the eddy currents of the Cold War between Western Democracy and Communist Russia. Because of concern over control of the Suez Canal and the Red Sea, which divides Africa from the Near East, Ethiopia was of interest because of its strategic location. In 1953 the United States opened a US military assistance group to aid Ethiopia in return for the establishment of a strategically important communications center in Ethiopia, the largest high frequency radio installation in the world at the time. The United States provided assistance to Ethiopia's developing airline, built a new international airport and a university in Addis Ababa, and supplied the Ethiopian Air Force with C-47 transports, T-33 jet trainers, and F-86 jet fighters. By the late 1960s, the high cost of the Vietnam War caused the United States to cut non-essential military spending. The US communications center in Ethiopia had become obsolescent with the advent of satellite communication. As a cost-cutting measure, the United States withdrew much of its previous activities and aid from Ethiopia.

When famine struck the country in the early '70s, Communist propaganda circulated by Communist sympathizers led Ethiopians to increasingly blame Haile Selassie and his government. In 1974 a group of young officers formed a Soviet-backed Marxist-Leninist junta led by Mengistu Haile Mariam. They deposed Haile Selassie in humiliating fashion, imprisoned him and his closest family members, executed over sixty of Selassie's family members, ministers, and military leaders, and established a one-party Communist state government called the Derg. No word whatsoever concerning the emperor was made public. Haile Selassie died under questionable circumstances. In a press release, the Derg stated the emperor had died of a heart attack while walking in a palace garden and there would be a private burial.

Under Mengistu, hundreds of thousands died during the Red Terror conducted by the Derg with direct military action and the use of hunger as a weapon. Cuban troops of Fidel Castro and Soviet-supplied military hardware were used to help Mengistu put down an uprising in what was called the Ogden War. (During that period, Count Gustaf von Rosen, who some years before had left Ethiopia for other adventures, was killed on the ground by guerrilla fighters near the Sudan border.)

In 1990 the collapse of the Soviet Union meant the end of Soviet support to the Derg. In 1991 Mengistu fled the country and found asylum in Zimbabwe. After a long trial in the High Court of Ethiopia that began in 1994 and ended in 2006, thousands of witnesses were called to testify; more than five thousand former members of the Derg were indicted. Mengistu and seventeen of his officers were convicted of genocide and sentenced to death. Ethiopia is conducting an ongoing, so far unsuccessful effort to have Mengistu extradited from Zimbabwe.

Information about the fate of Haile Selassie emerged after the fall of the Soviet-backed Communist Derg government. In 1992 during renovation of the palace, the body of Haile Selassie was found under a toilet facility where it had been thrown as a last gross insult by the Marxist regime. It is said to have been revealed by witnesses that Haile Selassie was tortured, then garroted in the basement of the palace on August 22, 1975. His remains were recovered and later buried with dignity and ceremony at the Holy Trinity Cathedral in Addis Ababa. Haile Selassie, who ruled Ethiopia for forty-four years, during which time he worked to modernize his ancient nation, will best be remembered for his impassioned speech before the League of Nations in 1936 which ended with the warning, "It is us today. It will be you tomorrow," words that rang hauntingly true three short years later, when Fascist Germany and Communist Russia crossed Poland's border and unleashed World War II.

With the fall of Mengistu's Communist government, relations with the United States and the United Nations were re-established. In 1994 under a new constitution, Ethiopia held its first multi-party elections to establish a federal republic. The people of Ethiopia continue to work toward modern economic development, world trade, and tourism. Mountainous terrain and lack of good roads still make land transportation difficult, but the Ethiopian Airlines John Robinson helped establish has one of the safest records of any airline. It serves thirty-eight domestic airfields and forty-two international destinations.

ACKNOWLEDGMENTS

The history of John Charles Robinson presented herein has been gathered by the author during an often difficult trail of investigation and original research stretching some thirty years. It is difficult to resurrect the history of any long forgotten hero. It is particularly challenging to piece together the history of a forgotten hero whose story never appeared in history books, an American hero who successfully pursued his seemingly impossible dream only to have his extraordinary achievements lost in chaos as war followed war in terrible succession, a hero who was black in the age of segregation.

Scores of the details within this book came from the contributions of individuals who knew John Robinson firsthand—while some of them are now deceased, I wish to pay tribute to them here. I am ever grateful to the following: Miomi Godine (who was the first to confirm to me that an African American pilot of the 20s and 30s named Robinson grew up in Gulfport, Mississippi—it was the beginning); Mrs. Bertha Stokes, Col. Robinson's sister of Queens, New York, an essential source; John Stokes and Andrew Stokes, Robinson's nephews whose recollections, photographs, and priceless recorded interviews with his contemporaries contributed greatly to this work; Al Key, record-setting Mississippi aviator; Cornelius Coffey, a partner in Robinson's school of aviation; Harold Hurd and Janet Waterford Bragg, both students and friends of Robinson; Inniss Ford and her son, Yosef Ford, who first met Robinson in Ethiopia; "Chief" Alfred Anderson, head of the school of Aviation at Tuskegee Institute; Harry Tartt and Katie Booth, who looked up to Robinson during school days in Gulfport; General Noel F. Parrish, Ret.; Curtis Graves of NASA who arranged interviews that otherwise might not have been open to me; Pick Firmin, former editor of the *Sun Herald* newspaper; and Tyrone Haymore, who helped organize the Robbins Illinois Historical Society and Museum.

Of special recognition is Jim Cheeks, a pilot who served with Robinson training Army Air Corps aviation mechanics at several bases in the United States and later flew with him in Ethiopia. Jim's input and photographs were primary sources for recording Col. Robinson's return to Ethiopia during World War II at Haile Selassie's request.

My friend and fellow flyer, Roland Weeks, retired publisher of the *Sun Herald* newspaper, arranged unlimited access of the microfiche archives of Robinson's hometown newspaper, the Gulfport/Biloxi *Sun Herald*, for the years 1935 and 1936. It was necessary to scan every page of every day of the paper for those years to find articles on Robinson. Though the paper did provide, with some pride, articles of his adventures during the Italo-Ethiopian War and his homecoming, one had to search the back pages to find them.

Additional institutions that supported my research include the Smithsonian Air and Space Museum (special thanks to Von Hardesty and Dominick Pisano); the National Archives; the Library of Congress; the Tuskegee University Library; the *Chicago Defender* Archives; the libraries of Harrison County and the University of Southern Mississippi.

No author's finished work stands as his or hers alone. The idea, the words, the style are more or less his or hers. But the finished book—tidy, free of awkward structure, grammatical errors, lapses in syntax, all the things that make a book acceptable to the reader—is aided by editors whose work often goes unsung. I hereby sing the praises of my editors, Jennifer McCartney and Herman Graf. Finally, this work may well have languished unread without the faith and hard work of my agent and friend, Jeanie Pantelakis.

I owe a debt of thanks to all the individuals and institutions listed above. I also thank my wife Kay, the love of my life, for her support and patience in putting up with cantankerous me and two no-account dogs.

Bibliography

(It should be remembered that the author did years of original research when there was very little printed information available on John C. Robinson. Much of the information gathered on Robinson was by personal interviews conducted by myself and by others on recorded cassette tapes at my request.)

National Archives

Library of Congress

Smithsonian Air and Space Museum

Archives of the Gulfport-Biloxi *Daily Herald* for the years 1934 through 1936.

Archives of the American Negro Press (ANP) for the years 1934 through 1936

The *Tuskegee Messenger*, Tuskegee, Alabama

Montgomery Advertiser, Montgomery, Alabama

The *Chicago Defender* Archives

The Associated Press (AP) 1935/36

The *Evening Star*, Washington, D.C.

Kansas City Call

Pittsburgh Courier

Hollis Burke Frissell Library, Tuskegee Institute, Alabama

Tuskegee University Library

Light Plane Guide, Vol. I, No. III, 1965

Travel & Leisure, Vol. 4, No. 1, 1965

World War II, Vol. 4, No. 4, October 1975

The Negro in American History, by the Board of Education, City of New York, 1965

The Ethiopian War by Angelo Del Boca, 1965

Rape of Ethiopia by A. J. Barker, 1936, Balantine

The Italian Invasion of Abyssinia by David Nicholle, 1997, Osprey

Haile Selassie's War by Anthony Mockler 1984, Random House

The Coming of the Italian-Ethiopian War, George W. Baer, 1967, Harvard University Press

CIA The World Fact Book, Ethiopia

TIME, Monday, May 11, 1936; Monday, May 18, 1936

Pan African Journal, Vol. V, No. 1, Spring 1972

US Department of State, Notes on Ethiopia

Various newsreel films of Italo-Ethiopian War available on the Internet (Italian, British, Dutch, Swedish, etc.)

The Italian film *Lo Squadrone Bianco*, 1936, directed by Augusto Genina

The Italian film *Il Cammino Della Heros*, 1937